MW01562928

PROGRESSIVE EXERCISES

IN THE

CHINESE WRITTEN LANGUAGE.

PROGRESSIVE EXERCISES

IN THE

CHINESE WRITTEN LANGUAGE

BY

T. L. BULLOCK,
Professor of Chinese in the University of Oxford.

KELLY & WALSH, LIMITED
SHANGHAI, HONGKONG, SINGAPORE & YOKOHAMA
1902.

PRINTED BY E. J. BRILL, LEYDEN (HOLLAND).

PREFACE.

At the present day most students of Chinese, before applying themselves to the Literary or Documentary Language, devote a good deal of time to the Spoken Language, which they learn with the aid of manuals and exercise books. In so doing they acquire the knowledge of a considerable number of written Chinese words, or characters. Thus equipped, they are able satisfactorily to commence their attack upon whatever book they may choose for the purpose of initiating themselves into the mysteries of Literary Chinese.

But very different is the position of the learner who wishes to begin his studies with the written language, and sets to work on, perhaps, the Classics, or, perhaps, a collection of Despatches, with absolutely no knowledge of any characters beyond the radicals. He is bewildered by the number of new words that he meets with in every line. He is not merely unable to grasp properly the construction of the sentences before him; but he is also hindered by the multiplicity of strange forms from learning even the characters themselves. It is specially to aid the beginner who wishes to go straight to the literary language, that these Exercises have been compiled; though it is hoped that other students may be able to work through them with advantage.

The written language of China comprises several different styles, from that of the ancient classics down to the documentary or business style, used for all official writings at the present day. The earlier Exercises contain a good many examples taken from the classics. But the long passages in the later Exercises belong distinctly to the modern documentary style, which is the branch that must be studied by every one who wishes to make practical use of the learning that he acquires.

The Exercises are progressive, commencing with the commonest characters and the simplest of sentences. In each of them the learner is introduced to a limited number of new words, never as many as twenty in one Exercise. If he will be content to proceed slowly, and to fix thoroughly in his memory every new character as he comes to it, he will find, when he reaches the end of the book, that without serious difficulty he has furnished himself with a considerable stock of simple words, and that he can proceed profitably to some more advanced work. Nor need he hesitate as to what book he shall select. Sir Thos. Wade's *Documentary Course* will be exactly what he requires. While studying it, he is recommended at the same time to read carefully through Dr. Hirth's *Notes on the Chinese Documentary Style*. These *Notes* are very valuable; but it would be a waste of time to attempt to study them before some progress in the language has been made. It will be seen that use has been made of Dr. Hirth's book several times in the explanatory notes attached to the Exercises in this volume.

ERRATA.

Page 5, Line 4 from bottom, for "af" read "of".
„ 24, Line 2 from bottom, for "itentionally" read "intentionally".
„ 29, Vocab., Col. 2, for *c'hi*^{1}, read *ch'i*^{1}.
„ 55, Vocab., Col. 2, for "seareh.' read "search".
„ 57, Text, Col. 2 from left, for 22 read 23.
„ 63, Vocab., Col. 2, for *teng*^{3}, read *têng*^{3}.
„ 78, Vocab., Col. 2, for *leng*^{3} read *lêng*^{3}.
„ 115, Vocab., Col. 2, after *lo*^{4} add "to fall, to sink down".
„ 170, Text, Col. 5 from right, for 巳 read 己.

TABLE OF CONTENTS.

I. INTRODUCTORY CHAPTER.

1. SPELLING.

For spelling Chinese words I have employed the system invented by Sir Thos. Wade. It represents the pronunciation heard in Peking. The system is not faultless; but it is the one most widely used, and is generally considered the best existing.

2. PRONUNCIATION.

These Exercises have not been compiled with the object of teaching any one to speak Chinese. But as the learner must pronounce the Chinese words in some manner, it will be well for him to attempt to do so with a moderate degree of accuracy. To assist him in this, a table of sounds is given below. As will be understood, the table does not claim to supply in every case an accurate description of the sounds. It merely furnishes the best advice as to pronunciation that one can give under the circumstances.

Consonants.

ch; as in *church.*
j; as in the French language, or as the *s* in the English *fusion.*
hs; this combination is said to represent a sibilant preceded by an aspirate; but the student is advised to content himself

with pronouncing it like *sh*. Note that *hs* is only found before the vowels *i* and *ü*.

ss; as *s*.

ts; as in *hits*.

tz; as *ts*.

y; this letter has its English, consonant sound; but it is very faint in *yen* and *yeh*, especially in the latter, which often sounds like *ieh*.

Other consonants as in English.

Vowels.

a; as in *father;* but when coming between *w* and *n* or *ng*, it is like the *a* in *want*.

ai; as in *aisle*, or in the French *paille*.

ao; a combination of the above *a* with the *ow* in *how*.

e; as in *yet* or in *hen*. It is only found after *i*, *ü* and *y*. See under *ie*.

ei; as the *ey* in *grey*.

ê; almost the German *oe*, and near the vowel sound in *turn*. *êrh*, something like *err*, but the *r* must not be rolled. *ên* and *êng*, as our *fun* and *hung*, without the initial consonant.

i; as the vowel sound in *flee*. *in* and *ing*, as in our *sin* and *sing*.

ia; a combination of the sounds *i* and *a*, as given above; but the *i* is pronounced lightly, as in *piano*.

iao; similar combination of *i* and *ao*.

ie; similar combination of *i* and *e*. It is only found with *h* or *n* following. For *ieh* take the *ie* in *siesta*, (the *h* does not affect the sound). For *ien* take the *ien* in *Sienna*.

iu; similar combination of *i* and of *u* as given below.

ih; there is much dispute as to the pronunciation of this sound. It is quite different from *i*. Some very good authorities hold it to be the same as *ŭ*, below. The student is advised to accept this theory, till he be in a position to judge for himself. He will then probably think that he can detect a difference.

o; nearly but not quite so broad as the *aw* in *law*.

ou; between the vowel sounds in *how* and *hoe.* The student is advised to adopt the latter for the moment.

u; as the vowel sound in *too.* In *un* and *ung* it is shortened. Thus *sun* is not exactly like *soon,* but its vowel sound resembles the *oo* in foot.

ua; uai; uei; ui; these are combinations of *u* with *a, ai, ei, i,* as given above; they come between *wa* and *oo-a, wai* and *oo-ai, wei* and *oo-ei, wi* and *oo-i,* sometimes the one sound sometimes the other seeming most nearly correct. *ui* may be said to be always *oo-i.* If one substitutes *oo* for *ew* in *dewy,* one has the sound of *ui.*

ü; like the French *u* in *du* or *tu.*

üa; only found with *n* following; in *üan* the *ü* keeps its ordinary sound, and the *an* is almost as flat as the English *an.*

üe; for this take the sounds given under *ie,* above, and substitute *ü* for *i.*

üo; a combination of *ü* and *o,* as above.

ŭ; this sound, which is only found after *ss* and *tz,* is very difficult to identify, and still more difficult to describe. For *ssŭ,* take the first syllable of *surrender,* as it is ordinarily pronounced, — of course without giving any weight to the *r.* The *ŭ* in *tzŭ* is the same.

In the Mandarin Language of Peking *ch* is very often found, followed by *i* or *ü.* But in Southern Mandarin (which in this is more in accord with the ancient language) instead of the *ch,* before those vowels, some words have a *k,* others *ts.* Thus, where a Peking man says *chin, chiang, ch'üan,* a southerner will say either *kin* or *tsin, kiang* or *tsiang, k'üan* or *ts'üan,* and so on. If one does hear *chin* in the south, it is for some word which is pronounced *chên* in the north.

Again, *hs* in the north represents either an *h* or an *s* in the south. Thus a Peking man says *hsia* and *hsün;* a southerner, *hia* or *sia, hün* or *sün.*

3. ASPIRATES.

It will be noticed that certain initial consonants are often followed by an inverted comma, *e.g.*, *p'ing*. The inverted comma denotes an aspirate. That is to say, the speaker must emit a breath as he pronounces these consonants. To a Chinese *p'ing* and *ping* are perfectly different sounds; while, though he says *ping* and not *bing*, his ear apparently recognizes no distinction between unaspirated *p* and *b*. The Russians, who speak Chinese well, always use *b*, *d*, instead of *p*, *t*, etc.

4. TONES.

The Tones are of the very highest importance in speaking Chinese. But it would be waste of time for the student to occupy himself with them, till he can learn the spoken language with a native teacher. Therefore no attempt is made here to explain them. Nevertheless, for the benefit af any reader who may have commenced the study of the spoken language, the tones of all words in these Exercises are marked according to Sir Thos. Wade's system, *e.g.*, *chien*^{1}, *tung*^{4}.

II. THE RADICALS.

The study of the Chinese written language should commence with the two hundred and fourteen radicals. The radicals are written words, or characters, having each their sound and meaning, and about three fourths of them being in use at the present day, while the remaining fourth are obsolete. But they differ from ordinary characters in that they are, or are supposed to be, primitive words, transformed hieroglyphs, as one may term them, and not compounded from simpler forms. Every other character in the language is supposed to have been framed by combination, and is said to consist of two parts, a radical and a non-radical part, which latter is generally called a phonetic. As the student will see for himself in time, the phonetic often gives some clue to the sound of the character, while the radical is usually connected with its meaning,

Again, the phonetic part itself is sometimes simply another radical, sometimes two or more radicals combined; or, at any rate, easily recognizable radicals in most cases enter into its composition. Any one, therefore, who is familiar with the radicals, will find the task of learning the phonetic part of the characters simplified in a wonderful degree.

Moreover a knowledge of the radicals is necessary to enable one to look out in the dictionary any word of which one does not know the sound. For all characters are indexed in the dictionary under the radical to which they belong.

The beginner should work at the radicals till he can recognize them all without fail, and can remember both their sound and their meaning. He should be able to write from memory all except, perhaps, a few of the most difficult ones towards the end of the list. His task will be rendered much easier, if he learns but a few characters at a time, and does not go on to new ones till he knows the old ones thoroughly.

It is very important to know the number of strokes in each radical. This will not give any trouble, as the radicals are arranged in the list in accordance with the number of their strokes.

It is not, however, always quite a simple matter to count the strokes in a character. As a general rule, a line in any direction is one stroke. But there are exceptions. If one line ends just where the line next to be written will begin, the two are made together, without the pen being lifted from the paper, and therefore they count as only one stroke. Thus it becomes important to know something of the order in which the strokes are written. As to this, the Chinese say 'left before right, above before below'; and so a character will be commenced ordinarily from the top left hand corner. Note also that all perpendicular strokes are written downwards, and all horizontal strokes towards the right; though among the slanting strokes there are some, more or less downwards, towards the left, and some upwards towards the right. Now, let us look at Radical 13. In writing this, first the left stroke is made, then the top and the right stroke, the last two being in one: total, two strokes. Radical 30 is formed in a similar way, with the addition, finally, of the lower horizontal: total, three strokes. Nos. 44, 72, 80, 102, 109 will afford further instances of the same. In Radicals 17, 28, 46, 80, the left hand and the bottom lines are written together, so as to form only one stroke. N°. 52 is made by two double strokes and then a dot. These instructions should be sufficient to explain how the majority of the characters are written; but there are a few which would require more detailed information than can conveniently be given here.

At the end of the List of Radicals there will be found a short table of modified or abbreviated forms. The student ought to pay careful attention to these, as many of them are very commonly used in the formation of characters.

---

1 stroke.

No.	Sound	Radical		Meaning
1	*i*	一		one.
2†	*kun*	丨		a down stroke.
3†	*chu*	丶		a point.
4†	*p‘ieh*	丿		a stroke to the left.
5	*i*	乙		a hook.
6†	*chüeh*	亅		a barb.

2 strokes.

No.	Sound	Radical		Meaning
7	*êrh*	二		two.
8†	*t‘ou*	亠		above.
9	*jên*	人	*	man.
10†	*jên*	儿		man.
11	*ju*	入		to enter.
12	*pa*	八		eight.
13†	*chiung*	冂		a limit.
14†	*mi*	冖		to cover.
15†	*ping*	冫		icicle.
16	*chi*	几		bench.
17†	*k‘an*	凵		receptacle.
18	*tao*	刀	*	knife.
19	*li*	力		strength.
20†	*pao*	勹		to wrap.
21	*pi*	匕		spoon.
22†	*fang*	匚		box.
23†	*hsi*	匸		to conceal.
24	*shih*	十		ten.
25	*pu*	卜		to divine.
26†	*chieh*	卩	*	a joint.
27†	*han*	厂		cliff.
28†	*ssŭ*	厶		selfish.

† The Radicals marked thus are obsolete, and are only found as portions of other characters. It is therefore less important than it is in the case of the rest of the Radicals, to remember their sound in addition to their form and meaning.

* The Radicals thus marked have modified forms, generally abbreviations, which are used for them in the composition of other characters. A table of these modifications is given at the end of the list of Radicals.

29	*yu*	又	also; again.

3 strokes.

30	*k‘ou*	口	mouth.
31†	*wei*	囗	to enclose.
32	*t‘u*	土	earth.
33	*shih*	士	scholar.
34†	*chih*	夂	to follow.
35†	*ts‘ui*	夊	to walk slowly.
36	*hsi*	夕	evening.
37	*ta*	大	great.
38	*nü*	女	woman.
39	*tzŭ*	子	son.
40†	*mien*	宀	a covering.
41	*ts‘un*	寸	inch.
42	*hsiao*	小	small.
43†	*wang*	尢 *	lame.
44	*shih*	尸	corpse.
45†	*ch‘ê*	屮	a sprout.
46	*shan*	山	mountain.
47	*ch‘uan*	巛 *	a stream.
48	*kung*	工	labour.
49	*chi*	己	self.
50	*chin*	巾	napkin.
51	*kan*	干	a shield; to concern.
52†	*yao*	幺	small.
53†	*yen*	广	projecting roof.
54†	*yin*	廴	to move on.
55†	*kung*	廾	hands folded.
56	*i*	弋	a dart.
57	*kung*	弓	a bow.
58†	*ch‘i*	彐 *	pig's head.
59	*shan*	彡	feathers.
60	*ch‘ih*	彳	a step.

4 strokes.

61	*hsin*	心 *	heart.
62	*ko*	戈	spear.

63	*hu*	戶	door.
64	*shou*	手*	hand.
65	*chih*	支	a branch.
66†	*pʻu*	攴*	to tap.
67	*wên*	文	literature.
68	*tou*	斗	a peck.
69	*chin*	斤	a pound; axe.
70	*fang*	方	square.
71†	*wu*	无*	negative.
72	*jih*	日	sun; day.
73	*yüeh*	曰	to say.
74	*yüeh*	月	moon; month.
75	*mu*	木	wood.
76	*chʻien*	欠	to owe.
77	*chih*	止	to stop.
78	*tai*	歹*	bad.
79	*shu*	殳	to kill.
80	*wu*	毋	do not.

81	*pi*	比	to compare.
82	*mao*	毛	hair.
83	*shih*	氏	family.
84†	*chʻi*	气	breath.
85	*shui*	水*	water.
86	*huo*	火*	fire.
87	*chao*	爪*	claws.
88	*fu*	父	father.
89	*yao*	爻	crosswise.
90†	*chʻiang*	爿	Radical 91 reversed.
91	*pʻien*	片	a slice or slip.
92	*ya*	牙	back teeth.
93	*niu*	牛*	ox.
94	*chʻüan*	犬*	dog.

5 strokes.

95	*hsüan* or *yüan*	玄	dark.
96	*yü*	玉*	jade stone.
97	*kua*	瓜	gourd.

98	*wa*	瓦	a tile.
99	*kan*	甘	sweet.
100	*shêng*	生	to produce; to live.
101	*yung*	用	to use.
102	*tʻien*	田	field.
103	*pʻi*	疋	a "piece" of cloth.
104†	*ni*	疒	disease.
105†	*po*	癶	back to back.
106	*pai*	白	white.
107	*pʻi*	皮	skin.
108	*min*	皿	dish.
109	*mu*	目*	eye.
110	*mou*	矛	lance.
111	*shih*	矢	arrow.
112	*shih*	石	stone.
113	*shih*	示*	to proclaim.
114†	*jou*	禸	footprint.
115	*ho*	禾	grain.

116	*hsüeh*	穴	cave.
117	*li*	立	to set up.

6 strokes.

118	*chu*	竹*	bamboo.
119	*mi*	米	rice.
120†	*ssŭ*	糸	silk.
121	*fou*	缶	earthenware.
122†	*wang*	网*	a net.
123	*yang*	羊	sheep.
124	*yü*	羽	feathers.
125	*lao*	老	old.
126	*êrh*	而	and; but.
127	*lei*	耒	plough.
128	*êrh*	耳	ear.
129	*yü*	聿	pen.
130	*jou*	肉*	flesh.
131	*chʻên*	臣	a minister.
132	*tzŭ*	自	from; self.

133	*chih*	至	to go to.
134	*chiu*	臼	a mortar.
135	*shê*	舌	tongue.
136	*ch‘uan*	舛	contradictory.
137	*chou*	舟	boat.
138	*kên*	艮	perverse.
139	*sê*	色	colour.
140†	*ts‘ao*	艸*	grass.
141†	*hu*	虍	tiger.
142	*ch‘ung*	虫	insect.
143	*hsieh*	血	blood.
144	*hsing*	行	to do, to go.
145	*i*	衣*	clothes
146	*hsi*	西*	west.

7 strokes.

147	*chien*	見	to see; to perceive.
148	*chüeh*	角	a horn.
149	*yen*	言	words; to speak.
150	*ku*	谷	valley.
151	*tou*	豆	beans.
152	*shih*	豕	pig.
153	*chai*	豸	reptile.
154	*pei*	貝	precious.
155	*ch‘ih*	赤	flesh colour.
156	*tsou*	走	to go.
157	*tsu*	足	foot; enough.
158	*shên*	身	body.
159	*ch‘ê*	車	cart.
160	*hsin*	辛	bitter.
161	*ch‘ên*	辰	time, period.
162†	*ch‘o*	辵*	to walk.
163	*i*	邑*	a city.
164	*yu*	酉	5 to 7 p. m.
165†	*pien*	釆	to distinguish.
166	*li*	里	a chinese mile.

8 strokes.

167	*chin*	金	gold; metal.
168	*chʻang*	長*	long.
169	*mên*	門	gate; door.
170	*fou*	阜*	mound.
171†	*tai*	隶	to reach to.
172†	*chui*	隹	short-tailed birds.
173	*yü*	雨*	rain.
174	*chʻing*	靑	blue.
175	*fei*	非	not; wrong.

9 strokes.

176	*mien*	面	face.
177	*ko*	革	raw hide.
178	*wei*	韋	leather.
179	*chiu*	韭	leeks.
180	*yin*	音	sound.
181	*yeh*	頁	leaf of a book.
182	*fêng*	風	wind.
183	*fei*	飛	to fly.
184	*shih*	食	to eat.
185	*shou*	首	the head.
186	*hsiang*	香	fragrant.

10 strokes.

187	*ma*	馬	horse.
188	*ku*	骨	bone.
189	*kao*	高	high.
190†	*piao*	髟	rough hair.
191	*tou*	鬥	to fight.
192	*chʻang*	鬯	fragrant herbs.
193	*li*	鬲	caldron.
194	*kuei*	鬼	spirits of the dead.

11 strokes.

195	*yü*	魚	fish.
196	*niao*	鳥	bird.
197	*lu*	鹵	salt.
198	*lu*	鹿	deer.

199	*mai*	麥	wheat.
200	*ma*	麻	hemp.

12 strokes.

201	*huang*	黃	yellow.
202	*shu*	黍	millet
203	*hei*	黑	black.
204	*chih*	黹	embroidery.

13 strokes.

205	*min*	黽	frog.
206	*ting*	鼎	tripod.
207	*ku*	鼓	drum.
208	*shu*	鼠	rat.

14 strokes.

209	*pi*	鼻	nose.
210	*ch‘i*	齊	even, equal.

15 strokes.

211	*ch‘ih*	齒	front teeth.

16 strokes.

212	*lung*	龍	dragon.
213	*kuei*	龜	tortoise.

17 strokes.

214†	*yo*	龠	flute.

MODIFIED FORMS.

9	人	becomes	亻
18	刀	"	刂
26	卩	"	㔾
43	尢	"	尣 兀
47	巛	"	川 巜
58	彐	"	彑 ⺕
61	心	"	忄 ⺗
64	手	becomes	扌
66	攴	"	攵
71	无	"	旡
78	歹	"	歺
85	水	"	氵 氺
86	火	"	灬
87	爪	"	爫

93 牛	becomes	牜	140 艸	becomes	艹
94 犬	„	犭	145 衣	„	衤
96 玉	„	王	146 襾	„	西
109 目	„	罒	162 辵	„	辶
113 示	„	示 礻	163 邑	„	阝
118 竹	„	⺮	168 長	„	镸
122 网	„	罒 ⺳	170 阜	„	阝
130 肉	„	月 月	173 雨	„	⻗

As the above table shows, the true 146th Radical is not *hsi, west*, but another character, namely *hsia* or *ya, to cover*. Practically, however, the obsolete *hsia* has been quite superseded by *hsi*.

Radical 95 had originally a dot at the bottom right hand corner, like Rad. 52; but is now always written without the dot, so that it has only four strokes. It was changed, in accordance with a common Chinese custom, out of respect to the Emperor Kang Hsi, part of whose personal name it is. For the same reason it is read *yüan* instead of *hsüan*.

RADICAL TEST TABLE.

The characters in the following table are arranged in order according to their radicals, *i.e.*, according to the radicals under which they are classified in the dictionaries. The beginner should work carefully through the table, not only noting the special radical of each character, but identifying as well as he can the other radicals which enter into the composition of the word. He should also pay special attention to the modified forms.

(1) 不上七 (2) 中 (3) 主 (4) 久之乎 (5) 九也乱 (6) 事了 (7) 五云 (8) 亦交 (9) 使今

以 (10) 兄 (11) 全內兩 (12) 六公兵 (13) 同
再 (14) 冠 (15) 冷冬 (16) 凡凰 (17) 出函
(18) 則分 (19) 加勸務 (20) 勿包 (21) 北化
(22) 匠 (23) 區 (24) 千南半 (25) 占卦 (26) 卽
危 (27) 原厄 (28) 去參 (29) 受取及 (30) 味
和各可 (31) 因四 (32) 地堡在坐 (33) 壯壬
壺 (34) 夆 (35) 夏 (36) 多外夜 (37) 天奇夾
(38) 好妥 (39) 字存孝 (40) 家寵 (41) 專對將
(42) 少尙 (43) 尤就 (44) 尺屋 (45) 屯 (46) 岸
島 (47) 州巡 (48) 左差 (49) 已巴巷 (50) 帳
布師 (51) 平年幹 (52) 幼玆 (53) 府 (54) 建
(55) 弄 (56) 式 (57) 引弟 (58) 彙彔彗 (59) 形
(60) 後 (61) 怕思愛忝 (62) 成我 (63) 所戾
(64) 把拏 (66) 放敢敲 (67) 斑 (68) 料 (69) 新
斧 (70) 於 (71) 旣 (72) 時是春 (73) 書更最
(74) 有朝望 (75) 根樂東 (76) 欲 (77) 正此歸
(78) 死 (79) 殺 (80) 毋每 (81) 毖 (82) 毡 (83) 民
(84) 氣 (85) 深永求 (86) 然災煩 (87) 爲爬
(88) 爺 (89) 爾 (90) 牆 (91) 牌 (93) 物牢 (94) 犯
獸 (95) 率 (96) 王瑞 (98) 瓶 (99) 甚甜 (100) 產
甥 (101) 甯 (102) 男由畫 (103) 疏疑 (104) 病
(105) 發 (106) 百皇 (108) 盡 (109) 眼相直眾
(110) 矜 (111) 知矣 (112) 碰磨 (113) 福禁
(114) 禽 (115) 私秦 (116) 空竄 (117) 端章豎
(118) 等管 (119) 粗 (120) 經累 (121) 缺 (122) 罪

罕罔　(123) 美羣　(124) 翎習　(125) 考耆者
(126) 耍耐　(127) 耕　(128) 聖聞聽　(129) 肆
(130) 服肯能　(131) 臨　(132) 臬　(133) 致臺
(134) 與舉舊　(135) 舍　(136) 舞　(137) 船　(138) 艮
(140) 草萬　(141) 虎號　(142) 蚊蛋　(143) 衅衆
(144) 衙　(145) 衫袋裏　(146) 要覆　(147) 親覺
(148) 觔　(149) 記誓　(150) 谿　(151) 豈　(152) 象
豬　(153) 貌　(154) 賊貫　(155) 赦　(156) 起
(157) 路蹇　(158) 躬　(159) 輕軍載　(160) 辜辦
(161) 辱農　(162) 道近　(163) 邦部　(164) 酌酒
(165) 釋　(166) 野量重　(167) 銀鏨　(169) 開
(170) 防陪　(171) 隸　(172) 雞隻雇　(173) 雪
(174) 靖靜　(175) 靠　(177) 靴　(179) 韮　(180) 韻
(181) 頭願　(182) 颳飄　(184) 飲養　(187) 駛驚
(188) 體　(190) 髮　(191) 鬧　(194) 魁魂　(195) 鮮魯
(196) 鴨鳳　(197) 鹹　(198) 麗　(199) 麵　(200) 麼
(202) 䵗黎　(203) 黔點　(210) 齋　(211) 齡。

III. EXERCISES.

Having mastered the radicals, the learner will be in a position to apply himself to these Exercises. In translating them, he should make sure that he understands the exact construction of each sentence word by word. This ought not to prove a difficult matter; as the English version is very literal; and free use has been made of brackets, in order to render it more intelligible. It seemed better that the compiler should expose himself to the charge of uncouthness, rather than run the risk of his translations not being understood. Wherever the rendering is not sufficiently exact, explanation has been given in the notes attached to the Exercises.

At the beginning of each Exercise there will be found a short list of Chinese characters, together with their sound and meaning. In this list are comprised all the words which are new to the learner in the accompanying Exercise. They should be studied most carefully.

One cannot impress too strongly on the beginner the necessity of fixing in his memory every character which he meets with in his lessons. It is not enough for him to 'get up' the translation of passages. He should be able to recognize each character when detached from its context, and to give its sound and principal meaning. Knowledge of characters is not by any means knowledge of Chinese; though a student who is not familiar with them is like a workman without tools: he will never accomplish anything. One constantly hears persons unacquainted with the Chinese language remark that they suppose its principal difficulty lies in the multitude of the characters. This is quite a mistake. At starting a certain amount of effort and persistence is required, in order to get a few hundred characters fixed in one's mind so firmly that they will not escape from it again. But once this has been effected, adding to one's stock becomes a comparatively simple task; and, the more one learns, the easier will it be to make further acquisitions. A man with very moderate powers of memory need have no apprehensions as to his ability, without excessive labour, to store in his mind as many characters as are needful for all ordinary work. But, long before he reaches this point, he will have discovered how many and how formidable are the other difficulties which the language presents to him who studies it.

EXERCISE I.

VOCABULARY.

三 *san*^{1}, three.
四 *ssŭ*^{4}, four.
五 *wu*^{3}, five.
六 *liu*^{4}, six.
七 *ch'i*^{1}, seven.
九 *chiu*^{3}, nine.
百 *pai*^{3}, hundred.
千 *ch'ien*^{1}, thousand.
爲 *wei*^{2}, to be, to do, to make.
wei^{4}, because of, for.
不 *pu*^{1}, not.

[1] 十七、九十、五十四、八十六、三十二。
[2] 七百六十五、八百、四百十九、三百一十七。
[3] 二千、九千五百、六千四百七十八。
[4] 六千三十五。

TRANSLATION.

1. 17; 90; 54; 86; 32.
2. 765; 800; 419; 317.
3. 2,000; 9,500; 6,478.
4. 6,035.

五[5]六十、七八千。七[6]月二十九日。四[7]斗米、七斤魚。五[8]六寸、八寸三。金[9]木水火土。麥[10]子、黍子、香瓜、黃麻、田禾。工[11]人、鼓手、文士、大臣、戶口。羽[12]毛、手巾、雨衣、瓦片、火石、白玉、大刀、弓矢。走[13]九里、一齊行、舟車。甘[14]心、骨血、口舌。干[15]戈、用力、欠雨、見鬼。

5. Fifty [or] sixty; seven [or] eight thousand.
6. The Seventh Month, twenty ninth day.
7. Four pecks [of] rice; seven pounds [of] fish.
8. Five [or] six inches; eight inches [and] three [tenths].
9. Metal, wood, water, fire, earth, (according to the Chinese, the Five Elements).
10. Wheat; a kind of millet; melon (fragrant gourd); jute (yellow hemp); growing corn (field corn).
11. A workman; a drummer (drum hand); a student (literary scholar); statesman or official of the highest rank (great minister); population (doors and mouths).
12. Feathers, or, down (feathers [and] hair); a handkerchief; a rain-coat; tiles, or pieces of tile; flint (fire stone); white jade; sword (big knife); bow and arrow, or, archery.
13. To go nine *li* (= 3 miles); to go together; boats and carts, (= means of conveyance).
14. Gladly (with pleasant heart); bones and blood, (a term for near relationship); altercation (mouth and tongue).
15. Shield and spear, (= war); to use strength, or, to exert oneself; to be short of (*lit.* to owe) rain; to see a ghost.

10. 子 here is merely a termination; *mai-tzŭ*, wheat; *shu-tzŭ*, millet.

11. 戶口, *lit.* doors and mouths, then, households and persons, and so, population.

12. 片, anything small and thin, slices, slips, flakes.

[16] 自辰至酉。
[17] 小鼻大目長耳。
[18] 山川谷穴。
[19] 山羊、鹿肉、龍爪、老鼠、長虫。
[20] 四方、三角、長方。
[21] 馬比犬大。
[22] 三七二十一。
[23] 青白赤黑黃爲五色。
[24] 爲首。
[25] 不爲人。
[26] 牙齒不白。
[27] 山不爲不高。
[28] 九九爲八十一。
[29] 不見日月。
[30] 人生七十。
[31] 力不足。
[32] 五百六十二疋。
[33] 四千三百里。

16. From 8 A. M. to 6 P. M.
17. A small nose, large eyes and long ears.
18. Mountains, streams, valleys and caves.
19. A goat (mountain sheep); venison (deer flesh); dragon's claws; a rat (old rat); a snake (long reptile).
20. Square; three-cornered; oblong (long square).
21. The horse is bigger than the dog (horse compared with dog [is] great).
22. Three sevens make twenty one.
23. Blue, white, red, black, yellow, are the five colours.
24. To be head, or, chief.
25. Not to be a man (not to play a man's part).
26. The teeth [are] not white.
27. The hill is not low (is not not-high).
28. Nine nines make eighty one.
29. [They did] not see sun [or] moon.
30. Man lives seventy [years].
31. [His] strength [is] not enough.

16. The Chinese day is divided into twelve periods of two hours each, the first period consisting of the hour before and the hour after midnight. *ch'ên* and *yu*, being the fifth and the tenth of these periods, correspond with our 7—9 A. M., and 5—7 P. M..

32. 562 "pieces".

33. 4,300 *li.*

32. 疋; a *p'i* is a complete, undivided web of cloth, silk, etc., as it comes from the loom.

As a general note, it will be well to remark, with regard to
1) the definite and the indefinite article,
2) conjunctions,
3) the copula,
4) pronouns, both personal and possessive,
5) signs of the plural for nouns and pronouns,
6) auxiliaries or signs of tenses in verbs,
that, though there are means of expressing these in Chinese, whenever the writer may think it desirable, still they are all very generally omitted, the reader being left to infer them from the context.

EXERCISE 2.

VOCABULARY.

有 *yu*^{3}, to have, to be, (not the copula).

知 *chih*^{1}, to know.

其 *ch'i*^{2}, pronoun of the third person, also a demonstrative pronoun.

此 *tz'ŭ*^{3}, this.

在 *tsai,* in, at; to be alive.

母 *mu*^{3}, mother.

無 *wu*^{2}, not, (especially as opposed to *yu,* no. 1, above).

我 *wo*^{3}, I.

皆 *chieh*^{1}, all.

之 *chih*^{1}, pronoun of the third person in the objective cases; a sign of the genitive.

可 *k'o*^{3}, may, can.

古 *ku*^{3}, ancient.

死 *ssŭ*^{3}, to die.

何 *ho*^{2}, what? how? why?

1. 有一人。
2. 人不知。
3. 知而不言。
4. 知人、知面、不知心。

TRANSLATION.

1. [There] is one man.
2. Men do not know.
3. To know but not to speak.
4. [When] you know men, you know their faces, you do not know their hearts.

知[5]有己、不知有人。鳥[6]食其肉。其[7]力不小。知[8]其一、不知其二。此[9]大有用。立[10]在門口。見[11]有二人、一在其首、一在其足。父[12]母在。父[13]不在。老[14]而無子。我[15]不知有無。人[16]皆知其無用。

5. To know [that there] is oneself, and not to know [that there] are [other] men, (*i. e.* to be selfish).
6. The birds ate his flesh.
7. His strength is not small.
8. To know the first [point] but not to know the second.
9. This is of great use (*lit.* greatly has use).
10. To stand in the door-way.
11. They saw there were two men, one at his head, the other at his feet.
12. [His] father and mother are alive.
13. [His] father is not alive.
14. Old and childless.
15. I do not know [whether there] be or not.
16. Men all know [that] it is of no use.

6. Taking these four Chinese words, as they stand, by themselves, one might translate them with equal correctness in many ways. There is nothing to guide one as to the tense of the verb; and, for *ch'i*, *his*, one might equally well say, *her*, *its*, *their* or *that*. I have, however, given to the words the meaning which they happen to bear in the passage from which they were taken; where, attention being paid to the context, there is no ambiguity at all. This remark will apply to many Examples in these Exercises.

8. 其 here is 'that' or 'the'; *ch'i i*, the first [point].

9. Adverbs precede the verb or adjective to which they are attached. *ta*, usually an adjective, is shown by its position to be here employed adverbially; and *yung*, ordinarily a verb, is here a substantive, the object of the verb that it follows. The student must be prepared at every moment to meet with words, which he knows as one part of speech, used as some other part. It has even been said that "a Chinese "character may in general be considered as conveying an idea without reference to "any part of speech; and its being used as a substantive, an adjective or a verb, "depends upon circumstances." This perhaps overstates the case; but it undeniably has a great deal of truth in it.

16. *ch'i*, it, *wu yung*, has not use.

西[17]土之人。不[18]知足。不[19]知足之人。走[20]石飛土之風。父[21]母之心、人皆有之。此[22]又可知。不[23]可不小心。有[24]心爲非。毋[25]爲小人。古[26]之人有言曰。有[27]古大臣之風。自[28]古皆有死。長[29]生不死。死[30]而爲鬼。我[31]不知其爲何人。

17. The men of a western land.
18. Not to know [that one has] enough; (*i. e.* to be discontented).
19. A discontented man.
20. A wind which rolls stones and makes earth fly.
21. A parent's heart, all people have it.
22. This also can be known.
23. One may not be careless.
24. To do wrong intentionally.
25. Do not be a small (*i. e.* a mean) man.
26. The men of old had a saying [which] stated that....
27. He has the spirit of an ancient statesman.
28. From old times all have (*i. e.* are subject to) death.
29. To live long and not die, (*sc.* to be immortal).
30. To die and become a ghost.
31. I do not know what man (*i. e.* who) he is.

17. 之, of. *chih*, when used to express the possessive or genitive case, is placed immediately after its substantive.

19. In this sentence 之 is attached not to a substantive, but to a whole phrase. As we have seen, the three words *pu chih tsu* mean 'to be discontented'. The addition of *chih* converts this phrase into an adjective or participle, 'discontented', qualifying the following word 'man'.

20. Observe the causative use of *tsou* and *fei*. The *chih* turns the verbs into participles, — a stone-moving and earth-blowing wind.

22. Note that the verb is in the passive voice.

23. *hsiao hsin*, to be careful, *lit.* to be minute in mind.

24. *yu hsin*, having the mind, = itentionally, *wei* to do, *fei*, wrong.

28. Death; *ssŭ*, usually a verb, is here a substantive.

[32]此爲何人之子。[33]何日無有。[34]父死母老。[35]有耳目之人無不知之。[36]父不知其子之心。[37]有我在此。[38]古之人皆用之。[39]牛有角。[40]我有子無女。[41]身無衣、口無食。[42]不見其面。

32. This is whose son?
33. It is an ordinary occurrence, (*lit.*, what day does one not have it?)
34. The father is dead, the mother old.
35. Those who have ears and eyes all know it.
36. A father does not know his son's heart.
37. I am here (*lit.*, in this place).
38. The men of old all used it.
39. Oxen have horns.
40. I have sons but not daughters.
41. Naked and hungry, (*lit.*, his body has not clothes, his mouth has not food).
42. Not to see his face.

35. *yu-êrh-mu-chih*, having ears and eyes, — a participle attached to *jên*, men. *wu pu*; the double negative makes a strong affirmative. One may fill up the ellipsis by saying, 'there are not [any of them who] do not know it'.

36. 其子, his son.

EXERCISE 3.

VOCABULARY.

民 *min*², the people.
語 *yü*³, words, to speak.
多 *to*¹, many, much.
過 *kuo*⁴, to pass; to transgress; a sign of the past tense.
王 *wang*², king, prince.
天 *t'ien*¹, the sky, heaven.
於 *yü*², in, at, with.
重 *chung*⁴, heavy, important.
學 *hsüeh*², to learn.

義 *i*⁴, righteousness; that which it is right to do.
年 *nien*², year.
幼 *yu*⁴, young.
貴 *kuei*⁴, honourable.
也 *yeh*³, a terminal particle; also.
命 *ming*⁴, fate, command, life.
福 *fu*², happiness, good fortune.
道 *tao*⁴, a path; the right way, truth, religion; to say.
君 *chün*¹, sovereign, ruler.

無[1]田之小民。四[2]方之民。其[3]無語。古[4]語又曰、士爲四民之首。不[5]多食、食不語。不[6]爲不多。在[7]此多有黃金。有[8]人走過。過[9]我門而不入。自[10]知其過。人[11]不知己過、牛不知力大。

TRANSLATION.

1. The small folk who have no land.
2. The people from [all] four quarters.
3. He had not one word [to say].
4. An old saying, again, has it (says) that the scholars are chief of the four [classes of] people.
5. He did not eat much. [When] eating, he did not talk.
6. It is not a few.
7. There is much gold here.
8. There was a man passed by.
9. He passed by my door and did not enter.
10. He himself knows his faults.
11. A man does not know his own faults: an ox does not know [that its] strength is great.

1. *wu t'ien* not to have fields; *wu t'ien chih*, landless.
2. *huang chin*, yellow metal, gold.
8. *tsou-kuo*, a compound verb, 'to go past'.
11. 己, of himself, his own.

12. 民立其爲王。

13. 天無二日、民無二王。

14. 此山西有赤水、赤水西有白玉山、玉山西有西王母山。

15. 人力不至於此。

16. 此言重大。

17. 金重於羽。

18. 人不學不知義。

19. 人生十年、日幼學。

20. 年幼無知。

21. 幼不學、老何爲。

22. 人命至重。

23. 爲天子父、貴之至也。

12. The people raised him up to be king.

13. The sky has not two suns: the people have not two kings.

14. West [of] these mountains is the Red Water (The Red Sea?); west [of] the Red Water is the White Jade Mountain; west [of] the Jade Mountain is the Mountain [of] the Western King's Mother.

15. Human strength does not attain to this.

16. This saying is important (*lit.* heavy and great).

17. Gold is heavier than (heavy [in comparison] with) feathers.

18. If a man does not learn, he will not know righteousness.

19. When a boy is ten years old (*lit.* when a man has lived ten years), he is called a young student.

20. He is young [in] years and has no knowledge.

21. If he learns not when young, what will he do when old?

22. Human life is extremely important.

23. To be the father [of] the Emperor is the extreme of honour.

14. *tzʻŭ shan hsi*, west *of* these mountains. A Chinese teacher would tell one to supply 之 between *shan* and *hsi*: a foreign grammarian would say that *shan* is "genitive by position". On every page we shall meet with instances of this genitive without *chih*.

22. 至, to reach to, to reach to the end, extreme, extremely.

23. *tʻien tzŭ*, the Son of Heaven, the Emperor: *tʻien-tzŭ fu*, the Emperor's father. 至, extreme; *kuei-chih chih*, extreme of honour. 也 is a terminal word, which is employed to mark the end of a sentence, or to make a pause in a sentence. In sentences such as this some grammarians translate *yeh* by 'is'. But there does not seem to be any authority for so doing; and *yeh* is constantly found appended

24 死生有命、福貴在天。

25 古有一人入山學道。

26 此非君子之道也。

27 小人不知君子之心。

28 大人不見小人之過。

29 君子不多言。

30 天黑走道。

31 老幼皆在。

32 此爲天大之福。

33 九百七十六年。

34 重三千五十八斤。

24. Death and life are ordained by fate (*lit.* have fate); fortune and honour rest with (*lit.* are in) heaven.
25. In old times there was a man [who] went into (went to live in) the mountains to learn religion.
26. This is not the conduct of a superior man.
27. The mean man does not know the superior man's mind.
28. The great man does not see the faults of the small man.
29. The superior man does not speak much.
30. To travel in the dark.
31. Old and young, all were there.
32. This is immense (heaven-big) good fortune.
33. Nine hundred and seventy six years.
34. Weighing three thousand and fifty eight pounds.

in cases where such a translation is quite impossible. It is better to consider that the copula is understood, just as it so often is, and that *yeh* has its ordinary force as a terminal word.

25. 一人; *i* has merely the force of the indefinite article.

26. 君子, a princely man, a man of noble nature, a superior man. The *chün-tzŭ* is the opposite to the 小人, or, mean man.

EXERCISE 4.

VOCABULARY.

事 *shih*[1], business; to serve; trouble.
使 *shih*[3], to use, to employ.
仁 *jên*[2], benevolent.
中 *chung*[1], the middle, within.
外 *wai*[4], outside.
內 *nei*[4], inside.
則 *tsê*[2], then; a pattern, rule.
愛 *ai*[4], to love.
出 *ch'u*[1], to go out, to send out.
安 *an*[1], peace, quiet.
信 *hsin*[4], to believe, sincere; a letter, news.
坐 *tso*[4], to sit.
欺 *c'hi*[1], to deceive, to cheat.
作 *tso*[4], to do, to make.
如 *ju*[2], as, like; if.

1 我有大事。
2 有大人之事、有小人之事。
3 君使臣、臣事君。
4 非其民不使、非其君不事。
5 不知其仁也。
6 心中有事。
7 仁在其中。

TRANSLATION.

1. I have important business.
2. There is the business of great men, and there is the business of small men.
3. The prince employs the minister; the minister serves the prince.
4. [If they were] not the [proper] people he would not employ them; [if it were] not the [proper] prince, he would not serve him.
5. I do not know that he is benevolent.
6. He has trouble in his mind.
7. Benevolence is in these things.

4. 其 is here a strong demonstrative: *the* people, *sc.* those that he had a right to employ; *the* prince, *sc.* the one that he ought to serve.

6. 中, like some other prepositions, follows the noun which it governs. In Examples 7 and 35 of this Exercise there are instances of combined prepositions, one preceding, one following the noun.

8 於水火之中。

9 知其外、不知其內。

10 中外大臣。

11 內則父子、外則君臣。

12 於一月之內。

13 父母愛子。

14 王有愛民之心。

15 君子學道、則愛人。

16 出入無門。

17 其土多出金玉。

18 此言出於無心。

19 出門見福。

20 出示安民。

21 人心不安。

22 我不信也。

23 君臣不信、民不安也。

8. In the midst of fire and water (in difficulty and danger).
9. To know the exterior, but not the interior.
10. The officials of high rank at the capital and in the provinces.
11. At home there is [the relation of] father and son; abroad that of prince and minister.
12. Within the space of one month.
13. Parents love their children.
14. The king has a heart full of love towards his people (*lit.*, a loving-his-people heart).
15. The superior man learns right principles, and then he loves people.
16. No means of entrance or exit (to go out, to go in, no gate).
17. That land produces much gold and jade.
18. These words proceeded from thoughtlessness.
19. To meet with happiness on going out at one's door.
20. To issue a proclamation tranquillizing the people.
21. Men's minds are disturbed.
22. I do not believe it.
23. If prince and ministers be not sincere [towards each other], the people will not be at rest.

8. 之; the insertion of *chih* makes it necessary to regard *chung* as a substantive governed by the preposition *yü*. Example 12 has a similar construction.

10. 中 and 外 are here adjectives — central and outside. 大臣, any one who serves his sovereign in a high capacity.

11. 則 is here untranslatable. It emphasizes the distinction between at home and abroad.

24 父坐子立。

25 坐立不安。

26 不欺人、心則安。

27 內不欺己、外不欺人。

28 天不可欺。

29 此爲何人作。

30 有不知而作之。

31 風雨大作。

32 愛民如子。

33 愛之如身不止如子。

34 見有一人坐作角弓、用手如飛。

35 在西門外山高又多。

36 面如土色。

24. The father sits, while the son stands.
25. Whether sitting or standing, to be not at ease.
26. If one does not deceive people, one's mind will be at peace.
27. Inwardly, not to deceive oneself; outwardly not to deceive [other] men.
28. Heaven cannot be deceived.
29. By whom was this done, (*lit.*, this was what man did)?
30. There are some who act without knowing why.
31. The wind and rain raged violently.
32. To love the people as one's children.
33. He loved him as himself, not merely as a son.
34. He saw there was a man sitting and making horn bows: he was using (*i. e.* moving) his hands as though they flew.
35. Outside the West Gate the hills are many and high.
36. His face was livid (*lit.*, like earth colour).

26. 則; this is a common use of *tsê*. Where in English we should put 'if' or 'when' before the first of two clauses, the Chinese often put *tsê* before the second, instead. We say, 'if you are good, you will be happy'. They say, 'you are good, then you are happy'. 而 is used in a similar way.

28. Observe that *ch'i* to deceive, is in the passive voice.

30. *lit.* There are those who do not know and do it. 之 is used indefinitely. Do it = do a thing, act.

33. *shên*, the body, is often used for 'self'. 止, only.

EXERCISE 5.

VOCABULARY.

善 *shan*⁴, good, virtuous.
謂 *wei*⁴, to say.
求 *ch'iu*², to beg, to seek for.
得 *tê*², to get; must.
失 *shih*¹, to lose, to err.
明 *ming*², bright, clear.
告 *kao*⁴, to tell.
爾 *êrh*³, thou.
理 *li*³, principle, right.
背 *pei*⁴, the back.
畏 *wei*⁴, to fear.
聖 *shêng*⁴, holy, saint; sage.
與 *yü*³, with, and.
上 *shang*⁴, above, on.
好 *hao*³, good; *hao*⁴, to love.
下 *hsia*⁴, below, under.
備 *pei*⁴, to prepare; complete.

[1] 十年行善不足。
[2] 有人謂其爲善人、有人謂其非善人。
[3] 求仁而得仁。
[4] 小民求而不可得。
[5] 求人不如求己、使口不如自走。
[6] 自知失言。
[7] 見人之得、如己之得、見人之失、如己之失。

TRANSLATION.

1. To practise good [works] for ten years is not enough.
2. There were men who said that he was a good man; and there were men who said that he was not a good man.
3. To seek for benevolence, and to obtain benevolence.
4. The common people ask and cannot obtain.
5. To seek from others is not [so good] as to seek from oneself; to use one's mouth (*sc.* to ask people) is not [so good] as to go oneself.
6. He himself knew that he had made a slip of the tongue (*lit.* a slip in his words).
7. To look upon other men's gains as though they were one's own gains; to look upon other men's losses as though they were one's own losses.

日[8]月有明。有[9]人告之
曰。此[10]事一一告知。我[11]
明告爾。爾[12]明知此理。
其[13]不知背面有人。無[14]
心失理謂之過、有心背
理謂之非。君[15]子之過
也、如日月之食、人皆見
之。君[16]子有三畏、畏天
命、畏大人、畏聖人之言。
古[17]之聖人三也。小[18]人
不知天命而不畏也。

8. The sun and moon are bright (*lit.* have brightness).
9. There was some one told him, saying . . .
10. He told them this matter point by point (*lit.* one by one).
11. I tell you plainly.
12. You well know this principle.
13. He did not know that there were men behind.
14. Unintentional misconduct is called a transgression (or, error); wilful offence against the right is called wickedness.
15. The faults of a superior man, they are like the eclipses of the sun or moon: the people all see them.
16. The superior man has three [things which he] fears. He fears the ordinances of Heaven. He fears the great men. He fears the words of the sages.
17. The holy men of old times were three.
18. The mean man does not know the ordinances of Heaven, and does not fear them.

10. By its position 事 looks as if it should be the subject of the sentence. The complete sentence, however, ran thus — *taking* this matter he told it to them, etc.. *kao chih*, told them, so that they knew.
12. *ming*, clearly, well.
13. *pei-mien*, behind.
14. 失理, a failure as to what is right, misconduct. 謂之, one calls it. 背, to turn the back on, to offend against.
15. 也 makes a pause in the sentence, and so gives emphasis. 食, an eclipse, from the old fable that the sun or moon at such times is being eaten by a dragon.

二[1]與一爲三。道[20]二、仁與不仁。不[21]可與言、而與之言、失言。我[22]心上有事。事[23]在我身上。上[24]好仁、而下好義。天[25]下有道。衣[26]食齊備可用。君[27]子不求備於一人。天[28]下有聖人。手[29]背之皮。人[30]有好有歹。

19. Two and one make three.
20. There are two paths, that of benevolence and its opposite.
21. To speak with a man whom one may not speak with, is to err with regard to one's words.
22. I have trouble in (*lit.* on) my mind.
23. The responsibility rests with me personally, (*lit.* the matter is on my body).
24. When those above (*i. e.* the rulers) love benevolence, those below love righteousness.
25. The empire has right principles.
26. Food and clothing have been made ready and can be used (are ready for use).
27. The superior man does not look for completeness (skill or knowledge on all points) in one man.
28. The empire has sages.
29. The skin on the back of the hand.
30. [Among] men there are good ones and there are bad ones.

21. One may not with [a man] speak, and one with him speaks, [this is] to err in one's words.

25. 天下, a substantive, 'that which is under the sky'. It is used both for the world and for the Chinese Empire, which to a Chinaman formerly seemed to be the same thing.

26. *ch'i pei*, ready, prepared.

27. 備, here a substantive, — completeness.

EXERCISE 6.

VOCABULARY.

未 *wei*^{4}, not, not yet.
能 *nêng*^{2}, can, able to.
今 *chin*^{1}, now, the present time.
者 *chê*^{3}, that which. (See notes).
吾 *wu*^{1}, I.
惡 *o*^{4}, or *ê*^{4}, wicked, bad; *wu*^{4} to hate.
惟 *wei*^{2}, only, but.
德 *tê*^{2}, virtue; moral nature.
必 *pi*^{4}, must, to be certain.
正 *chêng*^{4}, upright, correct.
勇 *yung*^{3}, brave.
欲 *yü*^{4}, to desire.
耕 *kêng*^{1}, to cultivate, to till.
野 *yeh*^{3}, waste land, wild.
本 *pên*^{3}, root, origin.
定 *ting*^{4}, to fix, to settle.

1 多日未見。 2 能知天命。 3 今日之事。 4 知者不言、言者不知也。

TRANSLATION.

1. I have not seen [you] for many days (for a long time).
2. He is able to know the decrees of Heaven.
3. The affairs of to day.
4. Those who know do not speak: those who speak do not know.

1. 未; *wei*, as here, very frequently conveys the idea of past time.

4. 知者, the knowing persons, those who know. 言者, the speaking persons, those who speak.

者; *chê*, like the possessive *chih*, 之, may be attached to one or to several words, and follows the word or words to which it is attached. It has been well described as the equivalent of .... 之人 or .... 之事; *e. g.* 知者 = 知之人. Again, it is said to give a participial force to the preceding verb; and in many cases it obviously comes very near the English termination *—ing*. Thus 學者 might be, (1) the learning man, or student, (2) the process of learning, (3) learning, knowledge acquired by study.

chê is very commonly styled a relative pronoun; and oftener than not it can best be translated by 'he who', 'those who', 'that which', etc.; but one should remember that each of these expressions is a relative together with its antecedent, which is a very different thing from a relative. One finds, however, a certain number of instances in modern Chinese, where it seems to perform the function of a pure relative, (*cf.* Ex. 22. 6).

子[5]曰、知之者不如好之者。子[6]曰、吾未見能見其過者。我[7]未見好仁者、惡不仁者。吾[8]未見力不足者。惟[9]天在上。惟[10]仁者能好人能惡人。其[11]可謂至德也。子[12]曰、吾未見好德如好色者也。有[13]德者必有言、有言者不必有德。

5. The Master said, those who know it (virtue) are not equal to those who love it.

6. The Master said, I have not seen any one who can see his faults.

7. I have not seen a lover of benevolence, nor a hater of the want of benevolence.

8. I have not seen any one whose strength is insufficient.

9. Only heaven [is] above [us].

10. Only the benevolent can love men, can hate men.

11. This may be called perfect virtue.

12. The Master said, I have not seen any one who loves virtue as he loves beauty.

13. Those who have virtue are certain to be able to speak (*lit.* to have words): those who can speak are not certain to have virtue.

5. 子 is used as a term of respect. It may be translated in many ways. It is here applied to Confucius by his disciples. 'The Master' is therefore a natural way of rendering it. *pu ju*, not as, not equal to.

6. 者 is here attached to the four preceding words, — the can-see-his-faults man.

7. *wu-pu-jên-chê*, the hating-the-not-benevolence man.

8. The three words *li-pu-tsu* are joined together and form an adjective, — strength-not-sufficient, = insufficient in strength: *li-pu-tsu-chê*, a man of insufficient strength.

10. 仁者, he who is benevolent, the benevolent man.

11. 至, *vide* Ex. 3. 22.

12. 色; *sê*, colour, is much used for beauty, and for the love of women. *chê*, attached to five words, the love-virtue-as-he-loves-beauty man.

我[14]非生而知之者。未[15]有己不正而能正人者。見[16]義不爲、無勇也。仁[17]者必有勇、勇者不必有仁。予[18]欲我何作。耕[19]者欲耕於王之野。耕[20]者生命之本也。古[21]之學者爲己、今之學者爲人。人[22]心不定。

14. I am not possessed of intuitive knowledge.
15. There has never been any one who is not correct (or, upright) himself and can correct others.
16. To see righteousness and not do it, is to want (*lit.* is not to have) courage.
17. The benevolent must have courage: the courageous are not sure to have benevolence.
18. What do you wish me to do, Sir?
19. The farmers wish to till [the soil] in the king's wastes.
20. Agriculture is the foundation (*i. e.* the main support) of life.
21. The learning of old times was for oneself (*i. e.* for one's own improvement): the learning of to day is on account of other men (*i. e.* for the sake of what they will say).
22. Men's minds are unsettled.

14. 生而, *etc.*, a born-and-know-it man. For 知之 *vide* Ex. 4. 30.

15. *chê* is attaehed to the seven preceding words.

18. 予. see Example 5. The question is put into the third person for the sake of politeness. "The gentleman wants me to do what?" This use of tbe third person is very common.

19. 耕者, the farming men, farmers. 野 is said in this passage merely to mean the country, the fields; but 'wastes' makes a very natural translation of it.

20. In this and in the next Example we have another use of *chê*. It here has the effect of turning the preceding verb into a substantive expressing the idea of the verb. *kêng* to farm; *kêng-chê*, that which is farming, the matter of farming, agriculture. 生命, life.

21. 爲; *wei*[4], because of.

[23] 定山之高者與川之大者。[24] 心者生之本也。[25] 王者舟也、民者水也。[26] 大人者、不失其赤子之心者也。[27] 耳長、命必長。[28] 此非野人之語也。

23. To determine the [relative] height of the mountains and size of the rivers.
24. The heart is the source of life.
25. The king is [like] a boat: the people are [like] the water.
26. The great man is he who does not lose his child-like heart.
27. If one's ears be long, one's life is sure to be long.
28. These are not the sayings of a wild (*i. e.* an uncultivated) man.

23. *lit.* to determine of the hills those which are high, *sc.* which are highest. Professor Julien gives this sentence as a specimen of one method of expressing the superlative degree, namely by an adjective in the positive degree, placed after a genitive case.

24. 心者, that which is the heart, = the heart. Here we have *chê* attached to a substantive. It belongs to a class of which Dr. Hirth says, "in explanations and "definitions *chê* is appended to the term to be defined, whereas the characters "forming the explanation are followed by 也, *yeh*." One may add that the *chê* and the corresponding *yeh* perform a useful office by marking with unmistakable distinctness the subject and the predicate of the sentence.

25. *chê* is used as in the last Example.

26. *ta jên chê*, the great man. *chê*, as in Nos. 24, 25. 赤子, *lit.* a naked baby, and so, a child. The *chê* at the end of the Example is simply 'he who'. It is worth while to note that this sentence has been explained by one Chinese commentator in a very different way. He makes the last half of it to be — he who does not lose the hearts of his children, *sc.* of his people.

EXERCISE 7.

VOCABULARY.

所 *so*³, that which; a place.	草 *ts'ao*³, grass, herbs.
及 *chi*², to reach to; to; and.	雖 *sui*¹, although.
矣 *i*³, a final particle.	亦 *i*⁴, also.

富 *fu*^{4}, rich.

以 *i*^{3}, to use, to take; by, with, according to; in order to.

存 *ts‘un*^{2}, to keep, to store.

莫 *mo*^{4}, not.

豈 *ch‘i*^{3}, interrogative particle, which expects the answer *No.*

[1] 人皆有所不爲。

[2] 其所言有信者。有不信者。

[3] 此爲天命所定。

[4] 無所不能、無所不知。

[5] 小人爲不善無所不至。

[6] 見善如不及。

[7] 非爾所及也。

[8] 自古及今未有能行之者也。

TRANSLATION.

1. Men all have that which they do not, *sc.* have something which they will not do.
2. There were some who believed, and some who did not believe what he said.
3. This was fixed by Heaven's decree, (*lit.* this is that which the decree of Heaven fixed).
4. He is omnipotent, omniscient, (*lit.*, he has not that which he cannot, has not that which he knows not).
5. When the mean man practises evil he will proceed to any extreme.
6. To look upon virtue as [something to which one] cannot attain (*i. e.* as requiring one's strongest efforts to reach it).
7. You do not attain to it, (*lit.* it is not that to which you attain).
8. From ancient times till now, there has not been any one able to do it.

1. 所; *so*, says Professor Julien, is a relative pronoun which is always placed after the subject and before the verb which governs it. This states the general rule very well; but in modern Chinese, at any rate, one occasionally meets with cases where *so* precedes an intransitive verb, of which it is evidently the subject. There is an instance in Ex. 25. 20, below.

2. *so*, that which, *ch‘i*, he, *yen*, said, *yu*, there were, *hsin chê*, believers of.

5. *wu so*, he has not that to which, *pu chih*, he does not go. Observe 所, that *to* which.

8. *tzŭ ku*, from old times, *chi chin*, to now, *wei yu*, there has not been, *nêng-hsing-chih chê*, a can-do-it man.

牛[9]馬食草。予[10]欲善、而民善矣、君子之德風、小人之德草。人[11]力所不爲而爲者天也。雖[12]死、其言至今。雖[13]聖人、亦有所不能。富[14]而不貴。富[15]與貴、人之所欲也。以[16]木作弓。

9. Oxen and horses eat grass.
10. If you, Sir, wish for what is good, the people will be good. The moral nature of the superior man is [like] the wind, that of the common people [like] the grass, (*i. e.* the latter is influenced by the former).
11. The doer of what human strength [can] not do, is Heaven.
12. Though he is dead, his words have come down to the present time.
13. Though he is a sage, he, too, has that which he cannot do.
14. Rich but not honourable.
15. Riches and honour are the object of man's desire.
16. To make a bow from wood.

10. 而, *vide* Ex. 4. 26. 矣 gives definiteness and decision to the statement. It can seldom be translated. 德 is used here in a vague sense, not positive virtue, but nature, or character, (Legge).

11. 而 is inserted here probably for euphony; as there is no conjunction required after 所.

15. The 之 here will puzzle the beginner. The explanation seems to be that the speaker regards *so yü* as a substantive. That which he desires = the thing desired. *chih* is thus the ordinary mark of the genitive. In practice it will be found that in such cases as this the translator may simply disregard the *chih.* 'Riches and honour are what men desire'.

16. The primary meaning of 以 is 'to use'. One might translate this sentence by 'to use wood and make a bow'.

所[17]謂大臣者、以道事君、不可、則止。所[18]能爲者、必爲之。君[19]子以仁存心。作[20]此、以存仁心。方[21]四十里、民以爲大。以[22]信義爲事。七[23]十者可以食肉。君[24]仁、莫不仁、君義、莫不義、君正、莫不正。豈[25]有此理。豈[26]非如此。

17. Those who are called great ministers serve their prince according to righteousness, and when [they find that] they cannot, then they stop (*i. e.* they retire).
18. That which I can do, I certainly will do it.
19. The superior man cherishes benevolence [in] his mind.
20. Do this, in order to preserve a benevolent mind!
21. [A park] forty *li* square, the people consider it great.
22. Make sincerity and righteousness your business!
23. Those of seventy [years of age] can eat meat.
24. When the prince is benevolent, all will be benevolent; when the prince is righteous, all will be righteous; when the prince is upright, all will be upright.
25. How should there be this principle? (= This is absurd!).
26. How should it be not like this, (how should it be otherwise)?

17. 所者; when these two words come into the same clause, take them together as a single relative, 'those who', etc.. *cf. Julien, Syntaxe Nouvelle*, Monographie de *so tche*.

19. *i jên, etc.*, to take benevolence and store [it in] the mind, = to store benevolence in the mind.

21. 以爲, to take [it] to be = to consider. The Chinese *li* is about one third of an English mile.

22. Take sincerity and righteousness to be (= as) your business. The phrase might be translated in other ways.

23. 可以, simply 'can'.

24. *mo pu*, *lit.* there will be none who are not.

27 豈不知人老必死。 28 多文爲富。 29 一日不見如三月矣。

27. How should he not know that when a man is old he must die?
28. Much literary knowledge is wealth.
29. One day without seeing her is like three months.

EXERCISE 8.

VOCABULARY.

將 *chiang*[1], to take; a sign of the future tense; *chiang*[4] a general.

問 *wên*[4], to ask, to investigate.

誰 *shui*[2], who?

由 *yu*[2], by, from; origin.

來 *lai*[2], to come.

去 *ch*^c*ü*[1], to go, to go away.

前 *ch*^c*ien*[2], before (in time or place).

後 *hou*[4], after, behind.

夫 *fu*[1], a man; *fu*[2], now; that.

乎 *hu*[2], an interrogative.

從 *ts*^c*ung*[2], to follow, from; *tsung*[4], a follower, an accessory.

孝 *hsiao*[4], filial, dutiful to one's parents.

敢 *kan*[3], dare.

異 *i*[4], different; strange.

地 *ti*[4], the earth, ground, place.

經 *ching*[1], the warp in a loom; to pass through, to manage; a canon, law; a sign of the past tense.

興 *hsing*[1], to rise, to begin, to prosper; to become.

將[1]仁存於心。

TRANSLATION.

1. Cherish benevolence in the heart.

1. 將. We have here a very common use of *chiang*. Sometimes a writer, when framing his sentence, prefers to place the object before the verb. In such case he inserts *chiang* before the object. This arrangement is most often seen when the object consists not of one but of several characters. In translating the sentence there is no need to give any equivalent of *chiang*; but one can do so if one wishes. 'Take benevolence and cherish it in the heart'. In the last Exercise (Ex. 7. 19) we saw *i* 'to use' similarly employed. But *chiang* is the regular word for the purpose.

[2]吾將問之。[3]其不知老之將至。[4]予爲誰。[5]大富由天。[6]誰能出不由戶。[7]問其所由。[8]不知其學問如何。[9]此人來去非我之力。[10]其來在前、我去在後。[11]有福死夫前、無福死夫後。[12]後生不信老人言。[13]吾誰欺、欺天乎。[14]有能一日用其力於仁矣乎。[15]從今而後可知其非孝也。

2. I will ask him.
3. He does not recognize the approach of old age.
4. Who are you, Sir?
5. Great wealth [comes] from heaven.
6. Who can go out except (*lit.* not) by the door?
7. Inquire into his motives.
8. I do not know what his learning is like.
9. This man's coming and going do not depend upon me.
10. He came before I went.
11. [A wife] who has good fortune dies before her husband; she who has not, dies after him.
12. Young men (the later-born) do not believe the old men's words.
13. Whom shall I deceive, shall I deceive Heaven?
14. Is there any one who can apply his strength for a single day to benevolence?
15. Henceforth (from now and afterwards) one may know that he is not filial.

2. *chiang* is here merely a mark of the future tense.
3. *chiang-chih*, about to arrive; as a substantive, 'the approach'.
7. *so* what, *chʻi* he (*i. e.* his conduct), *yu* springs from.
8. *hsüeh wên*, scholarship or learning. 如何, [is] like what, *i. e.* how good it is.
9. is not [a matter of] my strength; = I have no power concerning it. Observe *wo-chih*, my.
10. *lit.*, he came *tsai-chʻien* before, I went *tsai hou* afterwards.

吾[16]不從子之言、以至此矣。吾[17]從大夫之後、不敢不告也。敢[18]問其所以異。予[19]曰、我則異於人、無可無不可。此[20]天地之所以爲大。其[21]人未經過事。夫[22]孝者、天之經、地之義、人之行也。此[23]人來自內地。未[24]有來過如此之多也。未[25]經興工。興[26]則爲王。

16. I did not follow your words, Sir; and so I came to this [state].
17. I follow in the rear of the great officers, [and therefore] I did not dare not to tell [of such a matter].
18. I make bold to ask in what it differs.
19. The Master said, as for me, I am different from [other] men. I have no *cans* or *cannots*. (I am not irrevocably determined on any point).
20. This [is] that by which heaven and earth are great.
21. This man is inexperienced (has not passed through matters).
22. Now, filial piety is the law of heaven, the principle of earth, and the course of men.
23. This man comes from the interior.
24. So many as this have not come before.
25. They have not yet begun work.
26. If one succeeds, then one is a prince.

16. 以, by, whereby; *i chih*, whereby I came to.

18. 所以; *i*, by, *so*, what, = wherein, wherefore.

19. The force of *tsê* is fairly given by 'as for me'.

20. 之, vide Ex. 7. 15.

22. 夫, fu^2, now. *hsiao chê*, that which is filial, filialness.

24. 過, sign of the perfect tense: *lai-kuo*, has come; 如此, like this. 之 turns *ju tzʻŭ* into an adjective qualifying *to*. — It has not been that a thus-like many has come.

25. 經, sign of the past tense, *wei ching* have not.

上[27]老老、而民興孝。誰[28]能知未來之事。後[29]生可畏。無[30]所謂善、無所謂惡。

27. If the ruler treats his aged folk as he ought to treat them, the people will become filial.
28. Who can know the future (*lit.* things which have not yet come)?
29. Youths should be respected.
30. He is not what one would call good, nor what one would call bad.

27. Note 老 used as a verb, 'to treat as old'.

EXERCISE 9.

VOCABULARY.

改 *kai*^{3}, to change.
是 *shih*^{4}, that; is.
養 *yang*^{3}. to rear, to nourish.
教 *chiao*^{1}, to teach, doctrine.
舉 *chü*^{3}, to raise; to undertake.
共 *kung*^{4}, all, together.
衆 *chung*^{4}, crowd, all, many.
居 *chü*^{1}, to dwell.
北 *pei*^{3}, north.
星 *hsing*^{1}, a star.
路 *lu*^{4}, road, path.
成 *chʻêng*^{2}, to accomplish, to perfect.
視 *shih*^{4}, to see, to look at.
聽 *tʻing*^{1}, to hear, to listen.
聞 *wên*^{2}, to hear.
味 *wei*^{4}, taste.

有[1]過必改。過[2]而不改、是謂過矣。三[3]年無改於父之道、可謂孝矣。

TRANSLATION.

1. If one has faults, one must change (must correct) them.
2. [To have] faults and not correct them, that is called a fault, indeed.
3. [If a son] for three years does not change from the way of his father, he may be called filial, indeed.

學[4]者必由是而學。何[5]
以異於是。養[6]民之本
在於衣食。養[7]不教、父
之過。舉[8]善而教不能。
君[9]子不以言舉人。內[10]
外之臣皆舉其德。人[11]
所共知。衆[12]目共見。
如[13]天星之衆多。居[14]於
王所。北[15]辰居其所、而
衆星共之。上[16]天無路、
入地無門。

4. Learners must begin their studies with this (must [begin] from this and learn).
5. By what does it differ from this?
6. The source of the people's nourishment is in food and clothing.
7. To rear [children] and not teach them is a fault of the father.
8. To raise (promote) the virtuous and teach the incapable.
9. The superior man does not promote men on account of their words.
10. The central and provincial officers all exert their powers.
11. Known to every one, (what men all know).
12. Every one saw it.
13. Like the stars of heaven in multitude, (*lit.* like the numerousness of heaven's stars).
14. To dwell in the royal palace.
15. The Pole Star keeps its place, and all the stars bow to it.
16. No road up to heaven, no door into the earth, (no means of escape).

5. *ho i* = *i ho*, by what?
6. *lit.* the root of nourishing the people, etc..
8. 能, here, an adj., 'capable'.
12. *lit.* all eyes together saw it.
13. *chung to*, numerous; here a substantive.
14. 所, a place: *wang so*, the king's place, the royal palace.
15. 共, to salute, to bow to. It is in the third tone, and in modern Chinese it is written with the radical for *hand* at the side.

惟[17]君子能由是路、出入是門
也。居[18]仁由義、大人之事備
矣。所[19]作必成。事[20]雖小、不
作不成。足[21]見此事之必不
能成。視[22]其所爲。民[23]不聽
命。耳[24]聞不如目見。見[25]善
不信、聞惡則信。三[26]日不食、
耳無聞、目無見也。三[27]月不
知肉味。心[28]不在、視而不見、
聽而不聞、食而不知其味。

17. Only the superior man can go by this road, can pass in and out at this gate.
18. When he abides in benevolence and walks in righteousness, the business of the great man is complete.
19. What he is doing is sure to be accomplished.
20. Though a matter be small, if one does not do it, it will not be accomplished.
21. One fully sees the impossibility of accomplishing this matter (*lit.* this matter's impossibility of being accomplished).
22. Look at what he does.
23. The people will not listen to orders.
24. Hearing is not as good as seeing.
25. One sees virtue and does not believe it; one [merely] hears of wickedness and one does believe it.
26. For three days he did not eat, his ears had no [power of] hearing, nor his eyes of seeing.
27. For three months he did not know the taste of meat.
28. If the mind be absent, one looks but does not see, one hears but does not listen, one eats [things] but does not know their taste.

21. The words after *chih* must be looked upon as a substantive, 'impossibility of accomplishment'.

必由之路。[29] 此人語言無味。[30] 寸土皆是王地。[31]

29. The road by which one must go.
30. This man's talk has no flavour (is insipid).
31. Every inch of ground is the Emperor's land.

29. *pi-yu-chih*, the must-be-gone-by, — a participle attached to *lu*.

EXERCISE 10.

VOCABULARY.

同 *t'ung*^{2}, with, together, same.

樂 *lê*^{4}, pleasure, joy.

當 *tang*^{1}, ought; in, at. *tang*^{4}, to represent, stand for; to pledge.

時 *shih*^{2}, time, season.

謀 *mou*^{2}, to plot, to plan.

久 *chiu*^{3}, length of time.

相 *hsiang*^{1}, mutual, towards.

習 *hsi*^{2}, to practise.

初 *ch'u*^{1}, beginning.

遠 *yüan*^{3}, far.

性 *hsing*^{4}, nature, disposition.

近 *chin*^{4}, near.

順 *shun*^{4}, following, in accordance with.

名 *ming*^{2}, a name.

實 *shih*^{2}, true.

中西言語不同。[1] 與我同行之人皆亦見之。[2] 以善爲樂、何樂如此。[3]

TRANSLATION.

1. The languages of China and western countries are different.
2. The men who were going with me all also saw it.
3. To take pleasure in virtue: what pleasure is like this!

1. The ordinary name for China is *chung kuo*, the central country; while foreign nations are *wai kuo*, outside countries. *chung hsi*, Chinese and western, *yen yü*, words and speech, language.

3. 以, *etc.*, to take virtue and make it one's pleasure.

爲[4]民上而不與民同樂者、亦非也。豈[5]不知爲子當孝。非[6]所當爲之事。使[7]民以時。當[8]是時八年於外、三過其門而不入。我[9]力足以舉三百斤。得[10]百里之地而君之。謀[11]事在人、成事在天。君[12]子謀道不謀食。

4. To be the ruler of the people and not rejoice together with the people, is also wrong.
5. How could he fail to know that [he who] is a son must be virtuous.
6. It is not a thing which ought to be done.
7. To employ the people at the proper seasons.
8. At that time he was eight years away from home; and, though he thrice passed by his own door, he did not enter.
9. My strength is sufficient to lift three hundred pounds.
10. To obtain a territory of a hundred *li*, and rule over it.
11. Men plan things (it is in men to plan things), but heaven brings them about.
12. The superior man makes good principles his object, and does not make food.

4. In this instance the *chê* collects all the preceding words into a combined phrase, which forms the subject of the sentence. It equals .... 之事 and not .... 之人. The translation is not 'he who is the ruler', etc.; but 'the being the ruler', etc..

6. *lit.*, it is not a which-one-ought-to-do thing. The three words preceding *chih* are transformed by it into an adjective.

7. *i shih*, according to the season, *i. e.* not calling them out to mend roads in harvest time and so on.

9. *tsu i*, sufficient whereby I might lift. *chin*, the Chinese pound or *catty*. It varies in different trades and in different places, but it is about equal to $1^1/_3$ lbs. av..

10. 君, here a verb.

[13]古人有言、將在謀而不在勇。[14]天下之無道也、久矣。[15]父子不相見。[16]學而時習之。[17]五月初五、八月十五。[18]路遠知馬力、日久見人心。[19]人之初、性本善、性相近、習相遠。[20]聖人之所以同於衆者、性也。[21]好學近於知。[22]人見目前、天見久遠。

13. The ancients had a saying, that the [value of a] general is in his strategy not in his courage.

14. The empire's want of right principles, long has it been.

15. Fathers and sons [can] not see one another.

16. To learn [a thing] and constantly practise it.

17. The fifth day of the fifth month and the fifteenth day of the eighth month.

18. If a journey be long, one learns the strength of one's horse; and time shows (in a long time one sees) men's hearts.

19. [At] the birth of man, his nature is originally good; natures are near to each other (are similar), but practises are far apart.

20. That wherein the sage is similar to mankind in general, is his nature.

21. To be fond of learning is near to knowledge.

22. Men see [what is] before their eyes; heaven's vision is unlimited (sees long and far).

13. 將, *chiang*^{4}, a general.

16. 時, constantly.

17. *chʻu wu*, the 5th day. *Chʻu* is always placed before the numbers of the days of the month, up to the tenth inclusive.

19. For a different translation of the last part of this Example, *vide* Legge's *Analects*, XVII. II.

20. 所以者, that by which, that in which. This combination follows the same rule as *so chê*; *vide* Ex. 7. 17. For 之, *vide* Ex. 7. 15.

21. 知, *chih*^{4}, wisdom, knowledge.

[23]當順古人之道。[24]有其名、未有其實。[25]實心實力作之。[26]名不正則言不順、言不順則事不成。[27]久而自明。[28]順大道走。

23. One ought to follow the path of the men of old.
24. There is the name, but not the reality.
25. To do it with all one's mind and all one's strength (*lit.* with true mind and true strength).
26. If names be not correct, language is not in accordance [with the truth]. If language be not in accordance [with the truth], things will not be accomplished.
27. In time [it will make] itself plain.
28. To follow the high road.

EXERCISE 11.

VOCABULARY.

令 *ling*[4], to command, to cause.
勿 *wu*[2], do not.
利 *li*[4], sharp, profit.
對 *tui*[4], opposite, to match, to reply.
傳 *ch'uan*[2], to tell, to transmit.
法 *fa*[3], means, plan, law, example.
世 *shih*[4], an age, a generation, the world.
先 *hsien*[1], before, former.
師 *shih*[1], a teacher; a capital city.
良 *liang*[2], good.
賊 *tsei*[2], robber, brigand.
分 *fên*[1], to divide; *fên*[4], a share, one's lot, duty.
流 *liu*[2], to flow.
東 *tung*[1], east.
親 *ch'in*[1], parents, relatives, intimate, self.
平 *p'ing*[2], level, even, peaceful, ordinary.

1. 令人去。
2. 其身正、不令而行、其身不正、雖令不從。
3. 勿求富貴名利。
4. 二人所言不對。
5. 王勿異也、王問臣、臣不敢不以正對、王色定。
6. 好事不出門、惡事傳千里。
7. 天子之地方千里。
8. 爲法於天下、可傳於後世。
9. 先人作、後人傳。

TRANSLATION.

1. To order men to go.
2. If his own person be correct, he does not order, and [things] go on. If his own person be not correct, though he gives orders, people do not obey them. (When a prince's personal conduct is correct, his government is effective without the issuing of orders. If his personal conduct is not correct, he may issue orders, but they will not be followed. *Legge*).
3. Do not seek for wealth or honour, fame or gain.
4. The statements of the two men (what the two men say) do not agree.
5. "Let not your Majesty think it strange. Your Majesty asked me (*lit.* your servant), and I did not dare not to answer according to the truth." The king's countenance [became] composed.
6. [The report of] good deeds does not go outside the door: evil deeds are told for a thousand *li*.
7. The emperor's territory (domain) is a thousand *li* square.
8. He was an example to the empire, [and his story] could be handed down to after ages.
9. Former men act; later men tell. (Men recount the deeds of those of old times).

5. 異、here a verb, 'to think it strange', 'to be offended'. Notice, again, that the speaker uses the third person.
sê, colour, often means 'face', 'countenance'.

民[10]後義而先利。先[11]生何爲出此言。聖[12]人百世之師也。三[13]人同行、必有我師。良[14]法有利於民。今[15]之所謂良臣、古之所謂民之賊也。人[16]與人相愛、則不相賊。無[17]聖人之法、後人何以能立。不[18]分好歹。不[19]能分身。在[20]我本分之內。自[21]古三教流傳。風[22]自東北來。

10. The people put righteousness last and gain first.
11. Sir, why do you utter these words.
12. The sage is the teacher of a hundred generations.
13. If I walk with two men, one of them is sure to be able to teach me something. (*lit.* three men walking together, there must be my teacher).
14. Good laws benefit the people.
15. Those who at the present day are called good ministers, are what were formerly called robbers of the people.
16. If men love each other (if man with man mutually loves), they will not prey upon each other.
17. If they had not the example of the sages, how could the men of later times stand?
18. Not to distinguish between good and bad.
19. He cannot divide his body (*i. e.* be in two places at once).
20. It comes within my proper duty.
21. Three religions have come down [to us] from ancient times.
22. The wind is coming from the north-east.

11. *hsien shêng*, elder-born, — a term of respect. *ho wei*[4] for *wei*[4] *ho*, on account of what. *ho* is often placed before the word which governs it: *cf.* N°. 17 of this Exercise.

16. *tsei*, here a verb.

17. *ho i*, by what [means], how.

21. *liu ch‘uan*, have flowed and been transmitted, have come down.

水[23]流無分於東西也。無[24]不知愛其親。平[25]安無事之日。人[26]人親其親、長其長、而天下平。足[27]見其平日用心。東[28]風多雨。君[29]明臣良。古[30]者天子親耕。

23. Water in its flowing makes no distinction between east and west.
24. All know how to love their parents.
25. A time of peace and quiet and no trouble.
26. If every man would love his parents and show respect to his elders, the world would be at peace.
27. One fully sees that he was generally careful.
28. With an east wind there is much rain.
29. If the sovereign be intelligent, his ministers will be good.
30. In antiquity the Emperor himself ploughed.

26. *jên jên*, every one. The duplication of *jên* is a common method of saying 'all men'. Other substantives are duplicated in the same way. **親**, to treat as a parent, *cf.* Ex. 8. 27. **長**, when meaning 'to grow', or, as here, 'an elder', is read *chang*^{3}.

27. *p'ing jih*, generally, usually.

30. *ku chê*, an adverb, — anciently.

EXERCISE 12.

VOCABULARY.

禮 *li*^{3}, ceremony, politeness.
男 *nan*^{2}, male.
家 *chia*^{1}, home, family.
右 *yu*^{4}, right (hand).
左 *tso*^{3}, left (hand).
主 *chu*^{3}, master, lord.
國 *kuo*^{2}, country.
彼 *pi*^{3}, that.
海 *hai*^{3}, sea.
兄 *hsiung*^{1}, elder brother.

弟 *ti*^{4}, younger brother; *t'i*^{4}, the duty of a younger to an elder brother.

然 *jan*^{2}, but; so, yes.

諸 *chu*^{1}, all; a sign of the plural.

察 *ch'a*^{2}, search, examine.

殺 *sha*^{1}, kill.

君[1]子惡勇而無禮者。

曰、[2]學禮乎、對曰、未也、不

學禮無以立。母[3]生男

子。道[4]路，男子由右、女

子由左。不[5]知其君、視

其左右。一[6]人不能事

二主。家[7]有主、國有王。

國[8]雖小、而有君子亦有

野人。彼[9]此相問。彼[10]

國所見日月星辰無異

於中國。

TRANSLATION.

1. The superior man dislikes him who is bold but has not politeness.
2. He said [to me], 'have you learnt [the rules of] propriety?' I replied, 'not yet.' [He said] 'if you do not learn the rules of propriety, your character cannot be established,' (*lit.* you have not whereby to stand).
3. The mother gave birth to a male child.
4. On the road men take the right hand, women the left.
5. If you do not know the prince, look at his attendants.
6. A man cannot serve two masters.
7. The house has its master; the country has its king.
8. Though a country be small, still it has superior men and has also rustics.
9. They asked each other, (*lit.* that one, this one, mutually asked).
10. The sun, moon and stars which one sees [in] that country, are not different from [those in] China.

4. *nan-tzŭ*, often, 'boys', here simply, 'men': so *nü-tzŭ*, 'women'.
5. *tso yu*, those who stand on his right and on his left, his attendants.

天[11]下國家、天下之本在國、
國之本在家、家之本在身。
福[12]如東海。四[13]海之內皆
兄弟也。今[14]日之子弟又
爲將來之父兄。人[15]皆曰
然、我曰不然。食[16]天地自
然之利。察[17]明諸事。左[18]
右皆曰不可、勿聽、諸大夫
皆曰不可、勿聽、國人皆曰
不可、然後察之。殺[19]人如
草。

11. The empire, the state, the family; the root of the empire is in the state, the root of the state is in the family, and the root of the family is in the person.
12. Happiness [vast] as the eastern ocean.
13. All within the four seas are brothers.
14. The sons and younger brothers of the present day will also be the fathers and elder brothers of the future.
15. Men all say Yes, but I say No.
16. To live (to feed) upon the natural gifts (benefits) of the sky and earth.
17. To examine into all the matters.
18. When those in attendance [on you] all say, '[this man] will not do', do not listen to them; when the great officers all say, 'he will not do,' do not listen; when the people of your country all say, 'he will not do', after that examine into it (into the case).
19. To slay people as [one would cut down] grass.

13. *hsiung ti* is used sometimes for 'younger brothers', sometimes, as here, for 'brothers' generally.

14. *chiang lai*, the about to come, the future.

16. *tzŭ jan*, of itself so, naturally; *tzŭ-jan-chih*, natural. Sky and earth, = nature.

17. 明 is easy to understand, but is hard to translate here without giving it too much weight. *ch'a ming*, to examine and bring to light, to find out the truth about.

夫[20]子何以知其將見殺。
吾[21]今而後知殺人親之重也、殺人之父、人亦殺其父、殺人之兄、人亦殺其兄。
彼[22]此相親相愛。
道[22]德仁義非禮不成。

20. How did you know, Sir, that he was going to be killed.

21. Now and for the future I know the heavy [consequences] of killing people's near relations. If any one kills a man's father, that man will kill *his* father. If he kills a man's elder brother, that man will kill *his* elder brother.

22. They were intimate and affectionate with each other.

23. Religion, virtue, charity, righteousness, are not complete without ceremoniousness.

20. *fu tzŭ*, a term of respect, much like *tzŭ* alone. It is often applied to Confucius. His name was *K'ung*; and the word Confucius is merely *K'ung-fu-tzŭ*, latinized. 將, sign of the future; 見, to experience, throws the following verb into the passive voice.

21. *sha jên ch'in*; the mention of brothers, below, shows that *ch'in* here includes other near relations besides parents. 亦, also, in like manner.

EXERCISE 13.

VOCABULARY.

服 *fu*[2], to submit; to make to submit.

聲 *shêng*[1], sound, voice.

喜 *hsi*[3], joy, gladness.

忘 *wang*[4], forget.

姓 *hsing*[4], name.

歸 *kuei*[1], to return, to revert, to belong to.

窮 *ch'iung*[2], poor, exhausted.

離 *li*[2], to separate; from.

故 *ku*[4], cause, therefore; old; die.

望 *wang*[4], to look towards, to look forward to.

願 *yüan*[4], to wish, to be willing.

易 *i*[4], to change; easy.

銀 *yin*[2], silver.

錢 *ch'ien*[2], money; a "mace", or the tenth of a Chinese ounce.

達 *ta*[2], to penetrate, to progress.

王[1]問曰、何爲則民服。上[2]好義、則民莫敢不服。以[3]善養人、然後能服天下。有[4]理不在高聲。吾[5]非與之同時、親聞其聲、見其色也。子[6]路、人告之以有過、則喜。父[7]母愛之、喜而不忘。見[8]利忘義。忘[9]生敢死之心。百[10]姓聞王鼓之聲。

TRANSLATION.

1. The king asked saying 'what shall I do to make the people submissive'? (*lit.* do what, then the people will submit?)
2. If the ruler loves righteousness, the people will not dare not to be submissive.
3. If [a prince] nourish men by his goodness, afterwards he will be able to subdue the [whole] empire.
4. A man is not in the right because he talks loud.
5. I was not [living] at the same time with them, so as myself to hear their voices and see their faces.
6. *Tzŭ-lu* used to rejoice, when any one told him of his having a fault.
7. When his parents love him, a son rejoices and does not forget [them].
8. To forget righteousness when one sees gain.
9. A heart which forgets life and dares to die.
10. The people hear the noise of the king's drums.

4. *yu li*, to have reason, to be in the right, — being in the right does not consist in a loud voice.

5. 親, myself.

6. Tzŭ-lu was a favourite disciple of Confucius. *i yu kuo*, taking [the fact that] he had a fault, *kao chih*, told him. After *kao*, to tell, it is common to find the matter told preceded, as here, by *i*.

10. 百姓, always pronounced *po-hsing*, the hundred names, the people.

二[11]百年來、百姓相安無事。視[12]死如歸。其[13]身正而天下歸之。爲[14]不順於父母、如窮人無所歸。離[15]家不遠。士[16]窮不失義、達不離道、故民不失望。君[17]子上達、小人下達。此[18]事不可、何以故。四[19]海之內皆擧首而望之。不[20]願離家、遠居異地。

11. For two hundred years past the people have been at peace together, and without trouble.
12. To look upon death like going home.
13. If his person (his personal conduct) be correct, the whole empire will turn to him.
14. Because he was not in accord with his parents, he [felt] like a poor man [who] has no [place] to which to turn.
15. Not far from home.
16. The scholar when poor does not lose his righteousness; when prosperous he does not leave the proper path; therefore the people are not disappointed in their expectations (*lit.* do not lose their hopes).
17. The superior man progresses upwards, the mean man progresses downwards.
18. This matter will not do — for what reason?
19. All within the four seas raised their heads and looked towards him.
20. He was unwilling to leave his home and dwell far off in a strange land.

11. 來, up to the present time.
14. *wei*^{4}, because.
16. 達, to penetrate, hence, to make one's way, to succeed in life.
18. *ho i ku* for *i ho ku*, by what cause, for what reason.

前[21]日願見而不可得。天[22]命不易。古[23]者易子而教之。古[24]人不用金銀、以其所有易其所無。西[25]國以金銀爲錢、銀錢十當金錢之一。水[26]流千里歸大海。不[27]服水土。

21. On a former day I wished to see [you], but I failed to do so, (*lit.* could not obtain it).
22. The decrees of Heaven do not change.
23. The ancients exchanged children and taught them (*i. e.* used to teach each other's children).
24. The men of old did not use gold or silver: they bartered what they had for what they had not.
25. Western nations make money of gold and silver: ten [pieces of] silver money stand for one of gold money.
26. Water flows a thousand *li* and goes into the sea.
27. The climate disagrees with him.

24. *lit.*, using what they had, they exchanged [it for] what they had not.
27. *pu fu*; he does not submit to, 'he cannot stand', *shui t'u* the climate.

EXERCISE 14.

VOCABULARY.

直 *chih*², straight.
報 *pao*⁴, to requite; to report.
怨 *yüan*⁴, resentment, grievance.
或 *huo*⁴, perhaps, either, some one.
思 *ssŭ*¹, to think.
治 *chih*⁴, to govern.
修 *hsiu*¹, to repair, to put in order.
惑 *huo*⁴, doubt; to deceive.
若 *jo*⁴, as, like; if.
要 *yao*⁴, to want; important.
短 *tuan*³, short.

道[1]直如矢。以[2]是故知、善者有報、惡者有對。正[3]己而不求與人、則無怨。或[4]未見之、或見而不信。三[5]思而後行。安[6]上治民莫善於禮。西[7]國之禮、二人或行或坐、以右爲上。或[8]曰、以德報怨、何如、子曰、何以報德、以直報怨、以德報德。

TRANSLATION.

1. The road is straight as an arrow.
2. For this reason [you may] know that the virtuous have their recompense and the wicked have their requital.
3. If one rectifies oneself and does not seek anything from others, then one has no resentment.
4. Either they did not see it, or they saw it and did not believe it.
5. Think thrice and afterwards act.
6. To give rest to the ruler and to govern [well] the people there is nothing better than propriety.
7. [According to] the etiquette of western nations, when two men are either walking or sitting [together], the right hand side is considered the first place.
8. Some one said, what do you think of repaying injury with kindness? The Master said, with what [then] will you repay kindness? Repay injuries with justice, and kindness with kindness.

6. *an*, to rest, *shang*, the ruler.

8. **德** must here be taken as 'kindness'. **怨**, that which causes resentment; wrong, injury. If one had only the four words *i tê pao yuan*, they would be perfectly translated by 'do good for evil'. **何如**, what [is that] like? What do you think of that? **以直**, with justice.

[9] 君子不可以不修身、思修身、不可以不事親、思事親、不可以不知人、思知人、不可以不知天。

[10] 知所以修身、則知所以治人、知所以治人、則知所以治天下國家矣。

[11] 左道惑衆。

[12] 三十而立、四十而不惑、五十而知天命、六十而耳順、七十而從心所欲。

[13] 視人之家若視其家。

9. The sovereign cannot but cultivate his character (*lit.* put in order his own person). If he desire (think) to cultivate his character, he cannot but serve his parents. If he desire to serve his parents, he cannot but know men. If he desire to know men, he cannot but know Heaven.
10. If he know by what means to cultivate his character, he will know by what means to govern men. If he know by what means to govern men, he will know by what means to govern the Empire, [its] states [and its] families.
11. To deceive the multitude with false doctrines.
12. At thirty I stood firm: at forty I did not doubt: at fifty I knew the decrees of Heaven: at sixty my ears were obedient: at seventy I [could] follow what my heart desired (without transgressing).
13. To regard [other] men's families as one regards one's own family.

9. *chün-tzü*, the sovereign, (*Legge*); *pu k'o-i*, cannot, *pu hsiu*, not cultivate, etc..
10. *chih*, if he knows, *so i*, with what (= how), *hsiu*, to cultivate, etc..
11. *tso*, false or heretical.
12. This passage is part of an account of Confucius, given by himself.
13. *ch'i chia*, his family.

14 我要知彼人何姓何名、若長若短若中、若黑若白。

15 勿言人之短。

16 是爲至要。

17 何國不以得民心爲要。

18 世上無直人。

19 齊家、治國、平天下。

14. I want to know what is that man's surname, and what is his name: whether he be tall or short, or of medium height: whether he be dark or fair.
15. Do not speak of [other] men's shortcomings.
16. This is extremely important.
17. What nation does not consider it important to win the hearts of the people?
18. There are no upright men in the world.
19. To regulate the family, to govern the state, to give tranquillity to the empire.

14. *hsing* is always used by the Chinese for the surname; and *ming* for the personal name, equivalent to our Christian name.
16. *chih*, extreme; cf. Ex. 3. 22.
17. *pu i wei*, does not consider, *yao*, important, *tê*, to win, etc..
19. *ch'i*, even, regular; to make regular, to regulate.

EXERCISE 15.

VOCABULARY.

起 *ch'i*^{3}, to rise, begin.

念 *nien*^{4}, to think, to study, to read.

乃 *nai*^{3}, but, however, indeed.

宜 *i*^{2}, to be right, fitting, ought.

字 *tzŭ*^{4}, word.

他 *t'a*^{1}, other; (in spoken language, *he*).

肯 *k'ên*^{3}, to choose, to be willing.

費 *fei*^{4}, spend.

等 *teng*^{3}, a grade, class; a sign of the plural; to wait.

常 *ch'ang*^{2}, constant, frequent, usual.

忠 *chung*^{1}, loyal, faithful.

須 *hsü*^{1}, must, necessary.

亂 *luan*^{4}, disorder.

疑 *i*^{2}, doubt, suspicion.

自[1]明日起。一[2]日不念
善、諸惡自皆起。此[3]乃
爾皆宜思念。子[4]不學
非所宜。人[5]地相宜。
我[6]乃不願忘之。三[7]字
經與千字文、爲幼子所
念。先[8]有自己、後有他
人。雖[9]曰不肯費錢、必
有他故。小[10]人不肯爲
君子。其[11]爲平等之人。
爾[12]等明知此爲常事。

TRANSLATION.

1. Beginning from to-morrow.
2. If for a single day one does not think of goodness, all [kinds of] wickedness will spring up of themselves.
3. This, indeed, you ought all to reflect upon.
4. That a boy should not study, is not what he ought [to do].
5. The man and the place suit each other.
6. I, however, am not willing to forget it.
7. The Three-character Classic and the Thousand-character Composition are what children study.
8. Oneself comes first, other people come afterwards.
9. Though he says that [it is because] he does not choose to spend money, he must have other reasons.
10. The mean man does not choose to be a superior man.
11. He is a man of ordinary class.
12. You well know that this is a common occurrence.

1. *ming jih*, to morrow; so *ming nien*, next year.

5. This sentence is used with reference to officials and their posts.

7. These are two Chinese school-books, the first being in lines of three words each, the second consisting of exactly a thousand words, all different.

12. 等 here is simply a sign of the plural: *êrh têng*, you. In the next Example, N°. 13, it is again a sign of the plural, but with this difference, namely that it means 'and others'. In neither Example can there be any difficulty in deciding as to which of these two classes the *têng* belongs. In the first there is no reason whatever for inserting 'and others'; in the second the sentence would be nonsense without it. But the student will meet with passages where he must feel doubt as to

六[13]月初九等日。

九[14]世同居。

君[15]子有九思、視思明、疑思問、言思忠、見得思義。

為[16]子必孝、為臣必忠。

常[17]言道、要知山下路、須問過來人。

聖[18]人治天下、當察亂何自起。

亂[19]起不相愛、臣子不孝君父、所謂亂也。

13. On the ninth and other days of the sixth month.

14. Nine generations dwelt together.

15. The superior man has nine [things which] he thinks about: [in regard to] seeing, he thinks about distinctness: in regard to what he doubts, he thinks of questioning [others]: in regard to his speech, he thinks about honesty: when he sees gain, he thinks of righteousness; *etc.*, *etc.*.

16. He who is a son must be filial; he who is a minister must be loyal.

17. A common saying declares, 'If you wish to know the road at the hill foot, you must ask the men who come across'.

18. When a sage governs the empire, he must find out what disorder springs from.

19. Disorder springs from [people's] not loving each other: the minister's not being dutiful to the monarch, the son's not being dutiful to his father, are what is called disorder.

which meaning to take. The best rule for him will be that, wherever the word or words qnalified by *têng* either are necessarily plural, *e. g.* the names of two persons or things, or are capable of taking a plural, *e. g. ping*, a soldier, he should assume that the case is one of simple plural; *unless* something in the context shows him that 'and others' is the more reasonable interpretation. It is to be feared that this rule will not carry the student safely through the difficulty in every case; though it probably would so carry a Chinese well acquainted with the subject matter of the passage. (*Cf.* Dr. Hirth's *Notes on the Chinese Documentary Style*, *sub voce* '*têng*').

18. **何自**, from what.

19. **臣子**, the minister and the son.

[20] 王曰、我欲作大鼓、有能爲之者乎、衆臣對曰、臣等無能爲之者、有一臣常忠於上、前對曰、臣能爲之、當須大費。[21] 疑人不用、用人不疑。[22] 我不能等。

20. The king said, 'I wish to construct a large drum. Is there any one able to make it?' The ministers in general replied 'None of your servants can make it.' There was one minister, who was always loyal to his lord, [who came] forward and replied, 'Your servant can make it; [but] it will be absolutely necessary [to have] a large sum of money.'

21. If you suspect a man, do not employ him; if you employ a man, do not suspect him.

22. I cannot wait.

20. 有能...乎, *lit.*, is there a can-make-it man? *ch'ên têng*, *pl.*, ministers. [Among] your ministers there is not a can-make-it man. *tang hsü*, a strong 'must', — absolutely neeessary. 費, to spend, expenditure, money.

EXERCISE 16.

VOCABULARY.

兩 *liang*³, two, both; a Chinese ounce or "tael".

識 *shih*⁴, to know, recognize.

某 *mou*³, "a certain".

第 *ti*⁴, order, series.

次 *tz'ŭ*⁴, second, next; a time.

數 *shu*⁴, number, several.

萬 *wan*⁴, ten thousand.

少 *shao*³, few; *shao*⁴, young.

餘 *yü*², remainder.

始 *shih*³, beginning, first.

終 *chung*¹, end, last.

讀 *tu*², to read, to study.

書 *shu*¹, book, anything written or printed.

通 *t'ung*¹, penetrate, pierce through; wholly; understand.

熟 *shu*², ripe, cooked, experienced.

兩人相識。[1] 不識姓名之人。[2] 六兩七錢銀子。[3] 五百九十兩正。[4] 某月某日。[5] 多識於草木之名。[6] 第三次。[7] 又將此事次第告之。[8] 生而知之者上也、學而知之者次也。[9] 數十萬人。[10] 一百萬。[11] 萬無一失。[12] 目前事多人少。[13]

TRANSLATION.

1. The two men know each other.
2. A man, whose name is unknown.
3. Six ounces and seven tenths of silver, (six taels seven mace).
4. 590 taels exactly.
5. On a certain day in a certain month.
6. To have much knowledge of the names of plants and trees.
7. The third time.
8. Moreover he told him this matter point by point.
9. Those who are possessed of intuitive knowledge take the first place; those who know things by learning come next.
10. Several hundred thousand men.
11. A million.
12. Not one lost in ten thousand.
13. At the moment affairs are many and men few.

2. *lit.*, an unknown-surname-and-name man.

5. *mou* is used with reference to persons, places and other things, when the writer is unable or does not care to mention the name, place, etc..

7. Ordinal numbers are formed in Chinese by placing 第 before the cardinal numbers.

8. 將, cf. Ex. 8. 1. *ts'ü ti*, order, sequence, in proper order.

9. *vide* Ex. 4. 30 and Ex. 6. 14.

10. As this and the next Example show, the Chinese count numbers above ten thousand not by multiples of a thousand, but by multiples of ten thousand.

人[14]數至少有百餘。不[15]分老少。少[16]年子弟。彼[17]國水路至中國、有五萬餘里。生[18]死爲人之始終。事[19]有終始。經[20]書不可不讀。欲[21]知天下事、須讀古人書。通[22]古今若親目。治[23]人者食於人、天下之通義也。大[24]小麥一年一熟。如[25]此可得熟手。首[26]孝弟、次見聞、知某數、識某名、一而十、十而百、百而千、千而萬。

14. The number of men, at the very fewest, was a hundred and more.
15. Making no distinction between old and young.
16. The young folk.
17. The way from that country to China by water is over fifty thousand *li*.
18. Birth and death are the beginning and end of man.
19. Affairs have their beginnings and endings.
20. The Canons and Books cannot but be studied (must be studied).
21. If one wishes to know the affairs of the empire, one must read the books of the ancients.
22. To see through past and present, as though with one's own eyes.
23. That those who govern men should be supported by (live upon) men, is the universal principle of the world.
24. Barley and wheat have one crop in the year.
25. Thus one can obtain experienced hands (*sc.* men).
26. First filial piety and brotherly duty, next seeing and hearing

14. *chih* has its meaning of 'extreme'.

16. *tzŭ ti*, young fellows. *shao⁴ nien*, young in years.

20. These are the Five Canons and the Four Books, which are the most important classical works of China.

24. Barley is called *ta mai*, wheat *hsiao mai*. *i shu*, one ripening, *i.e.*, one crop.

26. This and the following Example will give an idea of the Three Character

[27] 爲學者必有初、小學終、至四書、孝經通、四書熟、如六經、始可讀。[28] 初次見面。[29] 學無老少、達者爲先。

(*sc.* the acquisition of knowledge); know certain numbers, learn certain names; one and ten, ten and a hundred, a hundred and a thousand, a thousand and ten thousand.

27. He who is a learner must have a beginning; when the Small Learning is finished, he proceeds to the Four Books; when the Canon of Filial Piety is understood, and the Four Books are thoroughly known, [works such] as the Six Canons can then be studied [by him].

28. To meet for the first time.

29. In learning there is no [distinction between] old and young: he who succeeds is first.

Classic (*cf.* Ex. 15. 7). Though it is extremely simple, still in it style and grammar are somewhat subordinated to metre and rhyme. 弟, *t'i*, brotherly duty.

27. 如, such as. In his notes to the *San Tzŭ Ching*, Dr. Giles assigns another meaning to *ju*. Six Canons, see Ex. 18. 9. 始, then, or, then only.

EXERCISE 17.

VOCABULARY.

號 *hao*⁴, name, mark, signal.	發 *fa*¹, to send, to send forth.
商 *shang*¹, to deliberate; to trade; name of a dynasty.	病 *ping*⁴, disease, fault.
講 *chiang*³, to discuss; to investigate.	最 *tsui*⁴, very, most.
論 *lun*⁴, to reason, discuss.	間 *chien*¹, space between, during.
運 *yün*⁴, to revolve, to transport.	冬 *tung*¹, winter.
	夏 *hsia*⁴, summer.
	春 *ch'un*¹, spring.

[1]國號商。 [2]不聽號令。 [3]講明經書。 [4]言道講理。 [5]不可講論人之好歹。 [6]無論遠近。 [7]日月運行。 [8]運米出口。 [9]文書未發。 [10]病發最重。 [11]天地之間無此法。 [12]冬日可愛、夏日可畏。 [13]上年冬間及本年春間。 [14]齊食齊有味。 [15]欠錢大王。

TRANSLATION.

1. The country was called Shang.
2. They do not listen to the words of command.
3. To explain (discuss and make plain) the Canons and Books.
4. To speak of reason and talk of principles.
5. One may not discuss people's good and bad [qualities].
6. Never mind (*or*, without taking into account) whether it be far or near.
7. Sun and moon proceed with their revolutions.
8. To export rice, (*lit.*, to convey rice out of port).
9. The despatch has not been sent.
10. His sickness is very severe.
11. Neither in heaven nor in earth is there this law.
12. The winter sun (the sun in winter) is pleasant; the sun in summer is to be dreaded.
13. During the winter of last year and the spring of this.
14. Eating together, and having (*i. e.*, enjoying) the taste together.
15. In the owing of money a great prince.

1. Shang, the name of an ancient Chinese dynasty. It has always been a common practice among the Chinese to call their country by the name of the reigning dynasty.

7. *yün hsing*, *lit.*, revolving proceed.

8. *k'ou*, a mouth, is commonly used (1) for a harbour or port, (2) for a pass through the mountains.

10. *fa* is here something like 'develop'.

11. *chien*, not 'between', but 'in the space of'.

[16]背理而行、以惡爲能。[17]願人有失、離人骨肉。[18]出言要順人心。[19]道吾惡者是吾師、吾好者是吾賊。[20]上天有路、無人走。[21]聽天所命、不念人過。[22]作千日鬼、無如作一日人。[23]事君要忠、親要孝。[24]一家養女、百家求。[25]一日爲師、終身爲父。[26]吾有一要言相告。

16. To act contrary to right, and to take wickedness to be ability.
17. To wish that men may have losses, and to separate near relatives.
18. In speaking one should be in accord with people's feelings.
19. He who tells [me] of my sins is my teacher; he who tells [me] of my virtues is my robber (robs me).
20. There is a road [leading] to heaven, but no men go [along it].
21. Listen to that which heaven commands; and do not think of men's faults.
22. To be a ghost for a thousand days is not so good as to be a man for one.
23. In serving a prince one wants loyalty; in serving parents one wants filial duty.
24. One family rears a daughter, a hundred families seek her.
25. One is a teacher for one day, a father [until] the end of one's life.
26. I have something important to tell you.

16. *pei*, to turn the back on.
17. *li jên ku jou*, to separate men's bones and flesh, to separate people who are as closely connected as if they were parts of the same body.
19. 是 is here the copula, 'is', and not, 'that man' [is].
22. *wu ju*, not as, not so good as.
26. 相, to [you]. It does not here mean 'mutually'.

不[27]可自存欺人之心。彼[28]此皆興大師。我[29]亦不敢從爾去也。三[30]十六萬八千九百七十四兩五錢二分。四[31]萬六千九百萬人。

27. One may not cherish in oneself the intention of cheating people.
28. They each raised a large army.
29. I also do not dare to accompany you.
30. 368, 974 taels, 5 mace, 2 candareens.
31. Four hundred and sixty nine million men.

28. *pi tz‘ŭ*, the one and the other, *chieh*, both. 師, an army.
29. *ts‘ung êrh ch‘ü*, following you to go.
30. 分, a candareen, the tenth part of a *ch‘ien*, or mace, and the hundredth part of a tael.

EXERCISE 18.

VOCABULARY.

甚 *shên*[4], very.	南 *nan*[2], south.
害 *hai*[4], harm.	秋 *ch‘iu*[1], autumn.
微 *wei*[1], minute, small.	云 *yun*[2], say.
議 *i*[4], deliberate, discuss.	詩 *shih*[1], poetry.

其[1]利非甚大、其害非甚微也。大[2]王當知、如此之病爲人所不能治。

TRANSLATION.

1. The gain is not very great; the harm is not very small.
2. Your Majesty must know that a sickness such as this, is what men can not cure.

1. 其, the, — emphatic.
2. *ju tz‘ŭ chih*; cf. Ex. 8. 24.

[3]利國利民之事、雖小必爲、害民病國之事、雖微必去。[4]兩事微有不同。[5]人心不定、議論最多。[6]彼此商議通商之事。[7]南風發於春間及秋間、冬時甚少、夏時最多。[8]日春夏、日秋冬、此四時運不窮。[9]三字經云、詩書易、禮春秋、號六經、當講求。[10]念過詩經。

3. Things which benefit the country and benefit the people, — though they be small, one must do them; things which harm the people and hurt the country, — though they be small, one must do away with them.
4. The two affairs have a slight difference [between them].
5. Men's minds are unsettled, and there is a very great amount of talk (*or*, of criticism).
6. They consulted with each other about matters of international trade.
7. The south wind blows in spring and in autumn: in the winter season there is very little of it, in summer time there is the greatest amount.
8. One speaks of spring and summer, one speaks of autumn and winter: these four seasons revolve unceasingly.
9. The Three Character Classic says: The Poems, The History, The Changes, The [two books of] Ceremonies, The Spring and Autumn [annals], are called the Six Canons: one ought to study them thoroughly.
10. He has studied the Book of Poetry.

6. *t'ung*, passing through; *t'ung shang* is the recognized term for trade between China and foreign countries.

8. *pu ch'iung*, unceasingly, *lit.*, not exhausted.

9. The Six Canons: these are now called *wu ching*, the Five Canons, there being only one Book of Ceremonies instead of two. *chiang ch'iu*; *chiang*, to investigate, *ch'iu*, to seek; *chiang-ch'iu*, to pay close attention to, to study diligently at anything.

詩[11]云、自東自西自南自北、無思不服。

自[12]己不正、安能正他。

最[13]愛論長論短。

人[14]云我亦云。

病[15]從口入。

害[16]人害己害自身。

前[17]事之不忘後事之師也。

近[18]水知魚性、近山識鳥音。

山[19]上有直木、世上無直人。

人[20]窮犬也欺。

天[21]下惟理可以服人。

一[22]人作事一人當。

11. The [Book of] Poetry says: from the east, from the west, from the south, from the north, none thought of not submitting.
12. If one be not upright oneself, how can one make others upright?
13. He is very fond of discussing people's merits and shortcomings (*i. e.* their characters).
14. What other men say, I also say.
15. Disease enters by the mouth.
16. When one injures people, one injures oneself, one injures one's own person.
17. Remembrance of the past is the guide for the future.
18. [He who lives] near water understands the nature of fish; [he who lives] near the mountains knows the notes of birds.
19. On the mountains there are straight trees; in the world there are not straight-forward men.
20. When a man is poor, even the dogs ill-treat him.
21. [Throughout] the world only right can make men submit.
22. One man performs an act, one man (*i. e.*, the same man) bears [the consequences].

12. *an*, interrogative — How?
16. *tzŭ*, of oneself, one's own.
17. *lit.*, the not forgetting of former matters is the teacher of future matters.
20. *yeh*, also, — the dogs too.

[23]存忠孝心、行仁義事。[24]人生一世、草生一春。[25]秋月分外明。

23. Keep a loyal and filial heart, perform philanthropic and righteous acts.
24. Man lives one term of life, grass lives one spring.
25. The autumn moon is exceptionally bright.

25. *fên*⁴ *wai*, beyond its share.

EXERCISE 19.

VOCABULARY.

應 *ying*¹, ought.
既 *chi*⁴, since, already.
難 *nan*², difficult; *nan*⁴, hardship, adversity.
但 *tan*⁴, only, but.
即 *chi*², then; near; at once.
罪 *tsui*⁴, crime, punishment.
犯 *fan*⁴, to offend, to transgress.
輕 *ch'ing*¹, light.
物 *wu*⁴, matter, thing.
情 *ch'ing*², feelings, affection, circumstances.
財 *ts'ai*², wealth.
合 *ho*², union, in accordance with.
受 *shou*⁴, to receive, to suffer.
禁 *chin*⁴, to prohibit, to prevent.
意 *i*⁴, thought, idea, intention.

[1]誰應爲王。[2]我應爲大。[3]爾既爲大、聽爾前行。[4]既有此風、必有大雨。

TRANSLATION.

1. Who ought to be king?
2. I ought to be chief.
3. Since you are chief, I will let you go in front.
4. As there is this wind, there will certainly be heavy rain.

3. *t'ing*, to hear, to acquiesce, to allow.

[5]上山甚難、下山甚易。[6]此
擧不但今年難行、卽將來
亦不可行。[7]不但小民、卽
大夫亦信其爲實。[8]衆人
卽行共議。[9]殺一無罪非
仁也。[10]天子犯法與民同
罪。[11]無論罪犯輕重。[12]此
人年輕。[13]無足輕重之物。
[14]物之不齊物之情也。[15]我
等情願同死。[16]小財不出、
大財難得。

5. To go up hill is very difficult; to go down hill is very easy.
6. This measure is not only difficult to carry out this year, but in the future also it will be impracticable.
7. Not only the common people, but the great men also believed it to be true.
8. The whole body of men then proceeded to consult together.
9. To kill a single innocent man is to be wanting in benevolence.
10. If the Emperor offends against the law, his guilt is the same as a private person's.
11. Never mind whether the offence committed be light or heavy.
12. This man is young.
13. A thing of no importance.
14. It is the nature of things to be unequal.
15. We are willing to die together.
16. If one will not spend small sums, great wealth is hard to acquire.

6. 卽 is not 'an adversative conjunction', though English idiom sometimes requires one to translate it by 'but'. Occasionally one is unable to express it at all in translation.

9. 罪; supply 人; *wu tsui jên*, innocent man.

13. *lit.*, not enough [for one to consider its] lightness or heaviness.

14. *lit.*, the inequality of things is the nature of things.

15. 情願, to wish, to be willing.

犯[17]有不法情事。生[18]
人不能一日無用、卽
不可一日無財。合[19]
而爲一。合[20]則不受
人欺。前[21]日之不受
是、則今日受之非也、
今日之受是、則前日
之不受非也。合[22]行
示禁。國[23]家立法之
意、不過教民爲善、禁
民爲非。

17. To have committed unlawful acts.
18. Living man cannot for a single day avoid using things, and therefore cannot for a single day be without funds.
19. To unite and become one.
20. If people unite, they are not ill-treated by others.
21. If your refusal to accept [a gift] on a previous occasion was right, your acceptance of one to day was wrong; if your acceptance of one to day was right, your previous refusal was wrong.
22. It is my duty to issue a proclamation forbidding [the practice].
23. The government's idea in enacting laws is nothing more than to cause the people to do good and to prevent the people from doing wrong.

17. *fan*, he is guilty of, *yu*, having (*sc.* doing), *pu fa*, unlawful, *ch'ing shih*, matters, acts. The construction of this sentence is explained in the above way by an accomplished Chinese gentleman. But, judging from the numerous instances that one finds in modern written Chinese of 有 following another verb, one would prefer to say, *fan yu*, to commit and to have, = to have committed.

20. 受; *shou*, to suffer, is one of the words used in Chinese to express the passive voice.

21. *lit.*, if the former day's non-acceptance [was] right, etc.; 是 is often used in opposition to 非, — right and wrong. 也; observe how each horn of the dilemma is terminated by *yeh*, and how the passage is simplified thereby.

22. 合; supply 理, right, principle. *ho*, it is in accordance with right, = it is my duty, *hsing*, to proceed, *shih*, to issue a proclamation, etc..

23. *kuo-chia*, the state, the government. *pu kuo*, is not beyond, is merely to.

24 事有如意、有不如意也。

25 兩人意見不同。

26 大難不死必有後福。

24. There are some things which are agreeable (are according to one's idea), some which are not agreeable.
25. The two men's views are different.
26. He who escapes from a great calamity (*lit.*, in great calamity does not die), must have future good fortune [in store for him].

25. 意；*i-chien*, view, opinion.

EXERCISE 20.

VOCABULARY.

恐 *k‘ung*^{3}, to fear.
活 *huo*^{2}, alive.
復 *fu*^{2}, back, again.
開 *k‘ai*^{1}, to open.
進 *chin*^{1}, to advance, to enter.
尚 *shang*^{4}, still, in addition to.
已 *i*^{3}, to finish, to stop; already.
查 *ch‘a*^{2}, to examine.
屬 *shu*^{3}, to belong to, to be.
凡 *fan*^{2}, all, whatsoever.
氣 *ch‘i*^{4}, breath, air.
官 *kuan*^{1}, an officer, an official; official.
雪 *hsueh*^{3}, snow.
連 *lien*^{2}, to connect, to join.
冷 *leng*^{3}, cold.
苦 *k‘u*^{3}, bitter, affliction.

1 恐不能活。

2 不知死活。

3 死者不可復活。

4 開門進內。

TRANSLATION.

1. I fear that he cannot live.
2. Not to know life from death, (Extreme stupidity).
3. Those who are dead cannot come to life again.
4. To open the door and enter.

[5]恐將來尙爲害也。

[6]以恐畏之故、不敢前進。

[7]一見此風、應卽改路、不可前進。

[8]已經出示開禁。

[9]未查者須先查、已查者又須復查。

[10]尙有一所至今尙未開工。

[11]事雖議定、實屬難行。

[12]七百口共食、凡屬一家一姓。

[13]字有出氣不出氣之分。

[14]凡有血氣者莫不愛親。

5. I fear that in the future it will still be a [cause of] harm.

6. By reason of their being afraid, they did not dare to advance.

7. Immediately that you meet with (*lit.*, once you see) this wind, you ought thereupon to change your course, and you must not go forward.

8. He has already issued a proclamation removing the prohibition.

9. The matters which have not been investigated must first be investigated; and those which have been, must be investigated again.

10. There still is one place, [where] up to the present they have not yet begun work.

11. Though the affair has been discussed and settled, it really is difficult to carry out.

12. Seven hundred persons took their meals together, all belonging to one family and being of one surname.

13. Words differ by being aspirated or being unaspirated.

14. Of all animate objects (*lit.* of all that have blood and breath), there are none that do not love their parents.

6. **以**, by, **故**, the reason.

8. **已**, *i*; note the difference in form between this character and **己** self. *i-ching*, a common sign of the past tense.

13. **出氣**, to put forth breath, — the Chinese term for what we call the aspirating of words. *lit.*, words have the difference of aspiration and non-aspiration.

14. **凡**; *fan* goes with *chê*, — all those which.

[15]忠君愛民之官。

[16]凡為地方官者。

[17]一經查出、卽將田地入官。

[18]下雨下雪、三日不已。

[19]一連數日南風大發。

[20]其色雪白、衆人所愛。

[21]連日大雪、其冷乃十餘年來所未經。

[22]多受苦難。

[23]天氣大冷、甚受辛苦。

[24]自相問言、世間之苦、何者爲重。

[25]天子爲百官萬民之主。

[26]人活一世、草生一秋。

15. Officers who are loyal to their sovereign and love the people.
16. All who are territorial officials.
17. As soon as ever [any such malpractices] are discovered, the land will immediately be confiscated.
18. Rain and snow fell for three days without stopping.
19. The south wind blew violently for several days in succession.
20. Its colour is snow white, which all men like.
21. For several days together there was a heavy snow fall, and the cold, indeed, was such as one had not experienced for ten years and more.
22. To suffer many hardships and troubles.
23. The weather was very cold, and we suffered greatly.
24. They asked each other, saying, of the afflictions in the world, which is the most severe.
25. The Emperor is the lord of all the officials and people (*lit.*, of the hundred officers and ten thousand people).
26. Man lives for one generation, grass grows for one autumn.

16. *ti fang*, place, territory.
17. 入官, (*verb. act.*), to make to enter the government, *sc.* to confiscate.
19. 一連, together, in succession.
23. *hsin-k'u*, bitterness, hardships.
24. *ho-chê*, which?

EXERCISE 21.

VOCABULARY.

省 *shêng*^{3}, province.
江 *chiang*^{1}, river.
河 *ho*^{2}, river.
府 *fu*^{3}, prefecture, or, department.
州 *chŏu*^{1}, sub-prefecture.
縣 *hsien*^{4}, district.
各 *ko*^{4}, each; every.
早 *tsao*^{3}, early.
岸 *an*^{4}, shore.
取 *ch'ü*^{3}, to take, to fetch.
免 *mien*^{3}, to avoid; to remit.
向 *hsiang*^{4}, towards.
刑 *hsing*^{2}, punishment.
貧 *p'in*^{2}, poor.
業 *yeh*^{4}, property; calling, occupation.
空 *k'ung*^{1}, empty.
補 *pu*^{3}, to patch, to fill up.

數[1]百年之久、中國分爲十八省。
江[2]西、山東、山西、河南、四川、皆省名。
若[3]論中國江河、其最大最長者、爲長江黃河。

TRANSLATION.

1. For some hundreds of years past China has been divided into eighteen provinces.
2. Kiangsi, Shantung, Shansi, Honan, Szechuan, are all names of provinces.
3. If one discusses the rivers of China, — the greatest and longest are the Yangtse and the Yellow River.

2. Kiangsi, Szechuan. In the case of these and many other common geographical names, almost all writers retain the old spelling which had become established before the introduction of Sir Thomas Wade's orthography.

3. 江, 河; both these words mean 'river'; but *chiang* is more in use in the south, and *ho* more in the north of China. *Chiang*, again, is more confined to large rivers. Neither of these rules, however, is of universal application. 長; *ch'ang chiang*, the long river, is the name by which the Yangtse is most generally known among the Chinese.

各[4]省分作府州、府州
又分州縣。知[5]府、知
州、知縣、皆爲地方官。
福[6]州府早經開爲通
商口岸。次[7]早水手
上岸取水。一[8]百取
五、自不少也。勿[9]取
他人之物。川[10]省一
百六十州縣。黃[11]河
故道北流入海。彼[12]
此各存意見。

4. Each province is divided into prefectures and sub-prefectures; prefectures and sub-prefectures, again, are divided into sub-prefectures and districts.

5. A prefect, a sub-prefect and a district magistrate are all territorial officials.

6. Foo-chow was long ago opened as a treaty port.

7. Early next [morning] the sailors went on shore to fetch water.

8. To take five per cent is, of course, not a small amount.

9. Do not take other persons' things.

10. The Province of Szechuan [contains] one hundred and sixty sub-prefectures and districts.

11. The old course of the Yellow River ran northwards into the sea.

12. The two men each kept their own opinion.

4. 府, 州, 縣 : There are many translations of these words; but those here given seem the most general. A *fu* is always a territorial division of a province, a *hsien* is always a division of a *fu*, or of a *chou*. A *chou* ranks between the *fu* and the *hsien*, and is of two kinds. It is in some cases, like a *fu*, a division of a province, and itself divided into *hsien*; in others it is, like a *hsien*, a division of a *fu*.

5. These are the titles by which the Chinese designate the officials who govern a *fu*, a *chou*, a *hsien*.

6. *fu-chou fu*; Every *fu*, or *chou*, or *hsien* has a chief city, bearing the same name as itself. Here *fu-chou fu* means the chief city of the *fu-chou*, or Foo-chow, Prefecture. *tsao ching*, *lit.*, early was. 口岸, a harbour and shore, *sc.* a port, *t'ung-shang* for international trade. These ports, having been established by treaty, are generally known in English as 'Treaty Ports'.

以[13]免意外之事。畏[14]法自不犯法、畏刑自可免刑。河[15]向東流。業[16]已向其告知。自[17]此富者不至於貧、貧者可至於富、安居樂業。問[18]其向來作何事業。無[19]田無業、實屬窮貧。東[20]門外多有空地。以[21]海外之有餘補內地之不足。此[22]爲空言、無補於事。君[23]子安貧。

13. In order to avoid any unexpected occurrence.
14. He who fears the law of course does not break the law, and he who fears punishment of course can avoid punishment.
15. The river flows eastward.
16. They have already told [it] to him.
17. Henceforth the rich will not come to poverty, while the poor can come to be rich, and live in peace, rejoicing in their occupations.
18. To ask him what had been his calling hitherto.
19. Without land, without property (or, without occupation); he really is poverty-stricken.
20. Outside the East Gate there is much vacant ground.
21. By means of the superabundance from beyond the sea to make good the insufficiency of our own country.
22. These are empty words, which are of no avail (do no filling up) in the matter.
23. The superior man [lives] contented in poverty.

16. 業; *yeh i*, or *yeh ching*, is a common sign of the past tense. *hsiang ch'i*, to him.

17. 自此, from this [time].

18. *hsiang-lai*, hitherto, *tso ho*, he did what, etc..

21. *i*, by, *hai wai chih*, beyond-the-sea's, *yu yü*, having superabundance. *nei ti*, generally the interior as opposed to the coast; but here the speaker's country in opposition to abroad.

EXERCISE 22.

VOCABULARY.

係 *hsi*^{4}, to be; to connect with, to concern.

處 *ch'u*^{4}, a place.

貨 *huo*^{4}, goods.

洋 *yang*^{2}, sea, foreign.

住 *chu*^{4}, to dwell, to inhabit.

往 *wang*^{3}, to go.

關 *kuan*^{1}, to shut; a gate, a pass, a custom-house; to concern.

單 *tan*^{1}, single; a sheet of paper, document.

散 *san*^{4}, to scatter, to disperse.

放 *fang*^{4}, to loosen, to issue.

丁 *ting*^{1}, a man.

會 *hui*^{4}, to meet; a society.

兵 *ping*^{1}, a soldier; a weapon.

武 *wu*^{3}, military.

帶 *tai*^{4}, a belt, a region; to lead, to bring.

案 *an*^{4}, a judge's table; a case at law.

並 *ping*^{4}, together; altogether.

恩 *ên*^{1}, kindness, favour.

[1] 不知其係何處人民。[2] 開口岸之時卽定二處、一係上貨、一係下貨。[3] 上海爲洋商居住之處。[4] 是年禁止工人前往南洋各處。[5] 關門、不令人進。

TRANSLATION.

1. I do not know to what place he belongs.
2. At the time when the port was opened, they then appointed two places; one was for landing, and one was for shipping cargo.
3. Shanghai is a place inhabited by foreign merchants.
4. This year they prohibited labourers from proceeding to the various places in the southern sea.
5. To shut the door, and not let people come in.

1. *ch'i hsi*, he is, *ho ch'u*, of what place, *jên min*, = *min-jên*, a private person.
4. *chin chih*, to forbid and stop. *ch'ien wang*, to go forward, to proceed.

[6]自開關以來地方之生意甚有起色、而洋人往此處居住者實不少也。[7]一人單住。[8]由海關發出免單。[9]亂定之後、使衆人散去。[10]將放過銀米各數、及丁口數目、開單會報。

6. From [the time of] the opening of the custom-house till now the trade of the locality has greatly improved; and the foreigners who have come to live at the place are really many in number.
7. One man, dwelling alone.
8. The Customs issued an Exemption Certificate.
9. When order had been restored, he made all the people disperse.
10. They drew up a paper and made a joint report of each quantity of money and rice which had been distributed, and of the numbers of the men and women [who had received them].

6. *i-lai*, up to the present time. 生意, business, trade. *ch'i sê*, to raise its colour, to improve. 洋人 . . . 者; in passages such as this, if one holds it absolutely necessary to preserve for *chê* the meaning of 'those who', one may explain the construction by supposing *yang jên* to be in the genitive case ('genitive by position'). The literal translation then would be, 'of foreigners those who came to this place to dwell were, etc..' But it appears more reasonable to regard *chê* in such sentences as having simply the force of a relative: *i. e.*, *yang jên . . . chê*, the foreigners who, etc..

8. 由; Sentences in this peculiar form are common in modern written Chinese. *Yu hai-kuan* manifestly means 'by the customs'; but one must not think that *fa-ch'u* is a passive verb and *mien-tan* its subject; for, if it were so, the order would be reversed, *sc. mien-tan fa-ch'u*. One may explain the sentence somewhat in this way, — by the customs there was an issuing of an Exemption Certificate. Though, even so, it may be objected that *fa-ch'u* is an active verb and not a verbal substantive. For practical purposes it is quite safe to omit the *yu* entirely in translating, and treat the words governed by it as the subject of the sentence. *mien tan*, *lit.*, an exempting [from duty] paper.

10. 將, *vide* Ex. 8. 1. In this case the eleven following characters are formally the object of *chiang*, and really the object of *hui-pao* at the end of the sentence. *fang kuo; kuo*, is a sign of the perfect tense. *ting k'ou*, men and women. *shu mu*, numbers. *k'ai tan*, to draw up a document. *hui pao*, to make a joint report: *hui* shows that the report was presented by two or more persons together.

目[11]不識丁。

手[12]下勇丁又不能治。

兵[13]丁多名會齊不散。

文[14]官治民、武官帶兵。

山[15]東一帶地方。

謀[16]害人命重案。

各[17]省教案同時並起。

勿[18]使其並在一處。

與[19]其並不來往。

此[20]事與我中土大有關係。

千[21]兵易得、一將難求。

11. He does not know the simplest character.
12. Moreover he cannot govern the soldiers under his orders.
13. A number of soldiers collected together and did not disperse.
14. Civil officials govern the people, military officers lead troops.
15. The region of Shantung.
16. A grave case of plotting against (*lit.*, to harm) a man's life.
17. Missionary cases occurred in all the provinces at the same time.
18. Do not let them be together in one place.
19. I did not associate with him at all.
20. This matter greatly concerns our land of China.
21. A thousand soldiers are easy to get; one general is hard to find (*lit.*, to seek for).

11. *lit.*, his eye does not recognize [the character] *ting*.

12. 勇. Soldiers belonging to the regular military establishment in China are called *ping*; and additional troops raised for special occasions are called *yung*. The latter word is often translated 'irregulars'; but ordinarily the *yung* are not irregular troops in our sense of the word. *yung ting*, soldier men.

13. *to ming*, many individuals. *hui ch'i*, to meet together.

15. *i-tai*, one 'stretch' of country.

17. 教, doctrine, religion, *chiao an*, religious cases, such as complaints laid before the authorities of ill-treatment of missionaries or converts. *ping ch'i*, occurred together.

19. 並 here merely strengthens the negative: *ping pu*, not at all, *lai wang*, coming and going, associating.

20. *kuan hsi*, to concern, to affect; consequences. *ta yu*, greatly has, *kuan-hsi*, consequences, *yü*, with, = seriously concerns.

會[22]同地方文武各官散放銀米。受[23]恩報恩。恩[24]不可忘。年[25]幼、尚未成丁。養[26]兵千日、用在一時。住[27]在東南門外。

22. To distribute money and rice in conjunction with the civil and military officials of the locality.
23. To receive kindness and repay kindness.
24. Kindnesses must not be forgotten.
25. He is young and has not yet become a man.
26. One supports soldiers a thousand days and uses them on a single occasion.
27. He lives outside the South East Gate.

22. 各 is often, as here, best translated by merely putting the following substantive into the plural.

EXERCISE 23.

VOCABULARY.

派 *p'ai*^{4}, to send officially.
員 *yüan*^{2}, an official.
辦 *pan*^{4}, to transact, deal with.
到 *tao*^{4}, to arrive.
新 *hsin*^{1}, new.
任 *jên*^{4}, a burden, an official post.
赴 *fu*^{4}, to go to.
該 *kai*^{1}, to owe, ought.
稟 *ping*^{3}, to petition.
照 *chao*^{4}, to reflect light; according to.
飭 *ch'ih*^{4}, to order.
核 *ho*^{2}, to examine, to consider.
委 *wei*^{3}, to depute; to employ on public duty.
領 *ling*^{3}, to receive; to lead.
拏 *na*^{2}, to take, to seize.
匪 *fei*^{3}, not; evil-doers, brigands,

兩[1]國各派大員會議近
事。派[2]員多帶兵勇前
往查辦。此[3]事如何辦
理、業已明論於前。路[4]
不行不到、事不作不成。
其[5]時新關尚未開辦。
新[6]派各員未能到任。
仁[7]以爲己任。業[8]經令
其各赴新任。該[9]員去
年在任病故。凡[10]事必
稟命而行。

TRANSLATION.

1. The two nations each despatched a high official to consult together about recent matters.
2. He sent an officer to take a large number of soldiers and to proceed [to the place, in order] to inquire into and deal with [the matter].
3. How this affair should be dealt with, has already been discussed and made plain beforehand.
4. If you do not make the journey you will not arrive; if the business be not done, it will not be accomplished.
5. At that time the New Custom-house had not yet been opened for business.
6. The newly appointed officers have not been able to reach their posts.
7. He took benevolence as his own task.
8. He has already ordered them each to proceed to their new post.
9. The said officer died of sickness last year at his post.
10. In all matters one must ask for orders and then act.

2. *ping yung*, soldiers, *vide* note to Ex. 22. 12.

7. *lit.*, taking benevolence, *wei*, he made [it] *chi*, his, *jên*, burden. *i* is frequently found following the word which it governs.

9. 該 is constantly used in referring to persons, places, etc., that have been previously mentioned: *kai yüan*, the said officer. It is also used of persons, etc., that have not been already mentioned: it then means 'concerned'.

各[11]事本應照案辦理。並[12]飭該道前赴各屬親查。自[13]應委員查核稟復。惟[14]各國領事官於此事大有不合之意。本[15]大臣當經照會該領事官、並派委員向其當面告知。

11. Each matter ought by rights to be dealt with according to precedent.

12. At the same time I ordered the said Taotai to proceed to each place in his jurisdiction and make personal investigation.

13. One ought of course to depute an officer to investigate the matter and report in reply.

14. But all the Consuls strongly disapprove of this proceeding.

15. I, the Viceroy, thereupon wrote officially to the said Consul, and at the same time sent a deputy to inform him of the matter personally.

11. 本, naturally, properly; *chao*, according to, *an*, previous cases.

12. 該道. *Tao* for *tao-t'ai*, an official ranking above a Prefect, but below the principal authorities of a Province. For want of a convenient equivalent in English, it is customary to keep the Chinese title and call him a Taotai. I have translated *kai tao* by 'the said Taotai', assuming, in the absence of the context, that he has been mentioned already. But if there has been no previous mention of him, the translation should be 'the Taotai concerned', *i. e.* the Taotai of that part of the country, the Taotai whose duty it is. 屬 is used of a place or person under one's jurisdiction. 親 oneself, in person.

14. *ling shih kuan*, a Consul. *ling* to lead: *ling shih*, a leader or director of affairs. 於, *etc.; lit.*, but the Consul of each country with this matter greatly has a feeling not in accord.

15. 本 has here the idea of 'self', 'personal'. In official communications the writer, when speaking of himself, does not use the pronoun 'I', but gives his title with *pên* prefixed to it. Thus a Consul will style himself *pên ling-shih-kuan*. 當, at [that time], *cf.* Ex. 10. 8. 經, sign of the past tense. *chao hui*, to write officially, or (subst.) the despatch thus written. It is the term formally adopted to denote official correspondence between Chinese and European officers. *wei yuan*, to depute an officer, or, as here, an officer deputed, a deputy. 向, *etc.*, to tell [it] to him, *tang mien*, face to face.

[16]應飭該縣立行查拏首要各匪。[17]賊匪殺害良民。[18]派委文武兩員、帶領兵丁一千餘名、前往該處查拏會匪。[19]查該員等所稟皆係實情、應如稟辦理、業經飭縣照數發銀、該員等卽行赴領。[20]改日領教。[21]春來秋往。

16. One ought to order the Magistrate concerned to proceed at once to search for and arrest the principal brigands.
17. The brigands are killing loyal people.
18. He instructed two officers, one civil and one military, to take with them a thousand and more soldiers and proceed to the place in question, in order to search for and arrest the banditti.
19. I find that the reports made by the said officers are all correct; and one should deal with [the matter] as they suggest. Orders have been given to the Magistrate to issue the money in accordance with the amount [stated]. Let the officers go at once [to his office] and receive it.
20. I shall have the pleasure of listening to you another day, (*lit.*, changing the day I will receive your teaching).
21. It comes in spring and goes in autumn.

16. *hsien* for *chih-hsien*, District Magistrate, a common abbreviation in writing. 立, *statim*, at once. *shou yao*, head and important, = chief, principal.

17. *sha hai*, simply, 'kill'.

18. *p'ai wei*, to despatch and depute, to instruct. 名, *cf.* Ex. 22. 13. 會 has here its meaning of ,a society', and shows that the persons to be arrested belonged to some unlawful association.

19. 查 is very commonly used in commencing a statement. Its meaning is, 'enquiring [into the matter, I find that]'. In such cases 'I find' is a convenient translation for it. 等, sign of plural. 所, *etc.*; those things which the said officers report all are true matters: one ought, *pan-li* to deal [with the question] *ju ping*, like, (in accordance with), their report. *chi hsing*, at once proceed, *fu*, to go, *ling*, to receive [it].

EXERCISE 24.

VOCABULARY.

防 *fang*², to guard, to guard against.
緊 *chin*³, tight, urgent, important.
回 *hui*², to go back, to send back.
被 *pei*⁴, to be the object of, to suffer.
藥 *yao*⁴, drugs, medicines.
形 *hsing*², form, shape.
悉 *hsi*², minute, fully.
着 *cho*², to order.
請 *ch'ing*³, to request.
部 *pu*⁴, a class, an office or department.
且 *ch'ieh*³, moreover, also.
務 *wu*⁴, business; must.
端 *tuan*¹, correct; doctrine.
盜 *tao*⁴, robber.
深 *shên*¹, deep.
船 *ch'uan*², a boat, a ship.
准 *chun*³, to sanction, to grant.

[1] 人言可畏、亦不可不防。
[2] 目前海防最爲緊要。
[3] 無關緊要之事、令其自辦。
[4] 我緊等多時。
[5] 其子在外、久未回家。

TRANSLATION.

1. Men's words are to be feared; and one cannot but be on one's guard against them.
2. At the present moment the marine defences [of the country] are most extremely important.
3. They ordered him himself to deal with matters which were not of serious importance.
4. I have been anxiously waiting [for you] for a long time.
5. His son is abroad and has not returned home for a long time.

2. *chin yao*, urgent, exceedingly important.
3. 關, to concern, *kuan chin yao*, of urgent concern.
5. 回 is also written 囘.

將[6]被拏之人立行放
回。小[7]民被欺必思
報復。良[8]藥苦口、利
於病。與[9]其病後求
藥、不如病前自防。
洋[10]藥有害民生、法所
當禁。欲[11]得熟悉海
外情形者。非[12]初學
所能知悉。着[13]照所
議辦理。着[14]照所請、
該部知道。

6. He immediately released the men who had been seized.

7. If the common people be ill-treated, they are sure to think of revenging themselves (*lit.*, of paying back).

8. Good medicines are bitter [to] the mouth, but beneficial for sickness.

9. Seeking for drugs after one is ill, is not so good as taking care of oneself beforehand.

10. Opium injures the lives of the people: it ought to be forbidden by law.

11. One wishes to get men thoroughly acquainted with conditions of things [in countries] beyond the sea.

12. It is not a thing which a beginner at learning can know well.

13. Let it be dealt with in accordance with what has been proposed.

14. Let [it be] as requested: [let] the Board concerned take note.

6. 被 is generally best translated by simply turning the following verb into the passive voice. *fang hui*, to release and let go home. *hsing*; *vide* Ex. 25. 4 Note.

9. This is a favourite way of instituting a comparison in Chinese. The general sense is plain, but it is difficult to bring the meaning exactly out of the words. 與, with, comparing with, 其, *the*: comparing [precautions] with the taking of drugs, [drugs] are not so good as precautions.

10. *yang yao*, the foreign drug, *sc.* opium. *fa so*, what the law, *tang*, ought.

11. *shu hsi*, well versed in, well acquainted with. *ch'ing-hsing*, forms of affairs, conditions of things, circumstances. *chê*, those who are.

13. 着, I order; but it is well rendered by the 'let' of the Imperative Mood. *chao*, in accordance with, *so*, that which, *i*, they have proposed.

14. 部; there are six great government departments at Peking, corresponding with our Treasury, War Office, etc.. They are known as the Six Boards (*pu*). *chih tao*, know, be aware of it, take note.

由[15]刑部行文地方官。且[16]該員久任九江、於洋務情形最爲熟悉、應請即飭赴任。異[17]端直如盜賊水火、且水火盜賊、害止及身、異端之害、害及人心。海[18]盜爲萬國所同惡、無論何國皆可拏辦。其[19]人學問深遠。其[20]深知水形、熟悉船務之水手。商[21]船出洋准帶火藥數斤。

15. The Board of Punishment sent a despatch to the territorial authorities.

16. Moreover, the said officer, having long held office at [the Treaty Port of] Kiukiang, is very well acquainted with the conditions of foreign affairs. One ought [therefore] to request that he be ordered immediately to proceed to his post.

17. Strange doctrines are just like robbers and brigands or fire and water. Moreover, in the case of fire and water, of robbers and brigands, the injury only affects (reaches to) the body; but in the case of the injury done by strange doctrines, the injury affects men's hearts.

18. Pirates are detested by all countries alike: any country can capture and punish them.

19. This man's learning is profound.

20. Those sailors who are well acquainted with the sea (*lit.*, with the water's form) and are thoroughly experienced in nautical matters.

21. Merchant vessels when going to sea are permitted to carry a few pounds of gunpowder.

15. 由; *vide* Ex. 22. 8.

18. *wan-kuo*, nations in general, all nations. *lit.*, pirates are that which all nations alike hate: never mind what country, all can, etc..

家賊難防。[22] 其意善且深矣。[23]

22. Thieves [among one's own] household are hard to guard against.
23. His idea is excellent and profound.

EXERCISE 25.

VOCABULARY.

奉 *feng*[4], to receive from a superior.
再 *tsai*[4], again, then.
俟 *ssŭ*[4], to wait.
滿 *man*[3], full.
底 *ti*[3], bottom.
期 *ch'i*[2], period, date; to expect.
記 *chi*[4], to remember, to record.
認 *jên*, to recognize, to acknowledge.
眞 *chên*[1], true, real.
計 *chi*[4], to calculate, to plan.
個 *ko*[4], a numerative, (see notes).
隻 *chih*[1], numerative of ships.
件 *chien*[4], a numerative.
據 *chü*[4], to grasp; proof; according to.

天[1]子奉天命平治天下。教[2]師同奉教之人。再[3]將前案悉行復核。俟[4]奉部核准再行開工。

TRANSLATION.

1. The Emperor having received the commands of heaven tranquillizes and rules the empire.
2. The missionaries together with the converts.
3. To take the former case again, and proceed to examine it thoroughly once more.
4. [We propose] to wait till we have been favoured with the Board's approval [of our scheme], and then to set to work.

2. *chiao shih*, the teachers of the doctrine; *fêng chiao*, [those who] receive the doctrine.

4. *ho chun*, to consider and approve, approve after due consideration. 行 *etc.*; then *to proceed* to begin the work: but *hsing* may often be omitted in translating.

其[5]聽此言即爲滿意。

聞[6]五月底定期開辦。

俟[7]年底期滿再行改新。

六[8]年七月不記日期。

當[9]將此事存記於心。

該[10]犯已經認罪。

此[11]言眞實。

各[12]該州縣務必認眞辦理。

我[13]兵殺賊不計其數。

該[14]口岸自通商以來、至今有四個月矣、其進口之洋船共計十七隻。

5. When he heard these words he immediately became contented.
6. I have heard that the end of the fifth month has been fixed on as the date for commencing business.
7. Wait till the time is up, at the end of the year, and then renew them.
8. In the sixth year and the seventh month; but on what day, I do not remember.
9. You ought to keep this matter in your mind.
10. The said criminal has already confessed his guilt.
11. These words are true.
12. Each Sub-prefect and Magistrate concerned positively must deal with the matter in earnest.
13. Our soldiers killed an unknown number of rebels.
14. It is now four months since the port in question was opened to international trade. The number of foreign vessels that have entered the port amounts in all to seventeen.

5. the two words *man-i* are used together as an adjective, 'contented'.

8. The sixth year, *i. e.* of the Emperor's reign. *jih ch'i*, the date of the day.

9. *ts'un chi*, store up and remember.

12. *wu* must, *pi* must; *wu pi*, positively must. *jên chên*, recognizing the truth, in earnest.

13. *tsei* is often used where we should say 'rebels'. *lit.*, our soldiers killed rebels, one did not calculate the number.

14. *lit.* [at] the said port from [the beginning of] international trade till now, up to the present there are four months.

[15]上人一個、下人一千。[16]此等案件亦甚少見。[17]若有緊要事件、自應稟報查辦。

15. The superior is one, the inferiors a thousand.

16. Cases of this class are also very seldom met with.

17. If there be affairs of urgent importance, they should of course be reported, [so that they may] be enquired into and dealt with.

個, (often written **箇**); *ko* is a numerative. What this means one can show more easily by examples than by definition.

In English, when we are speaking without reference to definite quantities or numbers, we can say *horses*, *knives*, *bread*, *sealing wax*; but, on the other hand, when we refer to definite quantities or amounts, though we may say *a horse*, *two knives*, we cannot say *a bread*, *two sealing waxes*, but we must use some such expression as *a piece*, or *a slice*, or *a loaf of bread*, *a piece*, or *a stick of sealing wax.*

The Chinese, in their colloquial language, when speaking indefinitely, say *horses*, *knives*, *bread*, *sealing wax*, just as we do; but when they come to speak with reference to definite amounts, not only must they say *a piece of bread*, of *sealing wax*, *etc.*, but they are also obliged to say *a piece horse*, *two pieces knives*, *etc.*.

The word thus inserted before a substantive is called by grammarians a numerative.

Some substantives have special numeratives of their own. Thus, *chih*, (the last word in this example), is the special numerative of *boats*, *birds*, *etc.*. While *ko* is used before all substantives which have no special numerative, and to some extent instead of the special numerative when there is one. Thus, for *a boat* one may say either *i chih ch'uan*, or, less elegantly, *i ko ch'uan.* It should be noted that, in expressions like *a pound of meat*, *an acre of land*, *pound* and *acre* act as numeratives.

The use of numeratives before substantives, under the circumstances described, is universal in the Chinese spoken language. And, amid the multitude of words and paucity of sounds, the employment of a special numerative assists the listener to understand what the speaker is talking about. But in the written language numeratives before substantives are exceedingly rare. They are, however, occasionally found. They are especially employed, as in this sentence, before the word *months.* This is doubtless because the names of the months are the same as their numbers, *e.g.*, *liu yüeh* is the recognized name of the sixth month; and therefore, when a writer means *six months*, he puts *liu ko yüeh.*

There are two more uses of the numerative which should be noticed: (1) it can be placed immediately after the substantive, e.g. *ch'uan chih*, which means *ships in general*: (2) it can be used without a substantive, as *chih* is in this example. Both these uses are common in the written language as well as in the spoken.

共計, one reckons altogether at, = amount in all to.

16. **件**, numerative of *an*, cases at law, of *shih*, business, etc..

據[18]該縣稟、上海一口往來船隻、是年失事甚少。應[19]飭地方官、立將良民被殺情形、據實稟明核辦。查[20]該縣任事一年、核計所出盜案、不及從前十分之一、實屬異常出力。凡[21]事認命。應[22]俟會面後、彼此議定、再行辦理。

18. According to the report of the said Magistrate, [among] the vessels coming and going at the port of Shanghai, the accidents have been very few this year.

19. It is my duty to order the local authorities immediately to furnish an accurate report concerning the slaughter which occurred of inoffensive people, in order that action may be taken after due consideration.

20. I find that the Magistrate in question has held his post for a year, and, having calculated the cases of robbery which have occurred, that they do not amount to one tenth of what they were before. This is really [a display of] extraordinary energy.

21. In all matters recognize the decrees [of Heaven].

22. We ought to wait till after we have met, and have consulted together and settled [the matter], and then [we can] proceed to take action.

18. 據, to grasp, to have in hand, to have received. 'According to' is often a convenient equivalent for it. 一口, the one port; but there is no stress on the *one*.

19. 立將, *etc.; lit.*, immediately to take, *ch'ing hsing*, the circumstances of, *liang min*, inoffensive people, *pei sha*, being slaughtered, [and] *chü shih*, grasping, *i. e.*, according to, the truth, *ping ming*, report [them and make them] plain, *ho pan*, [in order that one may] consider [them and] deal [with the case].

20. *ch'a; vide* note to Ex. 23. 19. *jên shih*, to be in charge of affairs. *ho chi*, to examine and calculate, to reckon up, *so ch'u an*, the robbery cases which have come out, *pu chi*, they do not come to, *ts'ung ch'ien*, [of] former [cases], *shih fên chih i*, in ten parts one, = one tenth. *shih shu*, truly [it] is, *i-ch'ang* different from usual, extraordinary, *ch'u li*, putting forth of strength, energy.

EXERCISE 26.

VOCABULARY.

曉 *hsiao*^{3}, dawn, bright; to know.
諭 *yü*^{4}, to command, to notify.
嚴 *yen*^{2}, strict, severe.
結 *chieh*^{2}, to tie a knot, to conclude.
交 *chiao*^{1}, to join; to hand to.
管 *kuan*^{3}, a tube; to control, to take charge of.
接 *chieh*^{1}, to receive, to take over.
公 *kung*^{1}, public; just.
給 *chi*^{3}, to give, to hand to.
每 *mei*^{3}, every.
完 *wan*^{2}, to finish; to pay.
稅 *shui*^{4}, customs duty.
半 *pan*^{4}, half.
收 *shou*^{1}, to receive.
細 *hsi*^{4}, fine (not coarse), small.

出[1]示曉諭嚴禁。 當[2]使學生通曉外國語言。 今[3]奉上諭嚴令各省大員將未結之教案即行辦結。 我[4]有何法與其結交。

TRANSLATION.

1. To issue a proclamation distinctly notifying the strict prohibition of....
2. One ought to make the students thoroughly acquainted with the spoken languages of foreign countries.
3. There has now been received an Imperial Decree, strictly ordering the high authorities of each Province at once to settle all out-standing missionary cases.
4. What means have I to become one of his friends?

1. 曉, clearly, distinctly.
2. *hsüeh shêng*, learners, students. *t'ung*, thoroughly, *hsiao*, know.
3. *shang yü*, a Decree of the Emperor. *wei chieh chih*, that have not been concluded. *pan chieh*, deal with and conclude, settle.
4. *chiao*, to join, unite; *chieh chiao*, form an union, *yü ch'i*, with him.

若[5]有罪犯在內、即應交出。此[6]歸何官管理。經[7]管之人早已回國、接辦者尚未來到。西[8]人有萬國公法一書。辦[9]理公務、應先面商、後以文件。每[10]有商船出洋、應由該管之官發給公文爲據。各[11]貨入口必須報關完稅。貨[12]入內地必完半稅。

5. If there be any criminals therein, they should immediately be delivered up.
6. What officer ought to see to this?
7. The man in charge went home long ago to his own country, and his successor has not yet arrived.
8. Europeans have a book [called] International Law.
9. When transacting official business, one ought first to discuss the matter at a personal interview, and afterwards to deal with it in writing.
10. Whenever a merchant vessel goes to sea, the officer in charge [of such matters] ought to issue to it an official document as a certificate.
11. All goods, when imported, must be reported to the custom-house and pay duty.
12. Goods when sent into the interior must pay a half duty.

5. *tsui fan*, men who have committed a crime.

6. *lit.*, this belongs to what officer, *kuan-li*, to take charge of and regulate.

7. 經, to transact, to manage: *ching-kuan-chih-jên*, the manager, superintendent. *chieh-pan chê*, he who takes over charge, a successor.

8. International Law, *lit.*, the public law of all nations.

9. *ying*, *etc.*; one ought first to consult face to face, afterwards to use documents; *chien*, numerative of *wên*, documents.

10. *mei yu*, every [time that] there is, = whenever. *ying yu*, there ought by the, *kai kuan chih kuan*, officer who ought to control, = officer in charge. *fa chi*, to send and give, to issue. *wei chü*, to be a proof.

此[13]案今經半年有餘並未完結。每[14]月收銀五兩。各[15]官離任時應將所有公文案件交給新任接收。其[16]餘各情、未能細知。到[17]底其數細微、可不論及。當[18]於收人入教之先、細察其人有無作惡犯罪之事、當收者收之、不可收者去之。立[19]法不可不嚴。

13. This case has now gone on for half a year and more, and yet it is still unfinished.
14. Every month he receives five ounces of silver.
15. Every officer, at the time of going away from his post, ought to hand over all the official documents and records to the new occupant.
16. The remaining matters, one has not been able to learn minutely.
17. After all, their number is [so] very small, [that] we need not discuss them.
18. Before accepting a man as a convert, [the missionary] ought to examine minutely whether he has done any thing wicked or has committed any crime; those who ought to be admitted, he should admit, and those whom he cannot [rightly] admit, he should reject.
19. When enacting laws one can not but be severe.

13. *yu yü*, and more. 並 strengthens the negative.

15. *so yu*, *lit.*, which there are, = 'the', or 'all the', agreeing with *kung wên*, *etc.*. *chiao chi*, deliver to, *hsin jên*, the new [occupant of the] post, *chieh shou*, [who will] receive [them].

17. *tao ti*, to come to the bottom, after all. *lun chi*, make one's discussion reach to them.

18. 於 ... 先, before. *shou jên ju chiao*, receiving a man into his flock. 有無, has or has not, 事, matters of, etc.. 收之, admit them.

中[20]秋寸草結子。年[21]到半百。

20. In mid-autumn the tiny (inch-high) herbs form (or, ripen) their seeds.
21. His age has reached fifty.

EXERCISE 27.

VOCABULARY.

舊 *chiu*[4], old.
因 *yin*[1], cause; because.
原 *yüan*[2], origin.
布 *pu*[4], cotton cloth; to spread.
稱 *ch'êng*[1], to say, to state.
便 *pien*[4], convenient; then.
客 *k'o*[4], a guest, a stranger, a traveller.
和 *ho*[2], harmony.
除 *ch'u*[2], to take away, to subtract.
做 *tso*[4], to do, to make.

當[1]念舊好、不念舊惡。凡[2]事必有因。因[3]何不可照舊辦理。乃[4]因天時嚴冷難以行工。原[5]色洋布。

TRANSLATION.

1. One ought to think of old kindnesses and not to think of old wickednesses (old injuries).
2. Every matter must have its cause.
3. Why cannot one deal with it according to the old [plan]?
4. However, on account of the severity of the weather, it was difficult to proceed with the work.
5. Unbleached foreign cottons.

3. *yin ho*, on account of what?
4. *t'ien shih*, weather, *yen lêng*, severely cold. *nan i*, difficult to, — a peculiar use of *i*: it is quite common, but it is not easy to explain in accordance with the ordinary meanings of *i*.
5. *yüan sê*, of their original colour, unbleached.

土[6]人喜用土布。天[7]主教布滿天下。該[8]原告赴縣稟稱。有[9]事、不便接客。客[10]商來往莫不稱便。此[11]事問人便知。兩[12]國業經失和。家[13]和萬事興。此[14]害不除、諸事無一可成。除[15]上海一口不計外、其餘各處今年來客甚少。百[16]川會海。

6. The people of a district like to use the cloth of the district.
7. The Roman Catholic Religion has spread throughout the Empire.
8. The said plaintiff went to the Magistrate's [office] and presented a petition, stating that....
9. He is engaged, and it is not convenient for him to receive visitors.
10. Travelling merchants, who come and go, all declare that [the system] is convenient.
11. As to this matter, ask people, then you will know.
12. A rupture has already occured between the two countries.
13. When a family [enjoys] harmony, every thing prospers.
14. If this [cause of] injury be not done away with, of all matters not one can succeed.
15. Leaving out the port of Shanghai, [which is] not counted, [one finds that from] the remaining places the travellers, [who have] come this year, are very few.
16. The numerous streams meet in the sea.

7. The Religion of the Lord of Heaven, — the name adopted in China for Roman Catholicism. *pu man*, to spread so as to fill.

8. *kao* means 'to lay a charge', or 'bring a suit against one'; so, *yüan kao*, a plaintiff, *pei kao* (*pei* to suffer) a defendant.

12. *shih ho*, to lose harmony, to go to war with each other.

15. **除 ... 外**. Observe this use of *ch'u* and *wai*, *ch'u* coming at the beginning and *wai* at the end of the clause, and the two together meaning 'with the exception of'.

黃[17]犬食肉、白犬當罪。前[18]世不修、今世苦。君[19]子雖貧、禮義常在。難[20]事細心求理。生[21]不帶來、死不帶去。有[22]路莫坐船。同[23]心合意。藥[24]治不死病。賊[25]目分外眞。小[26]人最難防。既[27]死不能復生。一[28]文錢六個字。滿[29]心滿意做好人。爾[30]做爾事、我做我事。

17. The yellow dog eats the meat, the white dog bears the blame.
18. In a former life he did not cultivate [his character], [therefore in his] present life [he has] hardships.
19. Though a superior man may be poor, his propriety and uprightness always remain.
20. In difficult matters seek carefully for the right.
21. At birth one brings nothing with one; at death one takes nothing away.
22. If there be a road, do not go in a boat.
23. Of the same mind and united in their ideas.
24. Drugs will cure diseases which are not mortal.
25. A thief's eyes are exceptionally accurate.
26. The mean man is very difficult to guard against.
27. When one has died, one cannot live again.
28. One cash has six characters [on it].
29. Be a good man with all your heart and all your mind.
30. You do your business, and I will do mine.

20. *hsi hsin*, with minute mind, attentively, carefully.

25. *fên wai*, *cf.* Note to Ex. 18. 25.

28. *ch'ien*, the copper coins of China, usually known as 'cash'; *wên* is here used as the numerative of 'cash'.

29. 做; this character is merely a vulgar form of 作 *tso*, to make.

EXERCISE 28.

VOCABULARY.

尊 *tsun*[1], to honour.

加 *chia*[1], to add, to apply.

傷 *shang*[1], to wound, to hurt.

章 *chang*[1], a document; a chapter; a regulation.

總 *tsung*[3], total, general.

盡 *chin*[4], to exhaust, to finish; entirely.

是[1]謂尊其道非尊其人。此[2]貨近有信來、法國將加重稅。不[3]得以利口傷人。不[4]可亂殺加害、以傷天地之和。自[5]第五章起。總[6]要小心照章辦理。舊[7]章之外又復加新。

TRANSLATION.

1. This [is] called honouring the doctrine, not honouring the man.
2. As to these goods, recently news has come that France is going to impose a heavy duty [on them].
3. One must not hurt people with a sharp tongue.
4. One may not impair the harmony of heaven and earth by indiscriminate slaughter and the infliction of injury.
5. Beginning from the fifth chapter.
6. In all cases one must be careful to act in accordance with the regulations.
7. Besides the old regulations, they are also adding new ones as well.

2. 將, sign of the future.

3. *pu tê*, one must not. 以, with.

4. *lit.*, one may not indiscriminately kill and inflict injury, *i shang*, whereby one hurts, etc..

[8]總共計有三百萬兩。[9]應派大員總管稅務。[10]書不盡言、言不盡意。[11]子欲報親恩於萬一、當內盡其心。[12]盡信書、莫若無書。[13]天地君親師、聖教所最尊者。[14]明人不用細講。[15]修身以俟死。[16]義不可背、貧不可怨。[17]世人結交須黃金。[18]凡事要存良心。

8. Altogether it amounts to (*lit.* one calculates that there are) three million taels.
9. [The government] ought to appoint an officer of high rank to take general (*or*, supreme) control of customs matters.
10. Books do not exhaust words; words do not exhaust ideas.
11. If a son wishes to repay a ten thousandth part of his parents' kindness, he ought, inwardly, to exhaust his mind (*i. e.* use his utmost mental efforts).
12. If one gives entire credence to books, one had better not have any books.
13. Heaven, earth, the sovereign, parents, teachers, are what the sacred (*i. e.* the Confucian) religion honours most.
14. To an intelligent man one need not explain things minutely.
15. Prepare yourself in order to await death.
16. One may not turn one's back upon righteousness, one may not murmur at poverty.
17. Men of [this] world, [if they are] to form friendships, require gold.
18. In all matters it is important to preserve a good conscience.

8. *tsung kung*, all together.
11. *yü wan i*, in ten thousand [parts] one [part].
13. 所者, that which, *vide* Note to Ex. 7. 17.
14. *pu yung*, one requires not, one need not.
17. 交, *chiao*, intercourse, friendship.

[19]君子愛財取之有道。[20]東南之地多水、西北之地多山。[21]做到老、學到老。[22]回心向道、改過自新。[23]田地深耕以養家。[24]人生不滿百。[25]求給田土以便安身。

19. If the superior man loves wealth, he acquires it in proper ways.
20. In the region of the South-east there is much water; in the region of the North-west there are many mountains.
21. Work till old age, study till old age.
22. Turn your mind back towards right principles, change your errors, and make yourself new (reform yourself).
23. Let your lands be deeply tilled, in order that you may nourish your family.
24. A man's life does not fill up a hundred [years].
25. I beg [you] to give me a plot of land, that I may find rest.

19. *ch'ü chih yu tao*, in getting it he has the [proper] path.

22. Notice 自, as is often the case, preceding the verb which governs it.

25. *i pien*, so as to be convenient for; so as to enable one; so that one may. *an shên*, rest one's body, repose oneself.

EXERCISE 29.

VOCABULARY.

違 *wei*¹, to disobey.

昔 *hsi*¹, former, formerly.

遵 *tsun*¹, to follow, to obey.

守 *shou*³, to keep; to guard.

約 *yo*¹, or, *yüeh*¹, to bind; an agreement.

條 *t'iao*², anything long and slender; a section, a clause

按 *an*⁴, to press down; according to.

保 *pao*³, to protect, to guarantee.

護 *hu*⁴, to help, to protect.

例 *li*⁴, a law, a rule.

錯 *ts'o*⁴, to err, be wrong.

彼[1]國認有違背公法之過。昔[2]時此理間有或違、今則莫不遵守。既[3]經定約、亦當遵守。爾[4]等各守本分。所[5]定之和約有十二條。中[6]國既准傳教、須必按照條約保護。發[7]給護照一事歸領事官經管。我[8]等性命亦恐難保。

TRANSLATION.

1. That country acknowledged that it had [committed] the offence of violating international law.
2. In former times occasionally there were perhaps [cases of] offending against this principle; now however all obey it.
3. A treaty having been concluded, one ought also to keep it.
4. Do you all mind your own duty!
5. The treaty concluded contains twelve articles.
6. China having sanctioned the preaching of [the Christian] religion, she must protect [missionaries and converts] in accordance with the treaty.
7. The Consul has charge of the business of issuing passports.
8. I fear that our lives, also, cannot be guaranteed.

1. *wei-pei*, offend against and turn the back on, *kung fa* public law; *kuo* transgression, offence.

2. 間, at intervals, occasionally. — occasionally there were perhaps [those who] offended.

3. *chi ching; chi*, since, *ching*, one has, *ting*, made, *yüeh*, an agreement.

4. 分, *fen*^{4}, lot, duty.

5. *ho yüeh*, a treaty of peace. Another term for a treaty is 條約, because a treaty is drawn up in *tʻiao*, articles.

6. *an chao*, according to.

7. *hu chao*, a protecting certificate, a passport. *chao*, is much used for certificates and such documents. *kuei*, belongs to, *ling shih kuan*, the consul, *ching kuan*, to manage and take charge of.

8. 難, difficult; frequently, as here, by meiosis for 'impossible'.

使[9]臣之身尊而不可犯、各
國定例力加保護。天[10]之
所命、人不能違。嚴[11]父出
好子。牛[12]能耕田、犬能守
戶。發[13]財受窮總由天。
衣[14]欲新人欲舊。豈[15]能盡
如人意。罪[16]上加罪。有[17]
利必興、有害必除。不[18]輕
用重刑。兄[19]弟和而家不
分。萬[20]事總要錢。做[21]錯
肯認錯、即此是好人。

9. The person of an ambassador is of [great] dignity and must not be violated. All countries make laws strongly protecting him.
10. What heaven commands, men cannot oppose.
11. A strict father produces good children.
12. The ox can plough the fields, the dog can guard the door.
13. The acquiring of wealth and the suffering of poverty come entirely from heaven.
14. Clothes, one wants new; men (friends, acquaintances), one wants old.
15. How can [one act] entirely according to [other] men's ideas? (One cannot do exactly what other people would like).
16. To add crime to crime.
17. If there be profit [in it], one must put it into practice; if there be harm, one must do away with it.
18. Do not lightly (without good reason) use severe punishments.
19. If brothers agree together, the house (*i. e.*, the patrimony) will not be divided.
20. In every thing there is an universal need of money.
21. After committing a fault, to be willing to acknowledge one's fault, this then is a good man.

9. *shih ch'ên*, a Minister employed [by the Emperor], *i. e.*, an envoy to a foreign state, whether an Ambassador or one of lower rank. 力加; *li chia*, strongly applying, *pao hu*, protection, = strongly protecting.

10. 之, *vide* Note to Ex. 7. 15.

[22] 愛民如子、保民若赤。

[23] 百姓莫察官府事。

[24] 自知失言、不敢出聲。

[25] 三千年前國人未明道理、甚愛異端、而國法禁之最嚴。

22. He loves the people as his children; he protects the people as though they were babes.
23. The people should not question the acts of the authorities.
24. He knew himself that he had made a mis-statement, and did not dare to utter a sound.
25. Three thousand years ago the people of the country did not yet understand right principles, and were very fond of strange doctrines; but the laws of the country forbade these very strictly.

23. *kuan fu*, an officer, a mandarin.
24. *shih yen*, to make a slip or error in one's words.
25. 異端, *cf.* Ex. 24. 17.

EXERCISE 30.

VOCABULARY.

擬 *ni*³, to propose, to intend.
否 *fou*³, not.
京 *ching*¹, a capital city.
設 *shê*⁴, to establish, to devise.
館 *kuan*³, a house, an establishment.
動 *tung*⁴, to move.
俱 *chü*¹, all.
泰 *t'ai*⁴, great, eminent.
詳 *hsiang*², details; minutely.

[1] 所擬辦法不知可否。

TRANSLATION.

1. One does not know whether the proposed procedure will do or not.

1. *pan fa*, the method of transacting, *so*, which, *ni* [they have] proposed. *k'o fou*, can [or] not = will do or not.

昔[2]人言必念京報
以識時務。在[3]京
師設立同文館。
擬[4]請按照同文館
之例、於上海又設
外國語言文字學
館。按[5]兵不動。
如[6]此、則動心否、予
曰、否、我四十不動
心。父[7]母俱存、一
樂也。民[8]教俱各
相安。

2. Men of former times [used to] say that one must read the Peking Gazette in order to be acquainted with the affairs of the day.

3. There has been established at the capital a College of United Literatures.

4. We beg to recommend that, in accordance with the precedent of the T'ung Wên Kuan, a school for the spoken and written languages of foreign countries should also be established at Shanghai.

5. Not to make any hostile movement.

6. "[In such a case] as this, would your mind be disturbed or not?" The Master said, "No. When I became forty years old, my mind was not [liable to be] disturbed."

7. That both one's parents should be alive, is one joy.

8. The common people and the converts were all on friendly terms.

2. *ching pao*, *lit.* metropolitan reports, or information. This is the official gazette, published daily at Peking, and consisting of (1) the Court Circular, (2) the Decrees of the Emperor, (3) Reports to him by officials, (commonly called Memorials).

3. *ching shih*, a capital city or metropolis. *t'ung wên kuan*; there is a college at Peking known by this name, where Chinese are taught foreign languages, while receiving a Chinese education as well.

4. We beg to recommend; *lit.*, we propose to request.

5. One meaning of 兵 is 'weapon'; and the literal translation of *an ping* is 'press down one's weapon'. It is here used metaphorically for keeping one's troops from advancing or attacking.

6. *tung hsin; tung*, to move, or, to be disturbed, *hsin*, as to one's mind, or, in one's mind.

8. *chiao*, [the people of the Christian] doctrine, converts. *chü ko*, all and each, one and all, *hsiang*, towards each other, *an*, are at peace.

泰[9]西各國俱無此例。爾[10]
等生在泰平無事之日。
請[11]飭戶部詳細查核、據情
定擬。其[12]詳不可得聞。
備[13]文詳稱。風[14]不來草不
動。遵[15]守天命。上[16]京求
名。事[17]雖議定不見舉動。
寸[18]草俱無。守[19]分、安命、順
時、聽天。父[20]曰、我死之後
爾等不宜分離、不如合力
相連。

9. No western nations have this law.
10. You are born in a time of great peace and freedom from trouble.
11. We beg that orders may be given to the Board of Revenue to examine minutely [into the matter], and in accordance with the circumstances to make proposals [for dealing with it].
12. One cannot learn the details.
13. To prepare (*i. e.* to write) a despatch minutely stating.
14. If the wind does not come, the grass does not move.
15. To obey and keep the commands of heaven.
16. To go to the capital to seek for fame.
17. Though the matter has been discussed and settled, one does not see any commencement being made.
18. Not even a blade of grass left.
19. Keep to your own lot (or, own duty), accept your fate, go with the times, and obey heaven.
20. The father said, after that I am dead, you ought not to separate: it is better to unite your strength, and be joined together.

9. *t'ai hsi*, the great west, Europe and America.
11. *hu pu*, the Board of Revenue, *lit.*, of households. *ting ni; ting*, to fix upon [a plan] and, *ni*, propose the same [for the Emperor's approval].
12. *pu k'o tê*, one cannot obtain that one, *wên*, should hear.
17. *chü tung*, to raise and move, to make a beginning.
19. 分, *cf.* Ex. 29. 4. 安, remain quietly in, 命, what has been ordained for you.

[21] 理當自食其力、不可坐食其金、食力無已時、食金當有盡。[22] 犬心不服、乃對主人曰、犬非故意放之、吾今已老矣、豈能如常、犬實心有餘、而力不足也。

21. One ought to support oneself by one's own efforts: one must not sit down and live upon one's gold. One may live upon one's efforts for ever, but living upon gold must have an end.

22. The dog felt himself unjustly treated, and thereupon replied to his master, "I did not let it go intentionally: I have grown old; and cannot [do] as I always [did]: I really have plenty of heart, but my strength is not sufficient."

21. *li*, [in accordance with] right, *tang*, one ought, *tzŭ shih*, to feed one self upon, *ch'i li*, one's strength.

無已時, *wu i shih*, has no time of ending. *tang yu chin*, must have exhaustion.

22. *ch'üan hsin*, the dog in his mind, *pu fu*, did not submit, *nai*, thereupon, *tui yüeh*, in reply he said, *chu jên*, to his master. 故意, *ku i*, on purpose, intentionally. 吾, *wu*, I, *chin i*, now already, *lao i*, am old indeed, *ch'i neng*, how can I, etc..

EXERCISE 31.

VOCABULARY.

爭 *chêng*[1], to dispute, to contest.
極 *chi*[2], extreme.
亡 *wang*[2], to die, to be lost.
急 *chi*[2], haste; urgent.
濟 *chi*[4], to help, to aid.
憂 *yu*[1], grief, care.
測 *ts'ê*[4], to fathom, to estimate.
厚 *hou*[4], thick, generous.
薄 *pao*[2], thin, mean.
勤 *ch'in*[2], diligent.
顧 *ku*[4], to look at, to regard.
臨 *lin*[2], to approach.
禍 *huo*[4], misfortune.
反 *fan*[3], contrary, to turn back.

彼[1]此相爭。君[2]子不與人爭。聽[3]者爭先恐後。富[4]到極處。天[5]動、而南北二極不動。亂[6]極必當復治。鳥[7]爲食死、人爲財亡。不[8]樂善道而亡其國。急[9]病而亡。何[10]濟於事。濟[11]人之急。遠[12]水難濟近火。君[13]子憂道不憂貧。樂[14]人之樂、憂人之憂。

TRANSLATION.

1. They disputed together.
2. The superior man does not wrangle with people.
3. The listeners strove to be first and were afraid (were unwilling) to be behind.
4. His wealth has reached an extreme point.
5. The heavens move, but the south and north poles do not move.
6. When disorder [comes to] an extreme point, there must be a renewal of order.
7. Birds die for the sake of food, men perish for the sake of wealth.
8. He did not delight in the path of virtue, and so he destroyed his kingdom.
9. [To take] a sudden disease and die.
10. What help is it in the matter?
11. To relieve the necessities of other men.
12. It is difficult with distant water to help (*i. e.* to put out) a fire close at hand.
13. The superior man grieves about truth, he does not grieve about poverty.
14. To rejoice at other men's joys; to grieve at other men's griefs.

1. *Lit.*, This man and that man mutually disputed.
7. *wei*^{4}, on account of.

既[15]取非常樂、須防不測憂。天[16]事不可測。常[17]人之心不足測此理。面[18]皮盡厚。面[19]皮薄。厚[20]於此而薄於彼。君[21]子常失於厚、小人常失於薄。大[22]富由勤。一[23]生之計在於勤。少[24]年須勤學。顧[25]前不顧後。顧[26]口不顧身。若[27]肯顧人之急。車[28]馬臨門。

15. When one has obtained more than ordinary pleasure, one must be on one's guard against unexpected woe.
16. The affairs of heaven are inscrutable.
17. The minds of ordinary men are not equal to fathoming this principle.
18. The skin of his face is extremely thick, (he is utterly brazen-faced).
19. The skin of his face is thin, (he is bashful).
20. Generous to this man, but mean to that one.
21. The superior man always errs on the side of generosity; the inferior man on the side of meanness.
22. Great wealth comes from diligence.
23. The plans of one's whole life (one's whole livelihood) are in (depend on) diligence.
24. The young must study diligently.
25. To regard the past and neglect the future.
26. To pay attention to the mouth (to food) and not to the body (not to clothing).
27. If you are willing to pay attention to other men's urgent needs.
28. Carriages and horses approach his door, (he is visited by rich people).

23. 計, *chi*, to plan.
24. *shao nien*, *vide* Ex. 16. 16.

[29]行善福報、行惡禍臨。[30]不臨谷不知地之厚。[31]病從口入、禍從口出。[32]有善者未得福、或反受禍。[33]不能害人、反害自己。[34]百姓早思作反。

29. If one practises virtue, happiness is one's recompense; if one does evil, misfortune will come.
30. If one does not go into a valley, one does not know the earth's thickness.
31. Disease enters by the mouth, misfortune comes out from the mouth.
32. There are [cases where] the virtuous have not obtained happiness: perhaps on the contrary they have suffered misfortune.
33. He could not injure others, but on the contrary injured himself.
34. The people long ago thought of revolting.

32. *shan chê*, those who are virtuous, the virtuous.
33. *tso fan*, to revolt, to rebel.

EXERCISE 32.

VOCABULARY.

寶 *pao*³, precious, a jewel.
志 *chih*⁴, resolution.
息 *hsi*², to stop; interest on money.
訓 *hsün*⁴, to teach, to instruct.
益 *i*², to increase; to benefit.
算 *suan*⁴, to calculate, to consider.
施 *shih*¹, to give, to bestow; to display.
落 *lao*⁴ (or, *lo*⁴).
壽 *shou*⁴, old age; long life.
歲 *sui*⁴, year.
閒 *hsien*², leisure, unoccupied.
擇 *tsê*², to choose, to pick out.
談 *t'an*², to talk, to converse.

出[1]洋多得寶石。士[2]爲國
之寶。不[3]寶金玉而寶善
人也。有[4]志者總能成。
爾[5]小生宜立志。不[6]違其
志。日[7]出而作、日落而息。
此[8]等惡習尚未盡息。每[9]
月按三分出息。人[10]求多
聞必學於古訓。違[11]父母
訓。訓[12]予弟以禁非爲、
有[13]益於民。不[14]但無益而
且有害。

TRANSLATION.

1. He went abroad and obtained many precious stones.
2. The scholar is the jewel of his country.
3. Do not value gold and jade, but value the virtuous man.
4. Those who have resolution (the resolute) can always succeed.
5. You young learners ought to fix your resolution (make up your minds).
6. Not to oppose their determination.
7. To work when the sun comes up: to rest when the sun goes down.
8. These kinds of evil practices have not yet entirely ceased.
9. Every month paying interest at the rate of three per cent.
10. If a man seeks for extensive knowledge, he must study the teachings of antiquity.
11. To disobey the instructions of one's parents.
12. To instruct the young, in order to prevent wrong doing.
13. It has advantage for (it is beneficial to) the people.
14. Not only is it of no benefit, but also it is harmful.

5. 生, here for *hsüeh-shêng*, a learner, student.
9. a *fên* is the tenth of a *ch'ien* (錢), a *ch'ien*, the tenth of an ounce or tael. *san fen* is thus three hundredths of a tael, three per cent.
10. *to wên*, to hear much, = much knowledge. *hsüeh yü* study at.
12. *Tzŭ ti*, *lit.*, sons and younger brothers.

[15]無益之書不必讀。

[16]人有百算、天有一算。

[17]有子無錢未算貧。

[18]講求天文算學者。

[19]施恩莫望報。

[20]樂善好施之人。

[21]己所不欲勿施於人。

[22]瓜熟自落。

[23]水落石出。

[24]五十以上謂之壽。

[25]多福多壽多男子。

[26]昔人壽極長、乃至數百歲。

[27]其人年六十七歲。

[28]自客歲以來閒住無事。

15. Useless books must not be read.
16. Men have a hundred calculations (plans), heaven has one calculation (one plan).
17. [He who] has sons but no money is not accounted poor.
18. Those who study astronomy and mathematics.
19. When you do a kindness do not look for repayment.
20. A man delighting in goodness and fond of giving.
21. What you do not wish [done to] yourself, do not do unto others.
22. When the melon is ripe, it falls of itself.
23. When the water sinks, the stones appear. (Then the truth is known).
24. Above fifty is called old age.
25. [May you have] much happiness, long life, and many sons.
26. Formerly men's lives were extremely long: they reached, indeed, to several hundred years.
27. That man's age is sixty seven years.
28. Ever since last year he has lived in retirement and has had no business.

18. *chiang-ch'iu*, *cf.* Ex. 18. 9; *t'ien-wên*, astronomy; *suan-hsüeh*, the study of calculation, mathematics.

21. 己, to yourself.

24. *wei chih*, one calls it; it is called.

26. *hsi*, here an adverb, formerly.

28. *k'o sui*, last year.

閒[29]談莫論人非。閒[30]人免進。勿[31]以此言爲常談。擇[32]日開工。擇[33]其善者而從之。鳥[34]擇木、木豈能擇鳥。

29. When talking at your leisure do not discuss other men's wrong-doings.
30. No admittance except on business.
31. Do not consider these words to be common-place talk.
32. To choose a day for beginning the work.
33. Choose the good and follow it.
34. The bird selects the tree (upon which it settles); how can the tree select the bird?

30. *Lit.*, let unoccupied men avoid entering.
33. *ch'i shan chê*, that which is good. The student should note the combination of *ch'i* and *chê* with one or more words between them.

EXERCISE 33.

VOCABULARY.

貪 *t'an*[1], to covet, to be greedy of.
功 *kung*[1], work accomplished, good services, merit.
酒 *chiu*[3], spirits, wine.
飲 *yin*[3], to drink.
戒 *chieh*[4], to refrain from, to avoid.
體 *t'i*[3], the body, the limbs.
賤 *chien*[4], mean; cheap.
別 *pieh*[2], to separate; different.
忍 *jên*[3], to bear, to endure.
猶 *yu*[2], still, yet; like.
勝 *shêng*[1], to sustain; adequate to; *shêng*[4], to conquer; victory.
敗 *pai*[4], defeat, ruin.
恭 *kung*[1], respectful.
敬 *ching*[4], to be reverent or respectful.

貪[1]財者無所不爲。莫[2]貪難得之利。貪[3]天之功爲己功。富[4]貴功名皆能有成。議[5]論多、成功少。酒[6]色傷生。少[7]飲酒不亂性。不[8]可不飲、不可多飲。戒[9]酒除色。戒[10]食牛犬。富[11]則貴、貧則賤。飲[12]食之人、人皆賤之。身[13]體平安。體[14]有貴賤、有小大、無以小害大、無以賤害貴。

TRANSLATION.

1. Those who covet wealth will do anything.
2. Do not desire profits which are difficult to obtain.
3. To desire that the merit of heaven shall be one's own merit, (to claim credit for what heaven has done).
4. Wealth, honour, rank, can all have accomplishment (all be obtained).
5. Much discussion and little effected.
6. Wine and pleasure injure life.
7. If one drinks but little wine, one will not disorder one's faculties.
8. One cannot but drink, but one should not drink much.
9. Beware of wine and put away (refrain from) pleasure.
10. Abstain from eating cattle and dogs.
11. If rich, one is honoured; if poor, one is held cheap.
12. Drinkers and gluttons, all men despise them.
13. May you enjoy peace and comfort!
14. [Among] the members of the body there are some honourable, some ignoble; there are some small, some great. [One must] not injure the great for the small, nor injure the honourable for the ignoble.

1. *wu*, have not, *so*, that which, *pu wei*, they do not.
4. *kung-ming*, official rank of any kind; *lit.*, merit, and reputation [coming therefrom].
13. *shen-t'i*, the body, one's person, — may your person have peace and rest.
14. 以, on account of, for the sake of.

其[15]人最愛體面。

心[16]無形體。

黑[17]白不能分別。

查[18]明有無別故。

心[19]中甚不忍別。

小[20]不忍、則亂大謀。

既[21]聞其聲、不忍食其肉。

急[22]急行善猶恐不及。

氣[23]猶風也、血猶水也。

經[24]目之事猶恐未眞。

仁[25]之勝不仁也、猶水勝火。

反[26]敗爲勝。

酒[27]能成事能敗事。

敗[28]者爲賊、成者爲王。

15. That man is very careful about his respectability.
16. The mind has no bodily form.
17. He cannot distinguish black and white.
18. To ascertain whether there be other reasons or not.
19. They felt quite unable to bear separation.
20. If one cannot endure in small matters, one will ruin great schemes.
21. Having heard its voice, he cannot bear to eat its flesh.
22. Do good with all speed, as if you were afraid of not being in time.
23. Breath is like wind, blood is like water.
24. Things which pass before the eyes, one still fears that they be not true, (how much more so, what one merely hears).
25. Humanity's conquering of inhumanity is like water conquering fire.
26. To turn defeat into victory.
27. Wine can make an affair succeed, and it can ruin an affair.
28. He who fails is a rebel, he who succeeds becomes a king.

15. *t'i-mien*, body and face, respectability.
19. *Lit.*, in their minds they very much did not bear to part.
21. *chi wên*, since he has heard.
22. *chi chi*; the repetition of the word gives it additional force. *pu chi*, not to reach to, not to be in time.

不[29]勝其任。恭[30]而有禮。在[31]家孝父母。恭[32]敬之心人皆有之。恭[33]敬不如從命。

29. He is not equal to [the duties of] his post.
30. Respectful and having ceremoniousness (and polite).
31. At home filial and reverential to one's parents.
32. The feeling of reverence, all men possess it.
33. Reverence is not so good as obedience to orders.

EXERCISE 34.

VOCABULARY.

惜 *hsi*^{1}, to spare, to pity.
筆 *pi*^{3}, a pen, a pencil.
紙 *chih*^{3}, paper.
寫 *hsieh*^{3}, to write.
頭 *t'ou*^{2}, the head.
尾 *wei*^{3}, the tail.
神 *shên*^{2}, spirits, divine.
畫 *hua*^{4}, to draw, to paint.
虎 *hu*^{3}, a tiger.
獸 *shou*^{4}, beasts, animals.
禽 *ch'in*^{2}, birds.
堅 *chien*^{1}, firm, strong.
祭 *chi*^{4}, to sacrifice to, to offer up.
才 *ts'ai*^{2}, talents, ability.
幹 *kan*^{4}, to transact; ability.

惜[1]衣得衣、惜食得食。非[2]言與筆所能盡。敬[3]惜字紙。

TRANSLATION.

1. He who is sparing of clothes obtains clothes: he who is sparing of food obtains food.
2. More than tongue or pen can express.
3. Respect and spare written paper.

2. *lit.*, [it is] not that which words or pen can exhaust.
3. *tzŭ chih*, word paper, paper with writing on it.

不[4]惜紙筆之費。白[5]紙上
寫黑字。能[6]寫不能筭。
和[7]約共寫三紙。頭[8]上有
青天。萬[9]事起頭難。從[10]
頭至尾。頭[11]尾相爭。神[12]
龍見其首不見其尾。敬[13]
鬼神而遠之。天[14]大過神。
此[15]字筆畫多少。畫[16]虎、畫
皮、難畫骨。虎[17]口取食。
虎[18]爲野獸之長。無[19]父無
君、是禽獸也。

4. Not to grudge the cost of paper and pens.
5. To write black words on white paper.
6. He can write but cannot calculate.
7. Of the treaty there were written altogether three copies.
8. Above one's head there is the azure sky.
9. In all things the beginning is difficult.
10. From head to tail, (from beginning to end).
11. The head and the tail strove together.
12. [Like] the Dragon Spirit, [of which] one sees the head, but does not see the tail.
13. Reverence spirits and keep aloof from them.
14. Heaven (or, God) is greater than the spirits.
15. This character has how many strokes?
16. When one draws a tiger, one draws the skin, it is hard to (one can not) draw the bones.
17. To take food from a tiger's mouth.
18. The tiger is the chief of wild beasts.
19. To be without father, without a prince, that [is to be] a bird or beast.

9. *ch‘i t‘ou*, to begin; the beginning.
12. *shên lung*, *lit.*, the spiritual dragon. *ch‘i*, its.
13. *kuei shên*, all sorts of spiritual beings. *kuei*, originally, the ghosts of the departed.
15. *pi hua*, strokes of the pen. *to shao*, how many?

[20]禽獸雖不能爲善、亦不能爲惡。[21]禽飛獸走。[22]世上無難事、人心自不堅。[23]心志堅乎過於石。[24]人宜堅其好善之心。[25]祭虎以爲神。[26]祭不在物而在心。[27]生不奉養、死祭無益。[28]大才小用。[29]何以識其無才。[30]每日幹事。[31]有能幹作、無能幹成。[32]其才幹未必實勝前人。

20. Although birds and beasts are unable to do right, they are also unable to do wrong.
21. Birds fly, beasts walk.
22. In the world there are no difficult matters; man's heart itself is not firm.
23. His resolution is more firm and steady than a rock.
24. A man ought to strengthen his love of goodness.
25. To sacrifice to a tiger as a god.
26. [The value of] a sacrifice is not in the thing [offered], but in the feeling.
27. [If, while one's parents are] alive, one does not serve and support them, it is no use to sacrifice to them when they are dead.
28. High talents in a humble post.
29. By what means did you know that he had no talents?
30. To transact business every day.
31. He has [sufficient] ability to work at a thing, but not to complete it.
32. It is not certain that his talents are really superior to those of former men.

24. 好, *etc.*, *lit.*, his virtue-loving feelings.
25. *i wei*, taking it to be, considering it.
27. *fêng*, to serve, *yang*, to nourish, to support.
32. *wei pi*, not certain.

[33] 詩云、自求多福。[34] 刑部公文業已到省。[35] 死君自是忠臣志。

33. The Book of Poetry says, seek for yourself much happiness.
34. The official despatch of the Board of Punishment has already arrived at the provincial [capital].
35. To die [for his] sovereign is naturally the faithful Minister's determination.

33. *tzŭ ch'iu*, seek for yourself.
34. *hsing pu*, *cf.* Ex. 24. 14. *yeh i*, already has.

EXERCISE 35.

VOCABULARY.

誠 *ch'êng*², sincere.
暗 *an*⁴, dark, secret.
裏 *li*³, inside, in.
遲 *ch'ih*², slow; late.
速 *su*², quick.
陽 *yang*², male; the sun; openly.
陰 *yin*¹, female; dark; secret.
根 *kên*¹, root.
雲 *yün*², clouds.
集 *chi*², to assemble.
怕 *p'a*⁴, to fear.
斬 *chan*³, to chop, to behead.
決 *chüeh*², to cut off; to decide; certainly.
說 *shuo*¹, to speak, to say.
話 *hua*⁴, speech, language.

[1] 一念之誠可動天地。[2] 君子必誠其意。[3] 誠恐法有難行。

TRANSLATION.

1. The sincerity of a single thought (a single sincere thought) can move heaven and earth.
2. The superior man must make his thoughts sincere.
3. It is really to be feared that this law will be hard to put into practice.

1. 念, *nien*, to think, a thought.

黑[1]暗中未能視明。明[5]人不做暗事。同[6]在一家裏。暗[7]裏須防人不仁。此[8]事不可遲。欲[9]速則不達。爲[10]惡無不報、遲速自有時。查[11]無陽奉陰違之人。陽[12]報陰報、遲報速報、終須有報。雪[13]山根底有向陽處、衆鳥雲集。陰[14]雲滿天。士[15]商雲集。集[16]衆公議。根[17]深不怕風。

4. In the darkness he was unable to see distinctly.
5. The man of light does not do deeds of darkness.
6. Together in the same house.
7. In the dark one must guard against man's wickedness.
8. This matter cannot be delayed.
9. If one aims at speed, one is not thorough.
10. The doing of evil is never without its reward: sooner or later the time of course will come.
11. To find out that there are no men who obey in public and disobey in private.
12. Open reward, secret reward, late reward, early reward; in the end there must be a reward.
13. At the foot of a snowy mountain there was a place facing the sun, and all the birds assembled there in flocks.
14. Dark clouds fill the sky.
15. Scholars and merchants assemble [there] in crowds.
16. To assemble every one and have a public discussion.
17. If its root be deep, it does not fear the wind.

6. 裏 is also written 裡.

9. 達, *cf.* Ex. 13.

[18]眞金不怕火。[19]衆人無
不害怕。[20]不分首從皆
斬。[21]斬草不除根、明春
又要發。[22]照例擬斬立
決。[23]議久不決。[24]卜以
決疑、不疑何卜。[25]能說
不能行。[26]路中說話草
裏有人。[27]直人說直話。
[28]說話少者實、說話多必
失。[29]世人每以大話爲
頭、使人常有大望。

18. True gold does not fear the fire.

19. The people were one and all afraid.

20. All shall be beheaded, without any distinction between leaders and followers.

21. If you cut down grass and do not dig out the root, next spring it will shoot again.

22. In accordance with the law to sentence to immediate decapitation.

23. To consult for a long time and not come to a decision.

24. One uses divination in order to determine one's doubts: if one doubts not, why divine.

25. He can talk but cannot act.

26. If one talks on the road, there will be men in the grass, (beware of listeners).

27. The straight-forward man speaks straight-forward words.

28. Those who talk little [say] the truth; if one talks much, one must make mistakes.

29. Men constantly begin by using grand language, and make people continually have great hopes.

19. *chung jên*, of all the people, *wu pu*, there were none who did not, *hai p'a*, fear.

20. 從, *tsung*[4], a follower, an accessory.

21. *ming ch'un*, next spring, *cf. ming nien*, next year, etc..

22. *ni*, to sentence, *chan*, to decapitation, *li* immediate, *chüeh* execution. As to *ni*, *vide* Ex. 30. 11.

29. *shih jên*, men of the world, *mei*, constantly, *i*, using, *ta hua*, big talk, *wei t'ou*, make a beginning.

[30]不但君擇臣、臣亦擇君。

30. Not only does the sovereign choose his minister, but the minister also chooses his sovereign.

EXERCISE 36.

VOCABULARY.

林 *lin*², a forest, a wood.

花 *hua*¹, flowers.

紅 *hung*², red.

果 *kuo*³, fruit; really.

步 *pu*⁴, a pace, step; a measure of five Chinese feet.

讓 *jang*⁴, to yield.

妻 *ch'i*¹, a wife.

賢 *hsien*², good, worthy, excellent.

恥 *ch'ih*³, shame.

羞 *hsiu*¹, shame.

悔 *hui*³, to repent.

愚 *yü*², stupid, clownish.

[1]單木不成林。

[2]如魚得水、如鳥得林。

[3]花香不在多。

[4]人無千日好、花無百日紅。

[5]雪花大片如手。

[6]今有匪犯、起意謀反、紅帶爲記、暗號定明。

TRANSLATION.

1. A single tree does not make a wood.
2. Like a fish that gains the water; like a bird that gains the grove.
3. The fragrance of flowers is not in their number.
4. Man has not a thousand days of good fortune, nor are the flowers red for a hundred days.
5. Snow flakes as big as one's hand.
6. There now are evil-doers and criminals, who have conceived

1. *tan*, single.

5. *ta p'ien*, *etc.*, *lit.*, great pieces like the hand.

6. 記, *chi*, to record, to remember, also a mark; 帶, *tai*, a girdle; 號, *hao*, a mark or signal of any kind.

無[7]花果。開[8]好花、結好果。若[9]該人果係良善。三[10]百六十步爲一里。離[11]北岸二百步有大竹林。讓[12]人前行。終[13]身讓路、不失百步。治[14]民者道之敬讓、而爭自息。男[15]子無妻、家無主。誰[16]無父母、誰無妻子。妻[17]賢夫禍少。敬[18]老尊賢。恥[19]惡衣惡食者未足與議也。不[20]怕羞恥。

the idea of plotting rebellion: red girdles are their mark, and secret passwords have been established.

7. The flower-less fruit, (the fig).
8. [The tree which] puts forth good flowers, will form good fruit.
9. If the said person really be a good man.
10. 360 *pu* make one *li*.
11. 200 paces from the north shore there is a large wood of bamboos.
12. To let a man go in front of one.
13. Give way all your life, and you will not lose a hundred steps.
14. Let him who rules the people, guide them to respect and deference, and quarrels will cease of themselves.
15. If a man has no wife, the house has no ruler.
16. Who has not father and mother, who has not wife and children?
17. If his wife be a good one, a man has few troubles.
18. Reverence the old and honour the worthy.
19. He who is ashamed of bad clothing and bad food is not fit to discourse with.
20. Not to fear shame and disgrace.

8. 結, *chieh*, to tie in a knot, here, to form.

11. A *pu* is a double pace, viz., the distance covered by one's foot from the moment of lifting it to when it is put down again.

14. *tao*, to guide, is in the third tone.

其[21]見羞恥滿面發紅。
貧[22]不足羞、可羞貧而
無志。悔[23]罪改過。
死[24]而無悔者。除[25]諸
病皆由於悔心。昔[26]
之所謂聖、今之所謂
愚也。一[27]毋之子、有
愚有賢。貪[28]愛財物、
謂之愚人。論[29]大計
不惜小費。幹[30]任大
事。

21. He, feeling his disgrace, blushed all over his face.
22. Poverty is not sufficient [cause] for shame: one may be ashamed of being poor and irresolute.
23. To repent of one's sins and reform one's errors.
24. He who dies without regret.
25. The removal of all faults comes entirely from repentance.
26. Those whom formerly one called saints, [are] those whom to day one calls fools.
27. Among the sons of one mother, some are stupid, some are capable.
28. He who is greedy of wealth and property is called a fool.
29. When arranging great schemes, do not be sparing of small expenses.
30. To manage and administer important affairs.

25. *ping*, moral diseases, faults. *yu yü*, arises from.
26. *hsi chih*, of former times, = in former times.
30. *jên*, a verb, — to administer.

EXERCISE 37.

VOCABULARY.

清 *ch'ing*[1], pure, clear.
冰 *ping*[1], ice.
熱 *jê*[4] (or, *jo*), hot.
靠 *k'ao*[4], to lean against, to rely on.
災 *tsai*[1], calamity.

旱 *han*⁴, dry; drought.
愼 *shên*⁴, careful.
快 *k'uai*⁴, quick; sharp; cheerful.
慢 *man*⁴, slow.
切 *ch'ieh*⁴, to cut; urgent; all.
屢 *lü*³, repeatedly.
似 *ssŭ*⁴, like, apparently.
旁 *p'ang*², side.

官[1]清民自安。
冰[2]清水冷。
如[3]走薄冰。
體[4]熱如火、心冷如冰。
發[5]冷發熱。
冰[6]山不可靠。
小[7]富靠勤、大富靠天。
靠[8]火之人先熱。
福[9]壽與禍災實是天所主。
水[10]旱之災。
水[11]旱之時早報災傷。
由[12]旱路進京。
言[13]不可不愼也。

TRANSLATION.

1. If the officials be pure, the people naturally will be tranquil.
2. Pure as ice and cold as water.
3. Like walking on thin ice.
4. His body was as hot as fire, his heart as cold as ice.
5. Hot and cold alternately.
6. Do not lean against (trust to) an iceberg.
7. The moderately rich man relies on his diligence, the man of great wealth relies on heaven.
8. The man who is near the fire is warm first.
9. Happiness and length of life, together with misfortune and calamity, truly are controlled by heaven.
10. Calamities [consisting] of floods and droughts.
11. In time of flood or drought, [the magistrate should] report the calamity and damage at an early date.
12. To go to the capital by the land road.
13. In one's words one cannot but be careful.

2. *ping ch'ing*, ice-pure, pure as ice.
5. [At one time] sending forth cold, *i. e.*, being cold, [at one time] hot.
9. 所, *etc.*, things which heaven controls.

當[14]官有三事、清愼勤。飛[15]災不入愼家之門。刀[16]雖快不斬無罪之人。快[17]樂常恐災禍。不[18]快不慢。慢[19]道如此。最[20]切最要之急務。一[21]切寶中人命第一。屢[22]經飭其切實查辦。屢[23]屢談及此事。若[24]不小心慢行、誠恐屢有傷害人口之事。清[25]似水。似[26]不能言者。相[27]似而不同。

14. In holding office there are three matters [to be observed], purity, carefulness, diligence.
15. Flying (sudden) calamities do not enter the door of a careful household.
16. Though the sword be sharp, it does not slay the unoffending man.
17. When joyful and glad always fear calamity and misfortune.
18. Not fast and not slow.
19. Be slow to (do not) speak thus!
20. Urgent affairs, very pressing and very important.
21. Among all sorts of precious things human life is the first.
22. He was repeatedly ordered to deal with the matter in earnest.
23. Again and again we have talked of this matter.
24. If they be not careful and go slowly, it is really to be feared that there will constantly be cases of injuring people.
25. Pure like (as) water.
26. [He appeared] like one who could not speak.
27. Like each other, but not the same.

21. 一切, one cut, = the entire lot, all. *ti i*, number one, first, most important.
22. *lü*, repeatedly, *ching*, did, *ch'ih*, order, *ch'i*, him, *ch'ieh shih*, in earnest, *ch'a pan*, to enquire and deal with.
23. *t'an chi*, in talking reached to.
27. *hsiang ssŭ*, mutually alike, like each other.

[28] 似木石之無知也。[29] 立在道旁。[30] 兄弟不和旁人欺。[31] 在旁無相干之人。[32] 彼國之人不殺生不飲酒。[33] 畫人難畫手、畫鳥難畫頭。

28. Like the insensibility of (as senseless as) wood or stone.
29. Standing by the side of the road.
30. If brothers disagree, others will cheat them.
31. People not concerned in the matter.
32. The men of that country do not kill living [creatures], and do not drink wine.
33. In drawing a man it is difficult to draw the hand; in drawing a bird it is difficult to draw the head.

30. *p'ang jên*, those at the side, outsiders, other men.

31. 干, to concern: *wu hsiang kan*, not concerned with [the affair].

EXERCISE 38.

VOCABULARY.

皇 *huang*², imperial, emperor.

帝 *ti*⁴, lord, supreme ruler.

負 *fu*⁴, to carry on the back; to turn the back on; ungrateful.

器 *ch'i*⁴, vessels, utensils, implements.

許 *hsü*³, to allow; excess, very.

械 *hsieh*⁴, weapons.

借 *chieh*⁴, to borrow, to lend.

眼 *yen*³, the eye.

虛 *hsü*¹, empty; false.

想 *hsiang*³, to think.

抵 *ti*³, to substitute, to make good; to arrive at.

兇 *hsiung*¹, savage, cruel.

忙 *mang*², hurried, busy.

大[1]清國大皇帝。天[2]高皇帝遠。皇[3]上念切民生。必[4]求上帝之恩。背[5]負重物、難於速行。虎[6]見其老人、負之背上。忘[7]恩負義。工[8]欲善其事、必先利其器。火[9]器例禁、不准人帶、此外防賊器械許其各備。

TRANSLATION.

1. The Emperor of China.
2. Heaven is high and the Emperor far off, (I can do as I please).
3. The Emperor thinks earnestly of (is very careful of) the lives of the people.
4. One must pray for God's favour.
5. Carrying on his back a heavy load, he had difficulty in going fast.
6. The tiger, seeing the old man, took him on its back.
7. To forget favours and be ungrateful for kindness.
8. If the artisan wishes to make good his work, he must first sharpen his tools.
9. Fire arms being prohibited by law, no one is allowed to carry them: with this exception, every one has permission to provide himself with weapons for defence against robbers.

1. *ch'ing* is the title which has been adopted by the dynasty now ruling in China and so is frequently employed as a name for China itself. 大, a complimentary epithet, often prefixed to names of countries and sovereigns: it need not be translated. *huang-ti*, or *huang-shang*, (上), Emperor.

4. *shang-ti*, God.

5. *pei fu*, on his back bearing.

6. 其, demonstrative, — the old man in question.

7. 義, goodness, good acts (of which one has been the recipient), kindness to one.

8. *kung*, a workman.

9. *lit.*, fire-arms, by law prohibited, it is not permitted to men to carry; outside of these, robber-repelling instruments and weapons, [I] permit them each to provide.

上[10]月有土民客民械鬥情事。一[11]切器物不許借與他人。若[12]要借銀、先須說明所借之數、所給之息。耳[13]聞是虛、眼見是實。眼[14]所未見、心所未想。世[15]人但顧眼前不想日後。不[16]信仁賢則國空虛。飛[17]禽走獸兩不相和、鬥無虛日。活[18]時常想死。如[19]無人保、不許再行出洋。

10. Last month fights with weapons occurred between the local people and immigrants.
11. No implements or articles are to be lent to other persons.
12. If one wishes to borrow money, one must first make plain the amount that one would borrow and the interest that one would give.
13. The hearing of the ears is false, the seeing of the eyes is true.
14. What the eye has not seen and the mind has not thought of.
15. Men of the world only look at what is before their eyes (only regard the present); they do not think of the future.
16. If the good and the worthy be not confided in, then the state will be empty and void (will be rotten).
17. There was disagreement between the birds and beasts, and fights took place every day.
18. In the time of (during your) life, constantly think about death.
19. If they have no man to stand surety for them, they will not be allowed to go abroad again.

10. *lit.*, last month there were local people stranger people weapon fighting, *ch'ing-shih*, occurrences. *k'o-min*, strangers, immigrants from other parts of China.

11. *i ch'ieh*, *vide* Note to Ex. 37. 21. *pu hsü*, are not allowed.

17. *lit.*, the flying birds and walking beasts, the two did not mutually agree: they fought not one empty day.

19. *tsai hsing*, again to do: *hsing* is redundant.

功[20]過似足相抵。水[21]手行兇、已非一日。該[22]犯兇惡異常。械[23]鬥兇殺、甘心抵命。急[24]忙作事。有[25]福之人不用忙。初[26]一日抵省、三日來發信辦事、忙不可言。

20. His merits and demerits are apparently sufficient to balance each other.
21. It is no new thing that junkmen should do acts of violence.
22. The said criminal was extraordinarily savage and wicked.
23. They fight with weapons and savagely kill people, and willingly give their lives in exchange.
24. To transact business in a great hurry.
25. The prosperous do not require to hurry.
26. On the first of the month I arrived at the provincial [capital]; for three days past [I have been] despatching letters and transacting business, and have been more busy than I can say.

21. *i fei i jih*, already is not one day.
22. *i ch'ang*, different from the common.
26. *san jih lai*, for the last three days. *hsin*, a private or unofficial letter, not a formal despatch.

EXERCISE 39.

VOCABULARY.

隨 *sui*[2], to follow; according to.
容 *jung*[2], to contain, to tolerate, to allow; easy.
歡 *huan*[1], to rejoice.
節 *chieh*[2], a knot or joint in grass; a section; limit; virtue, reputation.
壞 *huai*[4], to spoil; bad.
產 *ch'an*[3], to produce; property; livelihood.

種 *chung*³, a kind or sort; *chung*⁴ to plant, to till.

恒 *hêng*¹, permanent, regular.

宗 *tsung*¹, ancestral; a clan; a class.

羣 *ch'ün*², a flock; a crowd.

積 *chi*¹, to accumulate.

危 *wei*¹, danger.

化 *hua*⁴, to transform; to influence.

占 *chan*¹, to divine; *chan*⁴, to take by force.

改[1]悔福隨。

容[2]人各隨其意。

天[3]不容盜。

江[4]山容易改、人性最難易。

歡[5]喜快樂。

從[6]善改過、自得天歡喜。

歡[7]樂知節、則禍敗少。

壞[8]人名節、謀人財產。

彼[9]國無冬夏之異、田種隨意、無有時節。

TRANSLATION.

1. Reform and repent; and happiness will follow.
2. Allow people each to follow their own idea.
3. Heaven does not tolerate robbery.
4. Rivers and hills are easy to alter, but man's disposition is very hard to change.
5. To rejoice and feel glad.
6. If you follow what is good and reform your faults, you will obtain for yourself the joy of heaven.
7. In your rejoicing recognize the [proper] limit, and then your misfortunes and failures will be few.
8. To damage people's reputations; to plot against people's wealth and property.
9. In that country there is no difference of (no difference between)

4. *jung-i*, easy.
5. *huan-hsi*, to rejoice and *k'uai-lê*, be glad.
7. *pai*, defeat, failure.
8. *ming chieh*, reputation.
9. *shih chieh*, a time or season.

此[10]為公地、不准耕種。切[11]不可為壞事、切不可交壞人。生[12]前所作種種之惡、死後必有種種之報。有[13]恒產者有恒心。以[14]義為利、則財恒足。愛[15]人者、人恒愛之。該[16]處土產並無大宗。同[17]姓不同宗。有[18]神羣在人頭上。男[19]女不同羣。

summer and winter: the fields are cultivated according to one's idea (when it pleases one): there is no [special] season [for the work].

10. This is public land, and is not allowed to be cultivated.
11. On no account may one do bad acts: on no account may one associate with bad men.
12. If that which one does during one's life be every kind of wickedness, one is certain after one's death to meet with all kinds of retribution.
13. Those who have a regular livelihood have constant minds.
14. Take uprightness to be profit, and then your wealth will always be sufficient.
15. He who loves men, men always love him.
16. There is no principal class of local products at that place.
17. Of the same name but not of the same clan.
18. There is the crowd of spirits above men's heads.
19. Men and women do not assemble together.

10. *kêng chung*, to cultivate.
11. *ch'ieh*, urgently, = on any account. 交, *chiao*, to unite, to associate with.
12. *shêng ch'ien*, in one's life beforehand. *chung chung*, kind upon kind, all kinds.
13. 恒, also written 恆.
16. *kai ch'u*, of that place, *t'u ch'an*, the local products, *ping wu*, have not at all, *ta tsung*, a principal class, (or staple).

小[20]民積怨既深、羣思
報復。積[21]水防旱。
治[22]家者不在善積財。
危[23]中得濟。安[24]不可
忘危。危[25]人自安。
大[26]事化小事、小事化
無事。冰[27]化爲水。
百[28]歲之後化而爲土。
占[29]筭人命。占[30]人妻
女。古[31]人形似獸、心
有大聖德。

20. The accumulated resentment of the common people having become deep, there was a general desire for revenge.
21. To store up water as a protection against drought.
22. The management of a household does not consist in being clever at accumulating money.
23. To obtain assistance in the midst of danger.
24. In time of peace one may not forget danger.
25. To imperil others and keep oneself safe.
26. Great affairs turn into small affairs, and small affairs into nothing.
27. Ice melts and becomes water.
28. After a hundred years he is transformed into dust.
29. To tell by divination a man's fate.
30. To take men's wives and daughters by force.
31. The ancients in their form were like beasts, but in their hearts they had the virtue of the great sages.

20. *ch'ün ssŭ*, in a crowd they thought, *pao fu*, to pay back.
22. *chih chia*, to manage a household, *chih chia chê*, the managing of a household.
29. *chan suan*, to divine and calculate.
30. 占, when meaning 'take by force', is often written 佔.

EXERCISE 40.

VOCABULARY.

量 *liang*^{2}, to measure, to calculate; to consider.

淺 *chʻien*^{3}, shallow.

具 *chü*^{4}, to prepare.

類 *lei*^{4}, a class, a kind.

燒 *shao*^{1}, to burn.

滅 *mieh*^{4}, to extinguish.

跡 *chi*^{4}, foot prints, tracks.

勒 *lê*^{4} (or, *lo*), to constrain, to force.

索 *so*^{3}, to demand, to exact.

乘 *chʻêng*^{2}, to mount, to ride, to avail oneself of.

吉 *chi*^{2}, good luck; happy.

凶 *hsiung*^{1}, bad luck.

海[1]水不可斗量。與[2]其商量借錢之事。測[3]量其海道之淺深。由[4]近至遠、由淺至深。江[5]水如今淺落異常。情[6]願出具保結。所[7]具保結是實。

TRANSLATION.

1. The water of the sea cannot be measured with a bushel.
2. To consult with him about a matter of borrowing money.
3. To measure the depth of the channel.
4. To proceed from what is near to what is far, from what is superficial to what is profound.
5. The water in the river is now more than usually low.
6. He is willing to give a guarantee.
7. The guarantee which has been given is genuine.

2. *yü chʻi*, with him, *shang-liang*, to consult.

3. *tsʻê-liang*, to measure, *chʻi* the, *hai-tao-chih* sea-path's, *chʻien shên*, shallowness or depth.

5. *chʻien lao*, to become shallow and fall.

6. *chʻing yüan*, he is willing, *chʻu chü*, to issue and prepare, (= to prepare and issue, to execute), *pao chieh* a security bond.

7. *so chü*, which has been prepared, = which has been executed.

[8]具稟人係新安縣人、
年四十七歲。[9]聖人
人類之首。[10]犬與我
同爲獸類。[11]匪類各
處殺燒。[12]前世燒高
香。[13]病重、內外發燒。
[14]以水滅火。[15]自取滅
亡。[16]欲滅跡而走雪
中。[17]風聲不好、形跡
可疑。[18]勒令寫給錢
單。[19]向其索欠甚緊。

8. The petitioner is a man of Hsin-an Hsien, aged forty seven years.
9. The saint is the head of mankind.
10. (*The ass said*), The dog and I together are of (both belong to) the class of beasts.
11. The brigands are murdering and burning everywhere.
12. In his former existence he burnt good incense, (and therefore is favoured now).
13. His sickness is severe: he is burning hot internally and externally.
14. To extinguish fire with water.
15. To bring destruction on oneself.
16. He wishes to extinguish (to hide) his foot steps and yet he walks in the snow.
17. His reputation is bad and his conduct suspicious.
18. They forced him to give a promissory note.
19. They pressed him very urgently for [payment of] his debt.

8. *chü ping jên*, the maker of the petition.
11. *fei lei* the brigand class, brigands; *ko chʻu*, in each place.
13. *fa shao*, to send forth burning, to be burning hot.
15. *tzŭ chʻü* to bring on himself.
16. 跡, also written 迹 and 蹟.
17. *fêng shêng*, rumours about him, his reputation; *hsing chi*, his forms and traces, his conduct.
18. *lê ling*, they compelled him, *hsieh chi*, to write and give, *chʻien tan*, a money paper.
19. *so*, they demanded, *hsiang chʻi*, towards him, = of him, *shên chin*, very urgently, *chʻien*, his debt.

不[20]許向教民勒索用費。並[21]嚴禁河兵、凡河岸車道聽人行走、不得借端勒索。乘[22]車出門向東。即[23]乘小船上岸、欲問何處、不見人民行跡。乘[24]人不備。當[25]乘便再談。吉[26]星高照。日[27]月告凶。化[28]凶爲吉。有[29]凶報凶、有吉報吉。

20. It is not permitted to extort from converts [their share of] expenses.
21. [He should] at the same time give strict orders to the river guards that they [are to] allow people to go along all carriage roads on the river bank, and that they must not make pretexts for extorting money.
22. Riding in a cart, he went out of the gate in an easterly direction.
23. Then, getting into a small boat, he went on shore, wishing to ask what was the place; but he saw no traces of people.
24. Taking advantage of people's being unprepared.
25. We ought to take the opportunity to have another talk.
26. May a lucky star shine [upon you] from on high.
27. The sun and moon announce misfortune.
28. To transform evil fortune into good.
29. If there be evil [in store for me], announce to me evil; if there be good fortune, announce good fortune.

20. *chiao min*, people of the [Christian] doctrine, converts. *yung fei*, expenses, expenditure. It here has reference to the cost of public theatricals, idol processions, etc..

21. notice 禁, to forbid, here translated 'order'. *chieh tuan*, to borrow causes, to find pretexts.

23. *hsing chi*, marks of people walking, tracks.

25. 便, *pien*, convenient.

26. 照, *chao*, to shine on.

兵革[30]非不堅利。生事[31]之以禮、死祭之以禮。

30. Their weapons and armour were strong and sharp.

31. While they (your parents) are alive, serve them according to propriety; when they are dead, sacrifice to them according to propriety.

30. 兵, *ping*, weapons of offence; 革, *ko*, weapons of defence, *lit.*, articles made of hide, shields, jackets, etc.. *chien*, strong, *li*, sharp.

EXERCISE 41.

VOCABULARY.

邊 *pien*[1], a side, a border.

界 *chieh*[4], a limit, a boundary; the world.

迎 *ying*[2], to go to meet.

永 *yung*[3], everlasting, perpetual.

移 *i*[2], to remove, to change, to transmit.

全 *ch'üan*[2], all; complete.

庶 *shu*[4], multitude; so that.

變 *pien*, to change, to alter.

巧 *ch'iao*[3], clever, cunning.

妙 *miao*[4], excellent.

哉 *tsai*[1], an exclamation.

戲 *hsi*[4], to play; a theatrical performance.

奇 *ch'i*[2], extraordinary, curious.

皇上[1]愼重邊防。兩[2]國邊界尙未定明。世[3]界不好。國[4]民聞聖人來、俱出來迎。

TRANSLATION.

1. The Emperor pays great attention to the defence of the frontier.
2. The boundary between the two countries has not yet been fixed.
3. The world is evil.
4. The people of the country, hearing that the holy man had come, all came forth to meet him.

1. *shên chung*; *shên*, is careful about, *chung*, considers a serious matter.
3. *shih chieh*, the world, the present age, (a Buddhist term).

來[5]至海邊迎接新官。
不[6]准集衆迎神。分[7]明
地界、永遠遵守。永[8]永
如此不移。不[9]能移及
他人。並[10]望詳細移復。
全[11]家敗盡。回[12]空之船
全數入江。必[13]須設一
善法、永得保全、庶可安
生矣。自[14]王子至於庶
人。

5. They came to the sea shore to meet and receive (to welcome) the new official.
6. It is forbidden to assemble the people and have processions of idols.
7. [Let them] mark out the boundary, and keep to it for ever.
8. For ever and ever like this, without changing.
9. [Property which] one cannot alienate to others.
10. I also hope that you will give me a reply with full details.
11. The whole family is utterly ruined.
12. The boats which were coming back empty have all of them entered the Yangtse.
13. We must devise a good plan, [by which we may] for ever obtain security, so that we can live in peace.
14. From the king's son [down] to the common people.

5. 接, *chieh*, to receive.
6. *ying shên*, to meet the spirits, — a term for holding processions of idols.
7. *yung yüan*, for ever, *tsun shou*, to observe and keep.
10. *hsiang hsi*, minutely and detailedly, *i fu*, reply. 移 is a term used for despatches or communications between officials of equal rank.
12. *hui k'ung chih*, the returning empty, *ch'uan*, boats, *ch'üan shu*, the whole number of them, have, etc..
13. 保, to protect, 全, complete or perfect; *pao ch'üan*, security.
14. *chih yü*, to.

盜[15]匪無從進步、良民庶可安居。至[16]死不變。三[17]人同心、黃土變成金。巧[18]言變亂是非。此[19]法甚爲巧妙。妙[20]算無移、方能取利。衆[21]聽此言、即曰妙哉妙哉。我[22]等相好如初、豈不善哉。戲[23]無益、戒之哉。各[24]人着其戲衣、向火而坐。奇[25]巧新戲。不[26]存天理必有奇禍。

15. Brigands will be unable to make their way in, and so well-behaved people will be able to dwell in peace.
16. Unchanging until death.
17. If three men be of the same mind, yellow earth may be changed into gold.
18. Cunning words alter and confuse right and wrong.
19. This plan is very ingenious and excellent.
20. [Make] good calculations and do not change them, then you will be able to gain profits.
21. When all the people heard these words, they immediately said, Capital! Capital!
22. If we [become] friends together as [we were] originally, will not that be excellent?
23. Play is no good; beware of it!
24. Each man put on his theatrical clothes, and sat down facing the fire.
25. New plays, both curious and ingenious.
26. He who does not keep the principles of heaven is certain to have strange misfortunes.

15. *wu ts'ung*, will not have [means] whereby, *chin pu*, to advance their steps; *shu*, and so, *liang min*, good people, etc..
22. *wo têng*, we.
24. 着, *cho*, to put on; *hsiang huo* [turned] towards the fire, *êrh tso*, and sat.

以[27]此洋土爲奇貨。殺[28]人須抵命。莫[29]聽耳旁風。君[30]子恥其言過於其行。飛[31]虛空中。

27. Of this foreign dirt (opium) they make a rare commodity.
28. He who slays a man must give his life in exchange.
29. Do not listen to idle rumours.
30. The superior man is ashamed that his words should go beyond his acts.
31. To fly through the air.

29. Idle rumours, *lit.*, wind beside the ears.
31. *hsü k'ung chung*, in the empty void.

EXERCISE 42.

VOCABULARY.

幫 *pang*¹, to help.
助 *chu*⁴, to help.
累 *lei*⁴, trouble, embarrassment.
晚 *wan*³, late.
輩 *pei*⁴, a generation, a class.
勞 *lao*², toil, labour.
料 *liao*⁴, materials; to estimate.
減 *chien*³, to diminish.
增 *tsêng*¹, to increase, to add to.
靖 *ching*⁴, tranquil, peaceful.
盛 *shêng*⁴, flourishing, plentiful.
榮 *jung*², glory; prosperous.
辱 *ju*⁴, disgrace; insult.

幫[1]人之忙。助[2]人成事。

TRANSLATION.

1. To help men's hurry, (to help men when they are pressed for time).
2. To help a man to complete an affair.

一[3]家被盜、九家聞聲幫助。
無[4]故受累。初[5]一日晚間。
世[6]人每每不肯幫助他人、
累及己身、後悔晚矣。豈[7]
可准此累民累官之事。
早[8]上不知晚上事。教[9]訓
晚輩。下[10]賤之輩。勞[11]則
思、思則善。身[12]雖勞、猶苦
學。勞[13]心者治人。回[14]去
料理家務。惟[15]有人心不
可料。

3. When one household is attacked by robbers, [the other] nine households, hearing the noise, will give help.
4. To suffer trouble without cause.
5. On the first of the month, late in the day.
6. Men constantly do not choose to help others; but, when trouble comes to their own persons, repentance is too late.
7. How can one sanction this matter, which will trouble the people and trouble the officials.
8. In the morning one does not know the affairs of the evening (what will happen in the evening).
9. To teach the younger generation.
10. The low and worthless class.
11. If one toils, one will think; if one thinks, one will become virtuous.
12. Though their bodies toiled, (though they were doing manual labour), still they studied severely.
13. Those who labour with their minds rule men.
14. He went home to look after his family affairs.
15. There is only the human mind on which one cannot calculate.

3. *pei tao*, to suffer robbery, to be robbed.
5. *chien*, during, at the time of; *wan chien*, late.
6. *shih jên*, people of the world. *hou hui*, repentance.
14. *liao li*, to manage, to put in order.

木[16]料生意今年大減。積[17]
欠加增、日益苦累。新[18]定
稅則有減無增。爾[19]輩該
當日日讀書、以增見識。
自[20]應重稅外來之貨、而減
免本國貨稅。地[21]方大爲
不靖。殺[22]賊靖海。國[23]不
安靖、盜風日盛。百[24]年以
前洋錢尚未盛行。見[25]他
榮貴、願他流亡。

16. The timber trade has greatly diminished this year.

17. His accumulated debts increase, and every day he is in greater distress.

18. The new tariff is lower, not higher.

19. You ought daily to study in order to increase your knowledge.

20. One naturally ought to [put] heavy duties on goods coming from abroad, and to reduce or abolish the duty on native goods.

21. The region is very much disturbed.

22. To kill pirates and tranquillize the sea.

23. The country is not quiet, and the practice of brigandage increases daily.

24. A hundred years ago foreign money was not yet in general use.

25. Seeing others prosperous and honoured, he wishes them to become vagrants or die.

16. *mu liao*, wood materials, *shêng i*, trade,

17. *chia*, to add; *chia-tsêng*, increase; *jih*, daily, *i*, he has more, *k'u lei*, hardship and trouble.

18. *hsin ting*, the newly settled, *shui tsê*, duty rules (tariff), *yu chien*, have diminution, *wu tsêng*, not increase.

19. *êrh pei*, your class, you, *kai tang*, ought, *jih jih*, daily.

20. *shui*, here a verb, to impose duty. 免, *mien*, avoid, abolish.

24. 尙 *shang*, still, yet.

25. 流, *liu*, to wander.

[26] 人生榮辱皆由天定。

[27] 羞辱莫甚於此。

[28] 利重害深、榮盛辱大。

[29] 使民凶年免於死亡。

[30] 皇天不負苦心人。

26. Whether a man's life be glorious or dishonoured is in all cases fixed by heaven.
27. There is no shame or disgrace greater than this.
28. Where the profit is large, the injury is profound; where the glory is abundant, the disgrace is great.
29. To cause the people in calamitous years to escape from perishing.
30. Imperial Heaven does not turn away from the man whose heart is sad.

EXERCISE 43.

VOCABULARY.

捨 *shê*^{3}, to let go; to throw away.

圖 *t'u*^{2}, a map or plan; to plan, to aim at.

孰 *shu*^{2}, who?, which?, what?.

推 *t'ui*^{1}, to push; to put aside; to put forward.

私 *ssŭ*^{1}, private, selfish.

載 *tsai*^{1}, to contain, to load; *tsai*^{3}, a year.

斷 *tuan*^{4}, to cut off; to decide; certainly.

供 *kung*^{4}, to offer, to present; *kung*^{1}, evidence, a deposition.

賞 *shang*^{3}, to reward, to bestow on an inferior.

罰 *fa*^{2}, to fine; to punish.

遊 *yu*^{2}, to travel, to wander.

零 *ling*^{2}, broken up, fragmentary.

[1] 殺之無益、不如捨之。

TRANSLATION.

1. To kill it is no use: I had better let it go.

1. *pu ju*, not [as good] as, = I had better.

捨[2]舊而圖新。爾[3]等務當圖謀正業。他[4]日自當圖報厚恩。孰[5]肯捨生而取義哉。功[6]名與身命孰重。出[7]洋年久孰無故土之思。推[8]車子以爲生。吾[9]輩今日當推舉一人爲王。所[10]欲必推、所惡勿施。不[11]說人私情。官[12]有正條、民有私約。公[13]私皆有利益。將[14]貨載在船上。

2. To reject the old and aim at what is new.
3. You positively must endeavour to find a regular livelihood.
4. Another day of course I must strive to repay your great kindness.
5. Who is willing to throw away life and take righteousness?
6. Rank or life, which is the more important?
7. Having gone abroad for many years, who has not a longing for his old land?
8. He made a living by pushing a barrow.
9. To day we ought to raise up some one to be our king.
10. What you desire, you must cede to others; what you dislike, do not bestow upon them.
11. Do not talk of people's private affairs.
12. The officials have the regular laws, the people have their private agreements.
13. Public and private [interests] will both have benefit and advantage [therefrom].
14. He took the goods and loaded them on to a vessel.

3. *wu tang*, positively must. *t'u mou*, plan and scheme.
7. 故, *ku*, here means 'old'.
8. 以, whereby, *wei shêng*, to make a living.
9. *t'ui chü*, to put forward and to raise.
12. 條, *t'iao*, *lit.*, articles, sections.

載[15]在條約。與[16]其斷交。
斷[17]不忍爲此也。今[18]經
半載有餘、並未擬斷。
以[19]飲食供給行路人。
赴[20]縣供稱。賞[21]善罰惡。
賞[22]罰不平。賞[23]銀十兩。
不[24]用刑斬、有罪者、但罰
其銀。虎[25]鹿不同遊。
父[26]母在不遠遊。俱[27]係
已革遊勇、供認行兇屬
實。

15. It is stated in the treaty.
16. To break off intercourse with him.
17. I certainly cannot bear to do this.
18. There has now elapsed half a year and more, and he has not given any decision.
19. They supply travellers with food and drink.
20. Having gone to the Magistrate, he deposed and said.
21. To reward the good and punish the wicked.
22. The rewards and punishments are not just.
23. To bestow upon him ten taels of silver.
24. [The king of that country] does not inflict corporal punishments or the penalty of death: he only punishes offenders with pecuniary fines.
25. The tiger and the stag do not go about together.
26. While your parents are alive, do not travel far.
27. They all were vagrant soldiers who had been dismissed from the service, and they confessed that it was true that they had committed acts of violence.

18. 擬, to propose, *vide* Ex. 30. 11.

19. *kung chi*, to supply, to furnish.

24. *Lit.*, does not use punishments or beheading; those who have offences, he only fines them money.

25. 遊; this character and 游 are interchanged with each other.

27. 革, to skin, to strip, to cashier. *chü hsi*, all were, *i ko*, already dismissed,

[28] 所收零星無多。

[29] 五兩零。

[30] 本利共欠三千零二十兩。

[31] 王曰、何以利吾國、大夫曰、何以利吾家、士庶人曰、何以利吾身。

28. That which they received (their harvest) was in petty quantities and not much.
29. Five taels, odd.
30. For principal and interest he owed altogether 3020 taels.
31. If the king says, how shall I profit my kingdom, the great officers will say, how shall we profit our families, and the inferior officers and the common people will say, how shall we profit ourselves.

yu yung, wandering soldiers, *kung jên*, in their depositions they acknowledged that, *hsing hsiung*, practising violence, *shu shih*, was true.

28. *ling hsing*, fractional, fragmentary.

30. Wherever, in writing down numbers, we place a cypher between two figures, the Chinese invariably in speaking, but not generally in writing, insert the character 零.

31. *ho i*, by what, = how. 士 in classical Chinese often means officials.

EXERCISE 44.

VOCABULARY.

趕 *kan*³, to run after; to hasten.

確 *ch'üeh*⁴ (or, *ch'io*), firm; real, accurate.

奏 *tsou*⁴, to report to the Throne.

破 *p'o*⁴, to break, to tear, to ruin.

感 *kan*³, to touch the feelings; to be grateful.

毆 *ou*¹, to beat.

打 *ta*³, to hit.

恃 *shih*⁴, to rely on.

伸 *shên*¹, to stretch out, to straighten.

屈 *ch'ü*¹, to bend, to crouch; a wrong.

特 *t'ê*⁴, special.

票 *p'iao*⁴, a slip of paper, a document.

奪 *to*², to seize, to snatch, to decide.

元 *yüan*², beginning, original.

雙 *shuang*¹, a pair, double.

[1] 聞盜趕來、亦被重傷。

[2] 委員趕往查問明確。

[3] 確查情形、趕緊放銀。

[4] 着將所奏各節確切查明。

[5] 破壞器物。

[6] 破人之家、取其財寶。

[7] 爲窮人補破衣。

[8] 受恩不感。

[9] 孝心感動天地。

[10] 至誠感神。

[11] 感化人心。

TRANSLATION.

1. Hearing the robbers, he ran to the place; and he, too, was severely wounded.
2. I have given orders to an officer to hasten to the spot, and to find out the truth by careful enquiries.
3. To make careful enquiries into the circumstances, and to distribute money with all speed.
4. Let him take each point in the report and investigate it with the greatest thoroughness.
5. To break and spoil utensils and articles.
6. To ruin people's families and get possession of their wealth and valuables.
7. To mend torn clothes for a poor man, (to be a poor man's wife).
8. To receive kindness and not be grateful.
9. A filial heart will influence heaven and earth.
10. Perfect sincerity will move the spirits.
11. To touch and convert men's hearts.

1. 趕, also written 赶.

2. *ch'a*, to search, *wên*, to enquire, [so that it be] *ming*, clear and, *ch'üeh*, accurate.

3. *kan chin*, with haste and urgency.

4. *so tsou ko chieh*, each section which has been reported. *ch'üeh ch'ieh*, *lit.*, accurately and cuttingly.

7. 爲, *wei*⁴, for.

9. *kan tung*, to touch and move, to influence.

[12]妻不可毆。[13]毆死民人二命。[14]打犬欺主人。[15]打虎必須親兄弟。[16]勿恃富而欺窮。[17]犬之所恃者牙也。[18]兵勇恃衆毆打小民。[19]有屈必有伸。[20]屈道伸身。[21]伸手索銀。[22]如我之正直不屈、豈不快哉。[23]法外之特恩。[24]特示曉諭、各宜遵從。[25]特立借票爲據。

12. A wife may not be beaten.
13. They beat to death two persons.
14. If you beat a dog, you insult his master.
15. To hunt a tiger, one must have one's brothers [as companions].
16. Do not trust in your wealth and ill-treat the poor.
17. What a dog relies on are his teeth.
18. The soldiers trusting in their numbers beat the common people.
19. Where there is bending there must be a straightening out, (or, where there are wrongs there is sure to be a righting of them).
20. To bend principles and extend oneself, (to make one's principles subservient to one's interests).
21. He stretched out his hand and demanded money.
22. To be upright and unbending as I am, is it not delightful?
23. Exceptional and special favour.
24. [I issue this] special notification, giving you distinct orders: each man ought to obey and follow them.
25. We specially draw up this promissory note as proof.

13. *Lit.*, beat to death people, two lives.

15. 親; not only brothers, but cousins in the same generation as oneself are called *hsiung-ti*: *ch'in hsiung-ti*, are real brothers, in our sense.

17. For 之 and 所者 see Notes to Ex. 7. 15 and Ex. 7. 17.

22. *Lit.*, like my, *chêng chih*, uprightness, etc.,.

23. *fa wai*, beyond the law, exceptional.

25. *chieh p'iao*, a loan document, an acknowledgment of money borrowed.

26 出票拏人。

27 認票不認人。

28 君子不奪人之所好。

29 奪其食而速其死。

30 既無確據、實難定奪。

31 同治元年。

32 自上年水災之後、地方元氣未復。

33 忠義無雙。

34 福壽雙全。

35 不論雙單月。

36 天事奇奇難測。

26. To issue a warrant for the arrest of a man.
27. We recognize the note and not its bearer.
28. The superior man does not seize what others love.
29. To rob [them of] their food and hasten their deaths.
30. Since there is no distinct proof, it is impossible to decide.
31. The first year [of the reign] of T'ung Chih.
32. The district has never recovered itself since the floods of previous years.
33. In loyalty and uprightness without an equal.
34. May your happiness and your old age both be perfect.
35. Never mind whether it be an even or an odd month.
36. The affairs of heaven are most strange and are hard to divine.

32. 自 ... 後 from after, since, *shui tsai*, the water calamity, *ti fang*, the district's, *yüan ch'i*, original condition, or, health, *wei fu*, has not come back.

35. Even month, *i. e.* second, fourth, etc.: odd month, first, third, etc..

EXERCISE 45.

VOCABULARY.

婦 *fu*[4], a woman, a wife.
兒 *êrh*[2], a boy, a son.
孫 *sun*[1], a grandson.
朋 *p'êng*[2], a friend.
友 *yu*[3], a friend, a companion.
祖 *tsu*[3], an ancestor.
鄰 *lin*[2], neighbouring, neighbour.

曾 *ts'êng*², past, done; *tsêng*¹, to add to.
族 *tsu*², a clan, a family.
睦 *mu*⁴, friendly.
鄉 *hsiang*¹, a village, the country.
序 *hsü*⁴, order, series.
倫 *lun*², relationship.

[1] 夫婦之情深如海。
[2] 愛同兒女。
[3] 不讀書兒孫愚。
[4] 衣破難對人。
[5] 好兒不貪祖上業。
[6] 切勿說官府可恃。
[7] 在家靠父母、在外靠朋友。
[8] 所欠未曾結清。
[9] 此事不知曾否說於本家親族。
[10] 子孫之衆皆出祖宗一人之身。

TRANSLATION.

1. The affection of husband and wife is deep as the sea.
2. Love them like sons or daughters.
3. If you do not study, your sons and grandsons will be stupid.
4. When one's clothes are ragged, it is hard to face people.
5. A good son does not covet the property of his ancestors.
6. On no account say that the authorities can be relied on.
7. When at home put your trust in your father and mother; when abroad, in your friends.
8. He has not cleared off his debts.
9. I do not know whether he has, or has not, told this matter to his own family and relations.
10. The crowd of sons and grandsons (of descendants) all spring from the person of one ancestor.

5. 祖上, *tsu shang*, 祖宗, *tsu tsung*, (in Example No. 10), and 祖先, *tsu hsien*, (in No. 22), all mean ancestors..
6. *kuan-fu*, officials, authorities.
8. *so ch'ien*, what he owes, *wei ts'êng*, he has not, *chieh*, settled, *ch'ing*, clear.
9. *ch'in tsu*, relations, those descended from the same ancestor.

父[11]子不信家不睦。和[12]睦
鄰里親族。鄰[13]鄰和睦、婦
子歡樂。鄉[14]愚未明例禁。
是[15]可忍也、孰不可忍也。
分[16]序而坐。兄[17]則友、弟則
恭、長幼序。人[18]倫有五、夫
婦爲先。內[19]則父子、外則
君臣、人之大倫也。教[20]以
人倫、父子有親、君臣有義、
夫婦有別、長幼有序、朋友
有信。

11. If father and son do not trust each other, the household will not be in harmony.

12. On friendly terms with neighbours and kinsfolk.

13. Your village neighbours will be friendly with you, and your wife and children will rejoice.

14. The country dolts (the stupid country folk) did not understand the law's prohibitions.

15. If he can bear this, what cannot he bear?

16. To sit down in proper order.

17. Friendliness on the part of the elder brother, respect on the part of the younger brother, between old and young order.

18. The human relationships are five; that of husband and wife comes first.

19. At home there is the father and the son, abroad there is the prince and the minister: [these are] the great relationships of mankind.

20. He taught them the relations of humanity, that father and

12. *ho mu*, harmonious and friendly; *lin li*, neighbours; *lit.*, *lin*, those who dwell near, *li*, those living in the same *li*, street.

15. 是, *shih*, this.

16. 分序, dividing in proper order, or according to precedence.

17. *Lit.*, be he an elder brother, then let him be friendly, *etc.*.

20. 以, *cf.* Ex. 13. 6. Note. 別, *pieh*, separation of functions, *i. e.*, the wife must take charge of every thing in doors, the husband out of doors.

[21] 高曾祖、父而身、身而子、子而孫、自子孫至元曾、乃九族、人之倫。

[22] 敬天地、禮神明、奉祖先、孝雙親、守王法、重師尊、愛兄弟、信友朋、睦宗族、和鄉鄰、別夫婦、教子孫。

son [should] have affection, prince and minister should have uprightness, husband and wife should have separation [of functions], old and young should have order, friends should have fidelity.

21. Great-great grandfather, great grandfather, grandfather, one's father and oneself, oneself and one's son, son and grandson, from son and grandson to great grandson and great great grandson: these indeed, are the nine [degrees of] kindred, the relationships of man.

22. Reverence heaven and earth, perform rites to the spirits, worship your ancestors, be dutiful to your parents; keep the king's laws, honour your teachers and venerable persons, love your brothers and be faithful to your friends; be friendly with your kinsfolk, and in harmony with your neighbours, keep separate [the duties of] husband and wife, teach your sons and grandsons.

21. 高曾祖 here stand for 高祖, 曾祖, 祖 (= 祖父, grandfather), one's paternal ancestors for three generations. 曾 is read *tsêng*, and not *ts'êng*. 元曾 = 元孫, 曾孫: *tsêng sun* is great grandson, and *yüan sun* great great grandson, the two being transposed in the text for the sake of the rhythm. Note also that 元, *yüan*, is a substituted character, being used for 玄 (Rad. No. 95), which is now tabooed.

22. 神明, spirits; 宗族, kinsfolk; 鄉鄰, *lit.*, village neighbours, as in Example No. 13, above; 別, *vide* Example No. 20.

EXERCISE 46.

VOCABULARY.

買 *mai*³, to buy.

賣 *mai*⁴, to sell.

緣 *yüan*², cause, reason; because of.

慮 *lü*⁴, care, anxiety.

託 *t'o*¹, to request.

代 *tai*⁴, for, on behalf of; a generation.

允 *yün*³, to assent.

摺 *chê*², a report to the Emperor, a memorial.

抄 *ch'ao*¹, to copy.

蓋 *kai*⁴, to cover; for.

機 *chi*¹, machine; opportunity; secret.

密 *mi*⁴, dense; secret.

1 賣刀買牛。

2 舊商買賣不及新商百分之一。

3 緣此死命。

4 因何緣由。

5 人無遠慮必有近憂。

6 臨危託故人。

7 託人代筆。

8 一代不如一代。

9 各人允從。

TRANSLATION.

1. To sell their swords and buy oxen.
2. The trade of the old merchants did not amount to a one hundredth part of that of the new merchants.
3. Because of this he lost his life.
4. On account of what reason and cause, (= for what reason)?
5. If a man has not distant anxiety (anxiety for the future), he will be sure to have grief close at hand.
6. When going into danger, ask [the help of] an old friend.
7. To ask a person to write for one.
8. Each generation is worse than the preceding one.
9. Each man assented and complied.

1. Oxen, *i. e.* cattle for the plough.

2. *mai mai*, buying and selling, trade. *pu chi*, did not reach to [that of] the new merchants, one part in a hundred.

惟[10]此二條萬難應允。具[11]
摺奏明。抄[12]寫文書。青[13]
布蓋頭。蓋[14]世無雙。乘[15]
機敗賊。西[16]國各種機器。
密[17]厚朋友。某[18]人在彼閒
談見而幫助。當[19]燒之於
火盡滅其類。今[20]聞日本
國家派人至泰西各國買
取黃金、緣(2)日本近來改用
金錢、而(3)慮存金不多、故有
此舉。

10. Only these two clauses, it is quite impossible to assent to.
11. To present a memorial to the Emperor.
12. To copy a despatch.
13. With black cloths covering their heads, (wearing black turbans).
14. Over-topping the age, and without an equal.
15. Taking advantage of an opportunity, he defeated the rebels.
16. All kinds of European machinery.
17. Close friends.
18. A certain man, who was idly talking there, saw [what was happening] and gave help.
19. We ought to burn them in fire and destroy the whole tribe of them.
20. We now hear that the Japanese government is sending men to all European countries to buy gold. (2) The reason [for this is that] Japan has recently adopted gold coinage, (3) and she is anxious because her stock of gold is not great: therefore she has [taken] this step.

10. 應, *ying*⁴, to answer, to assent to.

11. *chü*, to prepare, *chê*, a memorial, *tsou ming*, reporting and making plain.

16. *chi ch'i*, mechanical implements, machinery.

19. *chin mieh*, entirely destroy, *ch'i lei*, their class.

20. *jih-pên*, Japan; *kuo chia*, the state, the government. *t'ai hsi*, *cf.* Ex 30. 9. *mai ch'ü*, to procure by purchase, to buy. It will be noticed that *mai*³, to buy, is frequently combined with some other verb, meaning 'to procure', 'to receive', which it is unnecessary to translate. Similarly, *mai*⁴, to sell, is joined with words meaning 'to send', 'to issue'.

(2) *kai yung*, to change to the use of. (3) 舉, *chü*, an undertaking or step.

[21] 如該國並無領事官、(2)准其託別國領事官代爲管理、(3)亦必須別國領事官允爲代管。[22] 今之學者多不知外情、(2)由於洋務摺予之不發抄、(3)不發抄之故、蓋慮機密重情爲外人所知也、(4)然數年來所謂密諭密摺(5)往往中人不及知、外人暗知之。

21. If the said country be altogether without a Consul, (2) it is permitted to her to request the Consul of another country to act on her behalf. (3) It is also necessary that the Consul of the other country should consent to act for her.

22. Students of the present day are for the most part unacquainted with foreign matters. (2) This originates in the withholding from publication of memorials on foreign affairs. (3) The reason of their not being published is because [the government is] anxious lest secret matters of importance should become known to foreigners. (4) But for some years past, [in the case of] what are called secret decrees and secret memorials, (5) [it happens] constantly that Chinese do not come to know them, while foreigners secretly do know them.

21. Consul, *vide* Ex. 23. 14.

(2) *tai-wei*, on [her] behalf to do, *kuan-li*, the taking charge [of affairs]. This redundant use of *wei* is very common: 允爲, just below, is another instance.

22. (2) *yu yü*, originates in, *pu fa ch'ao*, the not issuing for copying, *chih*, of, *yang wu chê-tzŭ*, memorials on foreign affairs. Decrees and memorials intended for publication are sent to a certain office to be transcribed, and the copies are then handed to the publishers of the *Peking Gazette*. *fa ch'ao*, to send out for copying, is thus equivalent to 'publish'. *cf.* Note to Ex. 30. 2.

(3) 蓋, for, because; *chi mi*, secret. 爲, *etc.*, *lit.*, be that which foreigners know.

(5) *wang wang*, constantly.

EXERCISE 47.

VOCABULARY.

賑 *chên*[4], to give relief or charity.
漸 *chien*[4], gradually.
籌 *ch'ou*[2], to calculate, to consider.
晝 *chou*[4], day-time.
夜 *yeh*[4], night.
忽 *hu*[1], suddenly.
遷 *ch'ien*[1], to move, to remove.
避 *pi*[4], to flee from, to escape from.
幸 *hsing*[4], fortunate.
損 *sun*[3], to injure.
資 *tzŭ*[1], means, funds; to help.

有[1]災必有賑。
賑[2]濟難民。
將[3]來教化日深、皆可漸爲良民、聖教可期漸興。
去[4]日漸多、來日少。
詳[5]細籌思。
籌[6]辦海防。
白[7]晝被盜。

TRANSLATION.

1. If there be a calamity, there must be a distribution of relief.
2. To give charitable assistance to people in distress.
3. In the future, as their civilization becomes daily greater, they may all gradually become law-abiding subjects, and one may hope that the holy doctrine (Confucianism) will gradually make progress.
4. The days that are gone [become] gradually more, the coming days [grow] fewer.
5. To consider the matter thoroughly.
6. To consider and arrange (to devise plans for) the maritime defence [of the country].
7. To be robbed in broad day.

3. *chiang lai*, in future; *chiao hua*, teaching and transforming, civilizing. 期, *ch'i*, to hope; 興, *hsing*, to rise, to prosper.

5. *hsiang hsi*, minutely and closely, *ch'ou ssŭ*, consider and think.

日[8]集夜散。晝[9]夜不息。

忽[10]然不見。忽[11]明忽滅。

民[12]日遷善。遷[13]移他鄉。

親[14]近有德、遠避兇人。

幸[15]得避罪。莫[16]不幸於不聞過。

弟[17]子所作巧妙、乃過於師。

甘[18]心應允、約期舉事。

有[19]益無損。

無[20]損於貧民、無傷於富商。

該[21]商資本厚重。

8. Assembling by day and dispersing at night.
9. Not stopping by day or night.
10. He suddenly disappeared.
11. At one moment shining, at one moment extinguished.
12. The people daily move [towards] goodness.
13. To remove to another village.
14. Be intimate with [those who] have virtue, keep far away from violent men.
15. He luckily succeeded in escaping punishment.
16. There is nothing more unfortunate than not to hear (not to be told) one's faults.
17. [The work] which the pupil did was skilful and excellent: indeed, he surpassed his teacher.
18. They gladly assented and arranged a time to undertake the work.
19. It is advantageous and not hurtful.
20. It will not cause injury to the poor people nor harm to the rich merchants.
21. The merchants in question possess substantial capital.

10. 然, *jan*, an adverbial termination.
14. *chʻin chin*, to be intimate and keep near.
15. *tê*, to get, to succeed in; *tsui*, the punishment for a crime.
16. *yü*, than.
17. *ti tzŭ*, a pupil, a disciple; *kuo yü*, superior to.
18. *ying*^{4}, to answer, to assent to.
21. *Lit.*, *kai shang*, of the said merchants, *tzŭ pên*, the capital, *hou chung*, is substantial.

籌[22]備工資、按戶出丁。所[23]慮、放賑之處、難得許多良官、誠(2)如聖諭、豈今之州縣勝於前人。

七[24]月初間江水漸長、即(2)籌備料物、晝夜防護、經七(3)月十六日晚間、忽起大風、水高於岸、先(4)經曉諭居民遷避高阜、幸(5)未損傷人口、

22. [They must] provide funds for wages, and every house supply a man.

23. Unfortunately, in the places where charity is distributed, it is difficult to get very many good officials. (2) It is really like [the words of] His Majesty's edict, "how should the Subprefects and Magistrates of the present day be superior to their predecessors."

24. In the early part of the Seventh Month the water of the River (of the Yangtse) gradually rose. (2) Thereupon [the authorities] took measures to provide materials, and kept watch by day and night. (3). On the 16th day of the Seventh Month, at a late hour, suddenly there arose a high wind, and the water became higher than the bank. (4) Before this distinct orders had been given to the people dwelling [thereabouts] to remove on to high ground, (5) and fortunately no harm occurred to any person. (6)

22. *ch'ou pei*, think about and prepare, *kung tzŭ*, labour funds, and, *an hu*, according to the households, house by house, etc..

23. *so lü*, what one feels anxious about, = unfortunately. 許; note the meaning of *hsü*, — very. 放, *fang*, to loose, to distribute.

(2) *shêng*, holy, is frequently used for Imperial. *chou hsien*, *vide* Notes to Ex. 21.4 and 5.

24. 間; *chien*, at the time of, *ch'u*, the beginning.

(2) 經, sign of the past tense. *liao wu*, materials and things, *i. e.* materials for strengthening the embankments and stopping breaches. *fang hu*, to guard and protect.

(4) *hsien ching*, before did, *hsiao yü*, clearly order, *chü min*, the people dwelling [there], etc.. *fou*, Rad. No. 170.

而(6)貧民口食無資、受苦難言、當(7)經該縣稟請照例散賑。

But the poor people, having no funds [wherewith to procure] food, suffered indescribable hardships. (7) Thereupon the Magistrate concerned made a report, requesting that in accordance with the law he might [be allowed to] distribute relief.

(6) *k'ou shih*, food.

(7) 當, at [that time], *cf.* Ex. 10. 8, where the complete expression is given. 散, to scatter, to distribute.

EXERCISE 48.

VOCABULARY.

試 *shih*⁴, to try, to test.

場 *ch'ang*², an area, a place.

考 *k'ao*³, to examine.

規 *kuei*¹, a pair of compasses; a regulation; a custom.

酌 *cho*², to consider, to deliberate.

靜 *ching*⁴, quiet, still, serene.

惰 *to*⁴, lazy, idle.

弊 *pi*⁴, malpractices.

屆 *chieh*⁴, to arrive at; a term.

差 *ch'ai*¹, to employ officially; *ch'a*¹, error, difference.

遣 *ch'ien*³, to send; to send away.

勿[1]以身試法。進[2]考場。當[3]場正法。

TRANSLATION.

1. Do not make trial of the law with your own person.
2. To enter the examination hall.
3. To execute on the spot.

1. 以, with.
2. 'hall', more correctly 'yard' or 'enclosure'.
3. *tang ch'ang*, on the spot. *chêng fa*, to carry out the regular process of the law, = to behead.

須[4]交規銀若干。酌[5]定
規條。身[6]靜心勞之事。
夜[7]靜書爲友。勿[8]始勤
終惰。教[9]不嚴師之惰。
務[10]期百弊盡除。災[11]賑
之弊非止一端、作弊之
人亦非一類。每[12]屆年
終。時[13]屆冬令、風高冷
嚴。飭[14]差嚴密查拏。
遣[15]派武官二名。特[16]遣
大員酌定諸事。

4. It is necessary to pay a fee of a certain amount.
5. [After due] deliberation to frame regulations.
6. Business which causes mental but not bodily labour.
7. In the quiet of the night books are one's friends.
8. Do not be diligent at first and idle at last.
9. To teach without strictness is laziness of the teacher.
10. I earnestly hope that all sorts of malpractices may be entirely got rid of.
11. The malpractices [attendant on] famine relief are not only of one kind; also the men who are guilty of the malpractices are not [only] one class.
12. Each [time] that we arrive at the close of the year.
13. The winter season has arrived: the wind is high, the cold severe.
14. He ordered his constables to make a strict search for them and arrest them.
15. To despatch two military officers.
16. [The Emperor] specially sent an officer of high rank to consider and settle all matters.

4. *kuei yin*, custom money, a fee; 若干, *jo kan*, so much.
5. *kuei t'iao*, regulation clauses, regulations.
6. *Lit.*, *shên ching*, body-quiet, *hsin lao*, mind-toiling business.
11. *i tuan*, one point, one matter.
13. 令, *ling*, a season; *lit.*, the time arrives at the winter season.
14. 差, for 差人, an official servant. *yen mi*, severely and closely.
16. 諸, *chu*, all.

[17]忽見縣差手挐傳票。
[18]推多取少、受辱不怨。
[19]再江南鄉試、入場士子皆能守場規、安靜無弊。
[20]一請按月考試以查勤惰也、(2)查在館學習人員果能盡力勤學、(3)自可日起有功、(4)惟其中勤惰之分、亦必隨時考察、

17. They suddenly saw a constable from the Magistracy, carrying in his hand a summons.

18. Cede much and take little; if affronted do not resent it.

19. Further, at the Provincial Examinations for Kiang-nan, the scholars who entered the [examination] hall were all able to keep the rules of the hall: they were peaceful and abstained from malpractices.

20. We beg that there may be a monthly examination [of the students] in order to discover their diligence or idleness. (2) We would remark that, if the official students in the college can really study diligently with all their might, (3) they of course can make progress day by day. (4) But it will be necessary to find out by examinations at the

17. *ch'uan p'iao*, a summoning paper, a summons.

19. Kiang-nan, a former province, now divided into Kiang-su and An-hui. *hsiang shih*, the country examination, that held in the capital of each province, as distinguished from the higher examination held for all the provinces at Peking.

20. 一, one, one rule. In drawing up regulations, etc., the Chinese head each regulation with the character for 'one', instead of giving consecutive numbers, 'one', 'two', etc., as we do. *an yüeh*, month by month.

(2) 查, *vide* Ex. 23. 19, Note.

tsai kuan, in the school.

hsüeh-hsi is an adjective agreeing with *jên yüan*; student officers, = official students, pupils at the Government College.

kuo nêng, really can, *chin li*, exhausting their strength, *ch'in hsüeh*, diligently learn.

(3) *Lit.*, naturally can daily rise and, *yu kung*, have merit.

(4) *Lit.*, but in them the difference of diligence and idleness, one also must according to the time (= at the time) examine and search.

今(5)議俟該員等學習半年之久、按月考試一次、又(6)議每屆三年、舉行大考一次、分別次第、高(7)等者、酌量差遣試用、下(8)等者、照常學習、俟(9)下屆考試、再行察視。

time whether they be diligent or idle. (5) We now propose that, after the pupils have studied for the length of half a year, they should be examined once every month. (6) We also propose at the end of every three years to hold a grand examination, in which their order will be determined. (7) Those [placed] in the higher class will after due consideration be given official employment on probation. (8) Those in the lower class will continue the ordinary course of study; (9) and, when the time comes for the next examination, we shall again proceed to enquire into [their progress].

(5) *chin i*, we now propose, *ssŭ*, waiting till (= when), *kai yuan têng*, the said officers (*i. e.*, pupils), *hsüeh hsi*, have studied, *pan nien chih chiu*, a length of half a year, *an yüeh*, month by month, *k'ao shih*, to examine, *i tz'ŭ*, one time.

(6) 舉, *etc.*; to institute a great examination, one time, *fên pieh*, to differentiate, *tz'ŭ ti*, their order.

(7) 等, grade. *cho liang*, considering and measuring, *ch'ai ch'ien*, officially employ and send (give official employment), *shih yung*, using on trial.

(8) *chao ch'ang*, as ordinarily.

(9) *hsia chieh*, the next occasion. *ch'a shih*, examine and look at.

EXERCISE 49.

VOCABULARY.

夥 *huo*^{3}, numerous; a partner, an assistant.

盈 *ying*^{2}, full; overflowing.

虧 *k'uei*^{1}, to fail; deficient.

協 *hsieh*^{2}, to harmonize; to assist.

稍 *shao*^{3}, somewhat, slightly.

垂 *ch'ui*^{2}, to hang down, to drop down.

憑 *p'ing*², to rely on; proof.
包 *pao*¹, to wrap; a bundle.
還 *huan*², to come back; to repay.
準 *chun*³, to determine; accurate.

先[1]在魚行幫夥。案[2]件甚夥。器[3]小易盈。萬[4]川歸海而不盈。月[5]滿則虧。欠[6]銀日久不還。如[7]數歸還、並無虧短。協[8]同料理行務。無[9]人協濟。入[10]夏以來雨水稍多。人[11]心稍定。垂[12]首視下。

TRANSLATION.

1. He was formerly an assistant at a fish-dealer's.
2. The legal cases are very numerous.
3. If a vessel be small, it is easy to fill.
4. The myriad streams run into the sea, and yet it does not overflow.
5. When the moon is full, then it wanes.
6. To owe money for a long period and not repay it.
7. He paid it back in full, and there was no deficiency at all.
8. To manage conjointly the affairs of the firm.
9. He has no one to assist him.
10. Ever since the beginning of summer the rainfall has been slightly excessive.
11. Men's minds were in some degree quieted.
12. To bow the head and look down.

1. 行, *hang*², a mercantile firm. *pang huo*, *lit.*, a helping assistant.
2. *chien*, numerative of *an*, a case or action at law.
3. Said of men of small ability.
7. *ju shu*, in accordance with the amount, in full, *kuei huan*, pay back, *ping wu*, there was not at all, *k'uei tuan*, loss and shortness.
8. *hsieh t'ung*, to act together, or conjointly. 行, *hang*, as in Example No. 1.

垂[13]手而等。

爾[14]有憑據否。

紙[15]裹不能包住火。

包[16]辦工料。

屢[17]次比對、皆屬準確。

今[18]因我等彼此見信、情願各出本銀五千兩、合夥生意、準(2)於一年期滿、公同結算、或(3)有盈虧、各人聽認、務(4)須協力同心、不得稍存私見、以垂永遠、

13. To wait with the hands hanging down, (without attempting to do anything).
14. Have you proof, or not?
15. One cannot wrap up fire in paper.
16. He undertook the supplying of labour and materials.
17. They have been compared together several times, and they all are absolutely accurate.
18. Now, because we feel confidence in each other, we are willing each of us to furnish capital [to the extent of] five thousand taels, and to form a partnership for trading purposes. (2) It is determined that at the completion of a period of one year we shall settle accounts together: (3) whether there be gain or loss, each man will acquiesce and acknowledge it. (4) In order that [our association] may continue perpetually, it is absolutely necessary that we unite our strength and be of one mind, and we must not be influenced in the least by our private interests.

14. *p'ing chü*, proof.
15. *pao chu*, wrap up.
16. 包 frequently means 'to undertake', 'to contract for'.
17. *pi tui*, to compare and place opposite, compare together.
18. *ho huo*, uniting as partners, *sheng i*, to trade.
(4) *shao ts'un*, slightly to preserve, *ssŭ chien*, private views. *i ch'ui*, in order that it may go down (go on), *yung yüan*, for ever.

(5)恐後無憑、立此合同、各存一紙。19今借到某某洋行規平銀五千兩正、(2)言明每月二分起息、(3)願將自已洋布四十包作爲按當、(4)準至本年十二月底本利清還、(5)如有過期、任聽將布變賣、(6)或有不足本利、惟保人補還、

(5) Fearing that afterwards there may be no proof, we have now drawn up the above agreement, [of which] each man retains one paper (one copy).

19. I have now received a loan [from] the foreign firm of Messrs — — of [the sum of] five thousand taels of Shanghai silver exactly. (2) It is stated explicitly that interest will be charged at the rate of 2 p.c. per month. (3) I am willing to give as security forty bales of foreign cottons belonging to myself. (4) It is determined that at the end of the Twelfth Month of this year the principal and interest shall be repaid in full. (5) If it should be that I overstep the limit, I will submit to [the creditor's] taking the cotton goods and selling them. (6) Should perchance it be that [the proceeds are] not equal to the principal and interest,

(5) 合同, an agreement.

19. *chieh*, he has borrowed, and *tao*, the money has actually come into his hands. *mou mou*, *vide* Ex. 16. 5.

規平; 5000 taels, or Chinese ounces of silver, according to the weights which are used for weighing silver in commercial transactions at Shanghai, these weights being known by the name of *kuei pʻing*: *pʻing*, literally, scales.

(2) 分, *vide* Note to Ex. 32. 9.

(3) *yüan chiang*, I am willing to take forty bales, etc., *tso wei*, and make them to be, *an-tang*, a pledge, (not a common expression).

(5) *jên tʻing*, allow. *pien*, convert into money.

(6) 惟 here does not mean 'only'. It emphasizes the words following, and it is best omitted in the translation. 補, *pu*, fill up [the deficiency] and, *huan*, repay.

恐(7)後無憑、特立此借票爲據。

the surety will make good [the difference]. (7) Fearing that afterwards there should be no proof, I specially execute this acknowledgement of the loan as evidence.

EXERCISE 50.

VOCABULARY.

舖 *p'u*[4], a shop.
境 *ching*[4], a region, a district.
搶 *ch'iang*[3], to take by force; to rob.
刼 *chieh*[2], to rob.
捉 *cho*[1], to seize.
倘 *t'ang*[3], if, but if.
拒 *chü*[4], to ward off, to oppose.
捕 *pu*[3], to catch, to seize.
格 *ko*[2], to correct; a pattern, a rule.
獲 *huo*[4], to seize, to arrest.
斃 *pi*[4], violent death.
恤 *hsü*[4], to pity; to relieve.

1 開設玉器舖。
2 皆爲舖夥。
3 邊境不靖。
4 入境問禁。
5 夜裏分路外出搶刼。
6 捉人勒銀。
7 派兵捕捉刼匪。
8 急水好捕魚。
9 倘敢故違、定行拏辦。

TRANSLATION.

1. To open a shop for [the sale of] articles of jade.
2. They all are shop assistants.
3. The frontier region is disturbed.
4. When you enter a territory, ask what is prohibited in it.
5. During the night they go out by different roads and commit robberies.
6. To make a man prisoner and extort money from him.
7. To despatch soldiers to arrest robbers.
8. Troubled water is good to catch fish in.
9. If they dare to disobey intentionally, I certainly shall proceed to arrest and punish them.

拒[10]捕殺差。拒[11]傷官兵。能[12]格君心之非。格[13]外施恩、以恤窮民。濟[14]急恤貧。有[15]犯必獲。今[16]年各種生意實獲厚利。一[17]夜羣盜入家。被[18]賊搶去財物、殺斃妻命。爲[19]此示諭舖戶居民人等知悉、境(2)內如有賊匪搶刼、爾(3)等務宜協同兵勇實力捉拿、倘(4)賊敢拒捕、許爾等格殺、照例無罪、

10. To resist arrest and kill the police officers.
11. To resist and wound the imperial troops.
12. He is able to correct what is wrong in the sovereign's mind.
13. To show extraordinary kindness, in order to compassionate the needy.
14. To help those in difficulty and to relieve the poor.
15. If there be offenders they must be arrested.
16. This year each kind of trade has really made substantial profits.
17. One night a gang of robbers entered his house.
18. He was robbed of his valuables and other property, and his wife was killed by the brigands.
19. Therefore [I issue] a notification bidding [you] shopkeepers and [other] inhabitants to know well that, (2) if there be brigands who plunder and rob within the district, (3) you must unite with the soldiers in making real efforts to capture them. (4) If the brigands dare to resist arrest, I permit you to kill them in self defence; and, in accordance

13. *ko wai*, beyond the rule, extraordinary; *shih ên*, to bestow favours, to show kindness, *e.g.*, to make a grant of food or money.

18. *Lit.*, he suffered that the brigands robbed him of valuables and property, and that they killed his wife: *ch‘i ming*, his wife's life.

19. *wei*^{4} *tz‘ŭ*, on account of this, *shih*, I notify, *yü* commanding, *p‘u hu*, shopkeepers and, *chü min*, resident people, — *jên têng*, merely a plural termination.

(3) 務宜, *wu i*, essentially ought, = positively must. 拿 = 拏.

(4) *ko sha*, to kill any one resisting lawful authority, to kill in self defence.

且[5]格殺一名、賞給花紅銀五十元、生[6]獲要犯一名、賞給花紅銀一百元、次[7]要犯、賞給五十元、被[8]賊拒傷、賞給藥資五元、傷[9]重者、賞二十元、若[10]因傷斃命者、賞給恩卹銀一百兩、如[11]有此等情事、由該處地保稟明、以憑核賞、決[12]不食言。

with the law, it will be no crime [on your part]. (5) Moreover, for the killing in self defence of one brigand, I will give a reward of fifty dollars. (6) For the capture alive of one important offender, I will give a reward of one hundred dollars. (7) For an offender of secondary importance I will give fifty dollars. (8) If any one be wounded by brigands who resist, I will give him five dollars as compensation. (9) To him whose wounds are severe, twenty dollars. (10) If [there should be] any one who dies on account of his wounds, I will give a compassionate gratuity of one hundred taels. (11) If there should be matters of this kind, let the *ti-pao* of the place concerned report the same, so that I may be enabled to examine [into the matter] and pay the reward. (12) I certainly will not eat my words (not break my promise).

(5) *shang chi*, bestow and give. *hua hung*, a reward, *lit.*, flowers and red. It is said that formerly it was the custom to present, as a public reward, a piece of red silk embroidered with flowers, and later the expression came to mean any reward. 元, *yüan*, a dollar: this character is often found with the meaning of 'dollar', being used in place of *yüan*, round, (for which see next Exercise).

(8) *pei tsei chü shang*, suffers that a brigand resisting wounds him. *yao tzŭ*, medicine money, money to buy medicines.

(11) 由, *vide* Note to Ex. 22. 8.

ti-pao, a headman or constable, who is appointed by the local authorities, and whose duty it is to report to them what happens in his village or district, as well as in some degree to maintain order. 以憑; *p'ing*, to depend on; in order that I may have something to go on, *ho*, in examining, etc..

(12) *chüeh*, positively, certainly.

EXERCISE 51.

VOCABULARY.

訪 *fang*^{3}, to search, to enquire.

項 *hsiang*^{4}, a kind, an item; sum of money.

巡 *hsün*^{2}, to patrol, to go the rounds.

繳 *chiao*^{3}, to hand in; to pay.

漏 *lou*^{4}, to leak; to evade payment.

承 *ch'êng*^{2}, to receive; to undertake.

炮 *p'ao*^{4}, a cannon.

充 *ch'ung*^{1}, to fill, to hold the place of.

捐 *chüan*^{1}, to subscribe money.

圓 *yüan*^{2}, round; a dollar.

矩 *chü*^{3}, a carpenter's square; a rule.

認[1]眞察訪。

各[2]項生意。

隨[3]時密訪、如有前項情弊、即行嚴拏重辦。

晝[4]夜巡防。

廵[5]察洋面、捕獲盜賊。

將[6]銀繳案。

TRANSLATION.

1. To search and enquire in earnest.
2. Each kind of trade.
3. [He is ordered] immediately to make close enquiries, and if there be any of the above kinds of malpractices, to proceed at once rigorously to arrest [the offenders] and deal with them severely.
4. Day and night to patrol and guard.
5. To cruise about and search the seas [in order] to capture pirates.
6. To take the money and pay it into court.

3. *sui shih*, following the time, immediately. 情弊, matters and malpractices, = malpractices.

5. 廵 is merely another form of 巡.

應[7]完之稅、如數繳清。
船[8]漏水入。船[9]到江
中補漏遲。子[10]承父
業。無[11]人承管之產。
買[12]得洋炮十尊。充[13]
當水手。鄉[14]愚貪利
想充勇丁。捐[15]資設
理義學。捐[16]助善舉。
明[17]月不常圓。規[18]矩
方圓之至。此[19]人無
規矩。

7. The duties which ought to be paid, have been paid in full in accordance with the amount.
8. The ship leaked, and the water came in.
9. When the boat reaches the middle of the river, it is [too] late to stop the leak.
10. The son inherits his father's property.
11. An estate which no one receives and takes charge of, (ownerless property).
12. He acquired by purchase ten foreign cannon.
13. To serve as a sailor.
14. The stupid countrymen in their greed for gain desire to serve as soldiers.
15. To contribute funds for the establishment of a free school.
16. To contribute to the support of a good undertaking.
17. The bright moon is not always round.
18. The compasses and the carpenter's square are the perfection of squareness and roundness.
19. This man has no manners.

7. 完, *wan*, to pay.

12. 炮, a common way of writing *p'ao*, a cannon: a more correct form is given in Ex. 67. 尊, *tsun*, numerative of cannon.

13. 當, to be, to hold the position of, *ch'ung tang*, to serve as.

14. *hsiang yü*, the country dolts. 想, *hsiang*, think, = desire. For *yung*, *vide* Ex. 22. 12.

19. *kuei chü*, a rule, a custom; also, as here, manners.

[20]殺人盈野、罪不容於死。

[21]訪得近日各州縣所設之巡船、每(2)隻皆要繳官府規銀二三千圓不等、方准承充、且(3)所用之巡船、及船上器械火炮、並各水手工食等項、俱(4)係該船上頭人捐資辦理、並非由官支給、是(5)以官府任從其走私漏稅、收受盜賊月規、

20. To kill people [in such numbers as] to fill the fields; death is not punishment enough for this.

21. We have discovered that of late [in the case of] the cruisers provided by each Sub-prefect or Magistrate, (2) for each vessel it is in every case necessary to pay to the authorities a fee varying from two to three thousand dollars, before it is allowed to serve. (3) Moreover, the vessels used, and the implements, weapons and cannon, together with the wages and food of the sailors, (4) are all supplied by the masters on the said vessels at their own expense, and are not paid for by government. (5) Therefore the authorities allow them to smuggle and evade [payment of] duties, [as well as to] accept monthly fees from pirates.

20. 罪, *etc.*, the guilt [is so great that it], *pu jung*, is not contained in death.

21. *fang tê*, to enquire and get, to get by enquiry, to discover.

(2) 隻, *chih*, numerative of vessels. *kuan fu*, the authorities, the Subprefects, etc., above mentioned. *pu têng*, not the same, varying; 方, then; *ch'êng ch'ung*, obtain and fill [the post].

(3) 及, and. 等項, such items, these items. 工, labour, wages.

(4) *chü hsi*, *etc.*, [in the case of] all [it] is the masters, etc., contribute funds, *pan li*, to supply them; *ping fei*, and not, *yu*, by, *kuan*, the government, *chih chi*, disburse [money].

(5) 是以, *shih i*, therefore, *kuan fu*, the authorities, *jên ts'ung*, permit, *ch'i*, them, the masters, *tsou ssŭ*, to smuggle.

每(6)賊一名每月交與規銀四圓、則隨便打刧、雖(7)有巡船明見、皆不捉拿。

(6) Each pirate every month pays a fee of four dollars, and then he commits piracies as he pleases. (7) Though a cruiser should see him distinctly, in no case does it arrest him.

(6) 交, *chiao*, to hand, *yü*, to; *chiao yü*, pay to them. *kuei yin*, a fee. *sui pien*, according to his convenience, as he pleases, *ta chieh*, practise robbery.

EXERCISE 52.

VOCABULARY.

抽 *ch'ou*^{1}, to pull, to draw out; to levy.

指 *chih*^{3}, a finger; to point.

華 *hua*^{2}, bloom; flowery; China.

氂 *li*^{2}, one thousandth part of an ounce.

符 *fu*^{2}, a tally; to agree; a charm.

仰 *yang*^{3}, to look up; humbly.

究 *chiu*^{4}, to examine, to investigate.

販 *fan*^{4}, to trade, to deal in.

概 *kai*^{4}, all, general.

隱 *yin*^{3}, secret; to conceal.

匿 *ni*^{4}, to hide.

抽^{1}身事外。刀^{2}利傷人指。先^{3}須指出憑據。榮^{4}華富貴眼前花。

TRANSLATION.

1. To withdraw oneself from (to get out of) the affair.
2. If a knife be sharp, it cuts men's fingers.
3. First you must point out the proof.
4. Glory and splendour, wealth and honour, are flowers before the eyes (flowers of the moment).

抽[5]釐、取之華商。善[6]爲
護身之符。查[7]出筆跡
不符。仰[8]求天恩。仰[9]
即遵照辦理。嚴[10]行究
辦。着[11]將各案公平究
結。販[12]馬之人。一[13]切
兵器概屬違禁、不准販
運。奏[14]明大概情形。
不[15]傳說主人隱事。匿[16]
怨而友其人。有[17]話明
說、不必隱匿。

5. In levying lekin, one collects it from the Chinese merchant.
6. Goodness is a charm which protects the person.
7. He discovered that the handwriting did not agree.
8. Humbly to pray for the heavenly favour, (the Emperor's favour).
9. I beg that you will at once act in accordance with [the instructions given].
10. To proceed stringently to investigate and deal with [the case].
11. Let him investigate and settle each case impartially.
12. A horse dealer.
13. Weapons of war of every kind are all contraband, and no one is allowed to trade in them.
14. To report to the Throne the broad facts [of the case].
15. Do not tell [people] the secret affairs of your master.
16. To conceal one's resentment and [pretend] to be friendly with the man.
17. If you have anything to tell, speak it out plainly; you must not conceal it.

5. Lekin (釐金): a tax on goods, originally, as its name shows, fixed at one thousandth part of their value.
7. *pi chi*, pen tracks, handwriting.
9. 仰, often used, by courtesy, when giving instructions to inferiors.
13. *wei chin*, offend against prohibition, contraband. *fan yün*, *lit.*, to convey for sale.
14. *tsou ming*, to report to the Emperor. *ta kai*, general, a general outline.
16. 友, *yu*, to be friendly.

[18]此貨在口岸內、無論或在
本行、或在買客之手、除[(2)]海
關進口稅外、一概不得向
其抽收。俟[19]貨出賣後、卽
向承買之華商抽收釐捐。
[20]爲此示仰往來客商、諸色
人等、知悉、爾[(2)]等如有請領
海關稅單、販運洋貨、一[(3)]到
所指之處、賣與華商、卽[(4)]應
報明、完繳內地釐金、以符
定章、

18. While these goods [remain] in the port; never mind whether they be in the [possession of the importing] firm itself, or whether they be in the hands of a purchaser, (2) with the exception of the maritime customs import duty, no one must levy any duty upon them at all.

19. [They must] wait till after the goods have been sold, and then collect the lekin from the Chinese purchaser.

20. Therefore [I issue] a notification, desiring [you] travelling merchants who go and come and all kinds of men to know well, (2) that, if you apply for and obtain custom-house transit passes, and convey foreign goods for sale, (3) as soon as [the goods] arrive at the place indicated [in the pass], and are sold to Chinese traders, (4) [the parties

18. (2) 除 . . . 外, *vide* Ex. 27. 15.
i kai, one and all, *pu tê*, one must not, *hsiang ch'i*, on them, *ch'ou shou*, levy.

19. 卽 向, *etc.; chi*, then, *hsiang*, upon the acquiring and purchasing Chinese merchant levy the lekin. 捐; *li chüan*, lekin contribution, another term for lekin.

20. 客 商; *k'o shang*, travelling merchants, *chu sê* and all kinds of, *jên têng*, men.

(2) *êrh têng ju yu*, if it be that you, *ch'ing ling*, ask for and receive. 稅 單, *shui tan*, *sc. nei ti shui tan*, inland duty papers, *i. e.* transit passes. According to treaty, foreign goods going inland, and, if owned by a foreigner, native goods coming from the interior to a treaty port for exportation, can be protected by a transit pass, and so freed from all liability to pay duties during their transit; for which favour they pay an extra half-duty at the port itself.

(3) 所 指 之, indicated.

(4) *wan chiao*, to pay.

(5)倘該商承買之後、有隱匿不報、(6)一經查出、定即將貨充公、分別究治。

concerned] ought at once to report [the sale] and pay the inland lekin, in order to be in accord with the rules laid down. (5) But if, after the said traders have purchased [the goods], there be concealment [of the fact] and failure to report it; (6) as soon as it has been discovered, [the authorities] assuredly will at once confiscate the goods, and punish the parties as each may deserve.

(6) 充公, *ch'ung kung*, make them become public property, confiscate, and, *fên pieh*, dividing and distinguishing, *chiu chih*, investigate and deal with.

EXERCISE 53.

VOCABULARY.

衙 *ya*², an office.
沿 *yen*², along; to continue.
途 *t'u*², a road; a journey.
刻 *k'ê*¹ (or, *k'o*) to carve. *k'ê*⁴, a short time, a quarter of an hour.
停 *t'ing*², to stop, to cease.
呈 *ch'êng*², a plaint; to present to a superior.
驗 *yen*⁴, to examine, to inspect.
追 *chui*¹, to pursue, to follow.
銷 *hsiao*¹, to melt; to cancel.
只 *chih*³, only.
仍 *jêng*², still, yet; again.
司 *ssŭ*¹, to control; an officer.

知[1]縣衙門。沿[2]海各處。

TRANSLATION.

1. The Magistrate's Yamen.
2. Each place along the coast.

1. A Yamen is the official residence and office of a Chinese Mandarin.

沿[3]江各州縣。死[4]於半途。應[5]顧前途。石[6]上刻字。不[7]任一刻停止。停[8]兵講和。爾[9]何日入呈。務[10]將護照呈驗。遣[11]員驗尸。追[12]趕馬賊。該[13]員虧短銀兩、着即嚴追。業[14]經銷案。只[15]怕此貨仍無銷場。只[16]可仍行稟明上司。應[17]請一人司理文件。

3. Each Sub-prefecture and District along the Yangtse.
4. To die half way on one's journey.
5. One ought to regard the road ahead (to pay attention to the future).
6. To carve words on stone.
7. Not to allow them to stop for a moment.
8. To stop one's troops and discuss peace.
9. What day did you enter your plaint?
10. You must present your passport for inspection.
11. To send an officer to examine the corpse (to hold an inquest).
12. To pursue the mounted brigands.
13. Let stringent measures be taken at once to recover the deficit in the accounts of the officer in question.
14. He has already closed the case.
15. Only I fear that these goods will still have no market.
16. I can only again report [the matter] to my superior officer.
17. We ought to engage one man to manage the documents (to act as secretary).

5. *ku*, to regard.

13. Supply 之 after 短, *tuan*, making the first four words into a participle attached to *yin liang*, — the silver ounces of which the said officer is deficient and short, *cho*, I order [the proper authorities] at once stringently to pursue.

14. *yeh ching*, already has.

15. *hsiao ch'ang*, a place where they can be got rid of.

[18] 洋炮能及遠而有準。

[19] 爲照會事、接(2)准總理衙門文開、總(3)稅務司議定、運照之貨聽其沿途發賣、只(4)須將運照在彼處呈官查驗、文(5)內又聲明、運照之貨、一到所指之地、卽刻將單繳銷、

18. Foreign cannon carry a long way and shoot straight.

19. In the matter of an official communication. — I have received a despatch from the Tsungli Yamen saying, (3) the Inspector General of Customs has decided that transit pass goods may be permitted to be sold [at places] along the route; (4) and that it is merely necessary to present the transit pass to the authorities for examination at that place, (*i. e.* at the place of sale). (5) In the [Tsungli Yamen's] despatch it is further stated, [with regard to] transit pass goods, that, as soon as they arrive at the place indicated [in the pass], [the merchant must] immediately hand in the pass

18. *Lit.*, *nêng*, can, *chi yüan*, reach far, and, *yu chun*, have accuracy.

19. 爲 . . . 事; A Chinese despatch begins with a sentence, of which the first word is *wei*[4] and the last is *shih*, "on account of [such or such] a matter". As to *chao hui*, *vide* Ex. 23. 15.

(2) 准, to receive a despatch from an equal or a superior; generally used without 接, *chieh*. Tsungli Yamen, the Chinese Board of Foreign Affairs; for its full title, see Ex. 70. 4 (2). *wên*, a despatch, *k'ai*, saying.

(3) The European Commissioner of Customs in each treaty port is called 稅務司, *shui wu ssŭ*, (superintendent of duty matters); and the head of the whole Customs Service, the Inspector General at Peking, is known as the *tsung shui wu ssŭ*.

運照, *yün chao*, a conveyance certificate. This is the ordinary term for a transit pass, *vide* Note to Ex. 52. 20 (2). *yün chao chih huo*, transit pass goods, *i. e.*, goods protected by a transit pass. *t'ing*, to permit.

其, them, *sc.* the merchants. *yen t'u*, along the route, (instead of waiting till their arrival at the spot named in the pass). *fa mai*, simply, 'to sell'.

(5) 卽刻, then immediately, *chiang tan*, take the pass and, *chiao*, hand it in, *hsiao*, [in order that it may] be cancelled.

一(6)經繳銷、便與無單之貨無異、等語、而(7)各洋商所領運照近來往往不繳、應(8)請貴領事官、諭飭各洋商、以(9)前不再追問、以後運照務宜隨到隨繳、如(10)仍然不繳、只可行飭稅務司、以(11)後何商不繳、何商停發也。

for cancelment, (6) and, as soon as it has been handed in and cancelled, then [the goods] will in no wise differ from goods which never had a pass. (7) But of late it has constantly happened that foreign merchants have not given up the transit passes which they have received. (8) I ought [therefore] to request you, Mr. Consul, to notify all foreign merchants that, (9) [as regards] the past no further enquiries will be made, but in the future transit passes must certainly be given up immediately on arrival [at the place indicated in them]; (10) and, if they still fail to give them up, I can only send instructions to the Commissioner of Customs, (11) that henceforth he must cease issuing passes to any merchant who fails to surrender them.

(6) *pien*, then, *yü*, with, *wu tan chih huo*, not-having-a-pass goods, *wu i*, [they are] not different. 等語, such words: this expression, which should not be translated, is merely inserted to mark the termination of the Tsungli Yamen's remarks. We shall meet with other very similar expressions, also used to show the conclusion of quotations.

(7) *êrh ko yang shang*, but all foreign merchants, *so ling yün chao*, the transit passes which they receive, *chin lai*, of late, *wang wang*, constantly, *pu chiao*, they do not deliver up.

(8) Mr. Consul; in Chinese the formal way of addressing an officer is to prefix *kuei* (honourable) to his official title. Honourable Consul, = you, Mr. Consul.

(9) 再, *tsai*, further, *chui wên*, follow up and enquire: *chui*, has often the meaning of reverting to what is past. 隨, *etc.*, according as they arrive, accordingly give up.

(10) 然, *jan*, is merely an adverbial termination.

(11) *Lit.*, in future what merchant does not give up, to what (*i.e.*, to that) merchant cease issuing.

EXERCISE 54.

VOCABULARY.

卑 *pei*[1], lowly, humble; oneself.
昨 *tso*[2], yesterday; recently.
閱 *yüeh*[4], to review; to peruse.
控 *k'ung*[4], to accuse; to bring an action.
堂 *t'ang*[2], a hall; a court of justice.
訊 *hsün*[4], to interrogate judicially.
阻 *tsu*[3], to hinder, to stop.
建 *chien*[4], to found, to establish.
造 *tsao*[4], to make, to build.
勘 *k'an*[4], to examine personally, to inspect.
列 *lieh*[4], to place in order; to set forth.
契 *ch'i*[4], a deed; a document.
美 *mei*[3], excellent; beautiful.

1 天尊地卑。
2 卑讓德之本也。
3 千年如昨。
4 昨去閱兵。
5 昨接來文、業已閱悉。
6 控追借欠之銀。
7 赴京呈控。
8 上有天堂。

TRANSLATION.

1. Heaven is exalted, earth is lowly.
2. Humility and meekness are the foundation of virtue.
3. A thousand years are as yesterday.
4. I went yesterday to review troops.
5. Your despatch, which I received yesterday, I have minutely perused.
6. To bring an action for the recovery of money borrowed and owing.
7. To go to the capital and lay a charge.
8. Above there is the hall of heaven.

1. 尊, *tsun*, honourable, venerable.
5. *lai wên*, an in-coming despatch.

未[9]曾坐堂訊問。訊[10]
供核斷。運[11]河淺阻、
米船難免停止。立[12]
國建業。造[13]作惡語。
其[14]欲建造學堂、誰能
阻止。勘[15]定邊界。
次[16]日復同道府往勘
河岸。今[17]將公議各
例列左。列[18]聖施恩。
查[19]明契據。特[20]立賣
契爲據。

9. He has not sat in court and examined [the parties].
10. To take the evidence, consider [the matter] and give a decision.
11. The Grand Canal is blocked by shallows, and it is difficult for the rice boats to avoid being stopped.
12. To found a kingdom and establish a dynasty.
13. To fabricate wicked stories.
14. If he wishes to build a school, who can stop him?
15. To inspect and determine the boundary line.
16. Next day again with the Taotai and the Prefect I went to inspect the river bank.
17. We now set forth below all the regulations as agreed upon at a public meeting.
18. Successive Emperors have bestowed favours.
19. To examine the documents and proofs.
20. We have specially executed a deed of sale as proof.

9. 曾, *ts'êng*, has.

10. 核, *ho*, to examine, to weigh the facts.

11. *yün ho*, transport river: this is the name of the Grand Canal, which runs from Hangchow to Tientsin, a distance of more than 600 miles. 淺, *ch'ien*, shallow.

14. Taotai; *cf.* Ex. 23. 12.

17. *lieh tso*, arrange on the left hand side of the paper, which, with the Chinese way of writing, is equivalent to our 'below': similarly, *yu*, the right hand, is used for 'above'. 公議, publicly discussed.

[21]何必捨近而走遠。[22]捐資成美、垂訓教人。[23]昨據卑縣教民王本善等赴縣稟(2)控某某等阻建教堂、呈請示禁、等情、該(3)教民等所稟是否屬實、應(4)俟飭差傳集兩造勘明訊斷。

21. What need is there to reject what is near, and go after what is distant.

22. Contribute funds to accomplish good [works]; hand down instructions to teach men.

23. Yesterday Wang Pên-shan and other converts of my District came to the Magistracy, (2) and charged certain persons with preventing them from building a chapel; they prayed that I would issue a notification forbidding [this conduct]. (3) [As regards the question whether] the complaint made by the said converts be true or not, (4) — that must wait till I have the two parties summoned before me together, and, after inspection of the site, interrogate them and give my decision.

22. 垂, *ch'ui*, hand down to future generations.

23. 據, is connected with *ping*, below; but it cannot conveniently be translated here. For its meaning *vide* Note to Ex. 25. 18. 卑, a self-depreciatory term for 'my'. The writer of the passage is evidently the Magistrate of the District; and as he uses *pei*, for 'my', he must be addressing a superior officer. *chiao min*, a Chinese who is a follower of the [Christian] doctrine. 等, and others.

(2) *ping k'ung*, petitioned charging. 等, here, (and again in Section (3)), a sign of the plural. *chiao t'ang*, doctrine hall, chapel. 呈, *ch'êng*, to address a superior, *ch'ing*, requesting.

等情, (*cf.* Ex. 53. 19 (6)) marks the close of the converts' statement: and the use of the word 情, (facts, matters), shows that the quotation is from something written by an inferior.

(3) *Lit.*, that which the said converts petition, *shih fou*, whether it be or not, *shu shih*, that it be true.

(4) *Lit.*, *ying ssŭ*, one ought to wait [till I], *ch'ih ch'ai*, order my police, *ch'uan chi*, to summon and assemble, *liang tsao*, the two parties, *k'an ming*, inspect and make plain, *hsün tuan*, interrogate and decide. 造 here has a special meaning: *liang tsao*, the two parties in a case.

24 查教士買產建造教堂、(2)契內只可載明、賣作本處教堂公產、(3)不得列傳教士及奉教人之名、(4)今閱抄契、係王本善承買為業、並非美國教堂公產。

24. I would remark that, when missionaries buy land [for the purpose of] building chapels, (2) it may only be inserted in the deeds that [the land] is sold to be the common property of the local mission (*lit.*, chapel): (3) one must not set forth the names of the missionaries or of the converts. (4) In the present case, looking through the copy of the deed, it is, (*i. e.* one finds that the words are), "Wang Pên-shan buys it to be his property", and not "the common property of the American mission".

24. (3) **列**, set forth. *ch'uan chiao shih*, preach-the-doctrine scholar, = the much commoner **教士**, missionary. **及**, and, or. *fêng chiao jên*, receive-the-doctrine men, converts.

(4) **抄**, *ch'ao*, to copy. *ch'êng mai*, receives and buys. *mei kuo*, America: the name by which the United States is generally known.

EXERCISE 55.

VOCABULARY.

旨 *chih*³, an imperial decree, or rescript.

滋 *tzŭ*¹, to make to grow; to excite.

希 *hsi*¹, to hope.

附 *fu*⁴, adjacent; to add to, to join.

毫 *hao*², a hair; extremely small, minute.

勸 *ch'üan*⁴, to exhort, to advise.

妨 *fang*¹, to impede; to matter.

礙 *ai*⁴, to obstruct; to injure.

誡 *chieh*⁴, to warn, to admonish.

浮 *fou*², to float; fleeting.

妄 *wang*⁴, reckless; false.

1. 遵旨籌辦防務。
2. 請旨定奪。
3. 望雨滋生田禾。
4. 希圖惑衆滋事。
5. 該錢多少希即示知。
6. 並據傳訊附近居民供稱。
7. 一毫之惡勸人莫作。
8. 買賣爭毫釐。
9. 派員前往附近各鄉勸捐。
10. 遲數日何妨。
11. 妨賢病國有礙於民。
12. 車多礙路。

TRANSLATION.

1. In obedience to a decree, to consider and deal with (*i. e.* institute) defence measures.
2. To request a decree deciding [the affair].
3. They are looking for rain to make the corn in the fields grow.
4. They aim at deceiving the people and stirring up trouble.
5. I hope you will at once notify me how much money I owe you.
6. Moreover the neighbours who were summoned and examined gave evidence stating....
7. Exhort men not to do the smallest amount of evil.
8. In trade one fights for the minutest sums.
9. He directed an officer to proceed to every village in the neighbourhood and exhort [the people] to give contributions.
10. What will a few days' delay matter?
11. It impedes the eminent, contaminates the state and causes injury to the people.
12. If carts be numerous, they obstruct the road.

4. *hsi t'u*, hope and scheme, *huo*, to deceive.

5. *kai*, to owe, *to shao*, how much.

6. *Lit.*, *ping*, at the same time, *chü*, he got from, *fu chin chü min*, the near dwelling people, *ch'uan hsün*, summoned for examination, *kung ch'êng*, statements declaring.

8. A *hao* is the tenth of a *li*, or the ten-thousandth part of a tael.

11. 礙 is often written 碍.

皇[13]上訓誡官民。出[14]示
勸誡屬民。浮[15]於水面。
浮[16]流無根之言。言[17]不
可妄。毆[18]斃平民、種種
妄爲。西[19]人來華傳教
係奉諭旨准行、本(2)省商
民與各教堂教士年久
相安、第(3)恐外來游民滋
生事端、希圖乘間搶刼、
(4)爾百姓無知利害、隨聲
附和。

13. The Emperor instructs and admonishes his officers and people.

14. He issued a proclamation advising and warning the people under his jurisdiction.

15. Floating on the surface of the water.

16. Floating rumours without foundation.

17. In one's language one may not be reckless.

18. He beat to death common persons and acted recklessly in all sorts of ways.

19. The coming of Europeans to China to teach their doctrine has been sanctioned by Imperial Decree. (2) The merchants and people of our province and the missionaries of each chapel have for many years been at peace with each other. (3) Only I fear that vagrant folk coming from outside may stir up trouble and create disorder, hoping to take advantage of the opportunity to plunder and rob; (4) and that you, the people, not knowing good from harm, may be led into joining them.

16. *fou liu*, floating and flowing, *wu*, having no, *kên*, root.

19. *Lit.*, that western men come to China to teach doctrine, *hsi*, is [a practice which has], *fêng*, received, *yü chih*, a Decree, *chun hsing*, authorizing it to be done.

(2) The merchants and people have been, 相安, mutually at peace, 與, with, etc..

(3) 第; note the meaning of *ti*, 'only'. 滋, *etc.*, stir up and produce affairs and matters. 間, space, space of time, opportunity; *ch'êng chien*, to avail oneself of the opportunity.

(4) *sui*, follow, *shêng*, the sound, *fu*, join and, *ho*, harmonize.

20 爾等當想、外洋各國教士、前來中國內地、各處設堂傳教、無(2)非勸人爲善、於(3)地方風土事宜、毫無損傷妨礙、爾(4)等務各嚴誡子弟族鄰、各守本分、各安恒業、切(5)勿輕聽浮言、妄生事端。

20. You ought to reflect that the missionaries from foreign countries, who come to the interior of China, in each place erecting chapels and preaching their doctrine, (2) do so merely for the sake of exhorting men to be virtuous, (3) and do not in the slightest degree injure or impair the *fêng-shui*, the soil or the affairs of the locality. (4) You must each of you severely admonish your young people, kinsmen and neighbours, that they should all of them keep to their proper duties, and all remain quietly in their regular occupations, (5) that on no account should they listen lightly to rumours, or recklessly stir up trouble.

20. (2) *wu fei*, it is nothing but.

(3) 風 here stands for 風水, the mysterious influences which, as the Chinese believe, affect the fortunes of persons and places. 土 = 土地, the soil or territory. 事宜, *lit.*, matters which ought [to be done]; but here the two words are practically equal to 事情, affairs. *hao wu*, not in the slightest degree, *sun shang*, do injury, *fang ai*, or be an impediment, 於, to, 地方, the locality's, *fêng-shui*, etc..

(4) *pên-fên*⁴, their proper part, lot, duty. 安, rest in. *hêng*, permanent.

EXERCISE 56.

VOCABULARY.

逾 *yü*², to cross, to pass beyond.

詐 *cha*⁴, to deceive.

納 *na*⁴, to pay.

卸 *hsieh*⁴, to unload; to resign, to hand over.

繞 *jao*⁴, to wind.

拆 *ch'ai*[1], to tear, to pull down. 揑 *nieh*[1], to fabricate.
偷 *t'ou*[1], to steal; clandestine. 區 *ch'ü*[1], a place.

不[1]可逾節。知[2]者詐
愚。過[3]關納稅。卸[4]
載貨物。繞[5]避水深
之區。拆[6]書讀之。
偷[7]得半日之閒。代[8]
人揑寫稟書。揑[9]控
某人占奪田產。能[10]
伸能屈。兵[11]力不可
恃。閱[12]書多傷眼。
只[13]得仍請概免釐、稅。

TRANSLATION.

1. One may not go beyond the [proper] limit.
2. A wise man pretending to be a fool.
3. On passing the custom-house one pays duty.
4. To discharge and to load cargo.
5. To go round and avoid places where the water is deep.
6. He opened the letter and read it.
7. To steal half a day's leisure.
8. To write an untrue petition for a man.
9. He brought a false charge against a certain man of seizing and occupying some agricultural land.
10. Able to expand or to contract.
11. Military strength can not (or, may not) be relied on.
12. Reading books much will injure the eyes.
13. We can only beg once more that they may altogether be exempted from lekin and duty.

2. 知, *chih*[4], wise. 4. *tsai*, to load.

6. 書, anything written or printed; here, a letter.

7. *t'ou tê*, to steal and get.

8. *tai jên*, for a man, *nieh hsieh*, to fabricate and write, = to write a false, *ping shu*, petition.

10. This phrase can be used of things; or it can be said of a man, 'able to stand erect or to stoop', *i. e.*, able to accommodate himself to circumstances.

萬[14]望容我片刻。酌[15]量情
形、隨時隨地、或增或減。
縣[16]差被控詐錢。以[17]身繞
木、三日無已。進[18]出口之
貨到中國邊關、即請查驗、
不(2)得逾十八個時辰、如逾
期不報、每日罰銀五十兩、
惟(3)此罰銀至多不得過二
百兩、凡(4)過關報貨時、若心
存欺詐、以多報少、希減應
納稅項、

14. Ten thousand times I hope (Most earnestly I pray) that you will be forbearing with me for a moment.

15. Taking into consideration the circumstances, according to the time and according to the place, perhaps increase, perhaps reduce it.

16. The Magistrate's servants have had an action brought against them for defrauding people of money.

17. (The snake) twisted itself round a tree, and did not cease (*i. e.* remained so) for three days.

18. When imports or exports arrive at a Chinese frontier custom-house, [the merchant] shall thereupon ask that they be examined. (2) He must not exceed thirty six hours. If he go beyond the limit without reporting, for every day he will be fined 50 taels; (3) but this fine at the most must not be greater than 200 taels. (4) Whenever a merchant reports goods for the purpose of passing them through the

14. 容, *jung*, to forbear with.

18. *chin ch'u k'ou chih huo*, *sc.*, *chin k'ou chih huo*, and *ch'u k'ou chih huo*, imports and exports.

(2) A *shih-ch'ên* is a period of two hours; *vide* Note to Ex. 1. 16.

(4) *fan shih*, at all times of, *kuo kuan*, passing the custom-house, *pao huo*, and reporting goods, *jo*, if, *hsin ts'un*, in his heart cherishing, *ch'i cha*, deceit and fraud, *i to*, taking a large amount, *pao shao*, he reports it as small, *hsi chien*, hoping to diminish, *ying na*, the ought-to-be-paid, *shui hsiang*, duty moneys.

查(5)有確據、即將貨物全罰入官、若(6)無該關准單、私自過關起卸、繞路拆賣、及(7)一切有心偷漏、等弊、亦(8)將貨物全罰入官、凡(9)有商人報關請辦內地稅單、心(10)存欺詐、或揑報貨物各色件數、並所出所往之區不符者、亦(11)將貨物全罰入官。

custom-house, if he fraudulently states them to be less than they really are, in the hope of reducing the amount of duty to be paid, (5) on enquiry being made, and there being conclusive proof, thc goods will all be confiscated to the government. (6) If, not having [obtained] the permit of the custom-house concerned, he secretly passes the custom-house and discharges [goods], or makes a detour [so as to avoid it] and opens [his packages] and sells things, (7) or intentionally evades payment of duty in any way, (8) [in such case] also all the goods will be confiscated. (9) Whenever a merchant applies to the custom-house for a transit pass, (10) and, through fraud on his part, there is a misstatement concerning the kinds or quantities of the goods, or their place of origin, or their destination, does not agree [with his statement], (11) [in this case] also, all the goods will be confiscated.

(5) *chi*, then, [the authorities], *chiang*, will take, *huo wu*, the goods, and *chʻüan*, all of them, *fa*, punishing, *ju kuan*, they will confiscate.

(6) 私自, privately and of himself, secretly. *chʻi hsieh*, to unload or discharge goods.

(7) 及, and, *i chʻieh*, all kinds of, *yu hsin*, intentional, *tʻou*, clandestine, *lou*, evasion of duty, *têng pi*, such malpractices.

(9) 凡 is connected with 者 at the end of section (10), and applies to all in between, — "in all cases where". *pao kuan*, reporting to the customhouse, *chʻing*, requests it, *pan*, to administer, to supply, *nei ti shui tan*, an inland duty paper.

(10) 或, perhaps, *nieh pao*, he makes a false report as to, *huo wu ko sê*, each kind of the goods, *chien shu*, or the number of articles; *ping*, and, *so chʻu so wang chih chʻü*, the places from which they come [or] to which they go, *pu fu*, do not correspond.

EXERCISE 57.

VOCABULARY.

聚 *chü*⁴, to collect, to assemble.
把 *pa*³, to take hold of, to take.
持 *ch'ih*², to seize, to grasp.
湖 *hu*², a lake.
俗 *su*², common.
遇 *yü*⁴, to meet with; to happen.
現 *hsien*⁴, now.
悌 *t'i*⁴, the duty of a younger to an elder brother.
汝 *ju*³, thou, you.
覺 *chüeh*², to perceive.
靈 *ling*², spiritual, intelligent.
農 *nung*², to till the soil; a farmer.
賈 *ku*³, shopman, trader.
位 *wei*⁴, a place, a seat.
象 *hsiang*⁴, an elephant.

是[1]故、財聚、則民散、財散、則民聚。

非[2]衆人無好義之心、不過一二把持公事之人、中有私求。

湖[3]南山多田少、有俗語云、三山六水一分田。

TRANSLATION.

1. Therefore, if wealth be accumulated, the people are scattered; if wealth be scattered, the people are gathered together.
2. It is not that the people have not hearts which love righteousness; it is merely that one or two men who monopolize public business, have private aims therein.
3. In [the Province of] Hunan the hills are many and the fields few: there is a proverb which says [of it], three tenths are hills, six tenths are water, and one tenth fields.

1. *shih ku*, [for] this reason, therefore.
2. *pa ch'ih*, to grasp, to get hold of, to monopolize.
3. The Province of Hunan derives its name from the fact of its lying south of the Tung-t'ing Lake.

合[4]行出示、曉諭各行
戶人等知悉、凡(2)遇買
賣貨物、務要現錢交
易。故[5]不孝與不悌
相因、事親與事長並
重、能(2)為孝子、然後能
為悌弟、能(3)為孝子悌
弟、然後在田野為善
良之民、在行間為忠
勇之士。汝[6]等當以
重生為第一要義矣、

4. It is my duty to issue a proclamation distinctly ordering all members of mercantile firms to take notice that, (2) whenever they buy or sell goods, they must be sure to give or take ready money.

5. Therefore the absence of filial piety and of brotherly duty follow the one from the other; to serve one's parents and to serve one's elders are both important. (2) He who can be a filial son, afterwards can be a dutiful brother. (3) He who can be a filial son and dutiful brother, afterwards will be a well-behaved person in the fields, or a faithful and brave soldier in the ranks.

6. You ought to make it your most important principle to value your lives. (2) The things in the world are infinitely various;

4. 合; *vide* Ex. 19. 22. 行, read *hang*², a mercantile house. *ko hang hu*, of every mercantile house, *jên têng*, the men, *chih hsi*, to know well, be well aware, = to take notice. For *hang hu*, *cf. p'u hu* in Ex. 50. 19.

(2) *fan yü*, on all [occasions when it] happens, = whenever. *wu yao*, positively must, *hsien ch'ien*, [for] ready money, *chiao-i*, trade.

5. 悌, *t'i*, brotherly: it is often written without the radical at the side. *Cf.* Ex. 16. 26.

(3) 行, *hang*, lines, ranks; *tsai hang chien*, in the ranks.

6. *ju têng*, you, *pl.; lit.*, you ought to take the giving of importance to life and make it your first important principle. First important = most important, — a common idiom.

(2)天下之物、萬有不齊、凡有知覺、莫不自重其生、(3)人爲萬物之靈、何不自重其生、汝等若知生之爲重、則當謀生計、(4)農工商賈、自食其力。7 一日各獸羣聚一處、(2)各道所長以爭王位、(3)虎則自稱力大、象則自認多謀、馬則恃其功高。

and, of all of them that have powers of perception, there are none that do not value their own lives. (3) Man is the most intelligent of all things. Why does he not value his own life? If you recognize the value of life, then you ought to make plans to get a livelihood; (4) and, farmers, artisans, merchants and shopmen, all support yourselves by your own efforts.

7. One day all the beasts assembled in a crowd in one place, (2) and each declared in what he excelled, in order to contend for the king's throne. (3) The tiger boasted of the greatness of his strength; the elephant asserted the magnitude of his intelligence; the horse relied on his high merits.

(2) *wan yu* = *yu wan*, have ten thousand inequalities. 知覺, knowing and perceiving. 自重, *etc.*; themselves value, *ch'i*, their, *shêng*, lives, = value their own lives.

(3) Most intelligent, *cf.* Ex. 6. 23. 生之, *etc.*; notice the *chih*, — life's being valuable. *shêng-chi*, a scheme or means of living.

(4) 自, *etc.*; feed themselves on their strength.

7. (2) *so*, in what, *chang*³, he was superior.

(3) *Lit.*, the tiger then said of himself that his strength was great; the elephant then recognized for himself his much scheming; the horse then, *shih*, relied on, *ch'i*, his, *kung kao*, merit's being high.

EXERCISE 58.

VOCABULARY.

幾 *chi*^{3}, how many; *chi*^{1}, nearly.

逢 *fêng*^{2}, to meet.

留 *liu*^{2}, to keep.

售 *shou*^{4}, to sell.

焉 *yen*^{2}, a terminal particle.

値 *chih*^{2}, value, worth.

價 *chia*^{4}, price, value.

張 *chang*^{1}, to draw a bow; to spread out; a sheet of paper.

較 *chiao*^{3}, to compare.

倍 *pei*^{4}, as much again.

廣 *kuang*^{3}, broad.

嗣 *ssu*^{4}, to continue, to succeed; after.

丈 *chang*^{1}, a measure of ten Chinese feet.

尺 *ch'ih*^{3}, a Chinese foot.

寬 *k'uan*^{1}, broad, wide.

[1] 洋船在通商各口上貨下貨、總須先領海關准單、(2)如違、即將貨物全行入官。

[2] 洋貨入口、完清海關正稅之後、在本口即無他項應完、(2)此貨如再完半稅、即可運往內地。

TRANSLATION.

1. When foreign vessels in a treaty port either land goods or ship goods, it is in all cases necessary that they first obtain a customs permit. (2) If they break the rule, the goods will at once all be confiscated.
2. When foreign goods are brought into a port; after the payment in full of the regular customs duty, they have then no other charges that they ought to pay in that port; (2) and

1. *chun tan*, a permitting paper, a permit.

(2) 即, *etc.*, [the officials] thereupon will take the goods and proceed to confiscate them all.

2. 淸, clear, to clear off; *wan ch'ing*, pay in full. 本; *pên k'ou*, this port, the port of entry.

無[3]論何貨、運入內地、幾次逢關、幾次納稅。洋[4]人之貨、一入華人之手、聽其或留或售、或用或不用、洋[(2)]人不得過而問焉。今[5]歲金銀進口無多、不必論、出[(2)]口往上海者、值關平銀三百萬兩。土[6]貨出內地、今年價值五萬七百餘兩、共[(2)]用運照六百四十九張。

if these goods further pay a half duty, they may then be conveyed into the interior.

3. Goods of all kinds, if conveyed into the interior, as many times as they arrive at a customs station, so many times must they pay duty.

4. When a foreigner's goods have once entered into the possession of a Chinaman, the latter can do as he likes about keeping them or selling them, about using or not using them: (2) the foreigner may not interfere in the matter.

5. This year the import of gold and silver is small, [so that] one need not discuss it; (2) but the export of them to Shanghai amounts to a value of three million Customs taels.

6. Native produce coming from the interior this year amounts in value to fifty thousand seven hundred taels and more; (2) and altogether there were used six hundred and forty nine transit passes.

4. *t'ing ch'i*, one allows him, he is allowed to.

(2) *kuo êrh wên*, to come across and ask, = to interfere. *yen* has no force, and is inserted only for the sake of the rhythm.

5. *Lit.*, this year the gold and silver entering the port are not much.

(2) *Lit.*, that which went out of the port to Shanghai.

chih, is worth; *kuan*, custom-house; *p'ing*, scales — is worth three million ounces of silver [weighed according to] the custom-house scales.

6. 土, native, local. *chia chih*, their value is worth. *yü*, more.

(2) *yün chao*, a conveyance certificate; *vide* Note to Ex. 53. 19 (3).

張, a sheet, here a numerative of transit passes.

7 近年進口洋貨、每歲值銀至八千萬兩以外、較(2)之十數年前幾加一倍。

8 西洋通商向止廣東一口、嗣(2)是沿海開口以及奉天、內達江西湖北。

9 原色洋布、不過九丈九尺、寬不過三尺每(2)疋抽稅四錢。

7. Of late years foreign imports have annually been worth over eighty million taels. (2) Comparing them [with those of] a dozen years or so previously, [one finds that] they have nearly doubled.

8. Trade with western nations was formerly confined to the one port of Canton. (2) Afterwards ports were opened along the sea [coast], and in Fêng-t'ien; [while] it (the trade) penetrated inland to Kiangsi and Hupei.

9. Unbleached foreign cottons, not more than ninety nine feet long, nor more than three feet broad, pay a duty of four mace per piece.

7. 進口, imported — an adjective agreeing with *huo*, goods. 至, up to, *i-wai*, beyond.

(2) *shih shu nien*, ten and some years. *chia i pei*, to add one fold, or, to add as much again, *i. e.* to double: so *chia êrh pei*, to treble; *chia shih pei*, to increase ten fold. 幾, nearly.

8. 向, formerly. 止, stopped at, was only at. 廣; *kuang-tung*; one must supply here *shêng-ch'êng*, provincial capital — the capital of the Province of Kuangtung. This is the city known to us as Canton. 'Canton' is merely '*Kuang-tung*' slightly mispronounced.

(2) 嗣; *ssŭ shih*, after this. 以及, *lit.*, thereby to. It simply means 'and'. Fêng-t'ien, the southernmost province of Manchuria. Kiangsi and Hupei, two Provinces on the banks of the Yangtse, the latter north of the Tung-t'ing Lake.

9. Unbleached, *vide* Ex. 27. 5.

(2) *mei p'i*, on every piece, *ch'ou shui*, they collect duty. As to *p'i*, see Note on Ex. 1. 32.

EXERCISE 59.

VOCABULARY.

調 *t'iao*², to blend, to adjust; *tiao*⁴, to move, to transfer.

涉 *shê*⁴, to ford; to be concerned in.

依 *i*¹, to rely on, to act according to.

逃 *t'ao*², to run away, to abscond.

申 *shên*¹, to extend, to put forth.

律 *lü*⁴, a law.

銅 *t'ung*², copper.

鐵 *t'ieh*³, iron.

光 *kuang*¹, light, brightness.

督 *tu*¹, to superintend, to lead.

撫 *fu*³, to soothe.

束 *shu*⁴, to bind together, to restrain.

徒 *t'u*², a varlet, a low fellow; empty; alone.

妥 *t'o*³, safe, satisfactory.

覆 *fu*⁴, to reverse; to reply; again.

[1] 兩國有不協之處、往往請友國從中調處、(2)其調處之法有三。

[2] 凡兩國交涉之事、係約所及者、依約而行、

TRANSLATION.

1. When two countries have matters on which they disagree, they often ask a friendly country to mediate between them. (2) The ways of mediating are three.

2. [As to] all international questions, — [in the case of] those which are regulated by treaty, one proceeds according to

1. *pu hsieh chih ch'u*, matters of disagreement, (*ch'u* here meaning 'points' or 'matters'). 往; *wang wang*, constantly. 從中, from the middle, = to come between them. *t'iao ch'u*, to adjust and settle, to arrange the difficulty, mediate. (*ch'u*³, to settle).

2. 凡; *fan* goes with *shih*, — all matters; 交涉, mutually concerned; — all matters in which two countries are mutually concerned. 所及者, those which the treaty reaches to. For *so . . . chê*, *vide* Ex. 7. 17.

條(2)約所不及者、據理而斷。中[3]國民人有犯罪逃至洋船、一經中國官員照會到、該領事即行交出。至[4]銀兩出洋、自應申明例禁、查(2)戶部則例內載、洋商將銀兩私運出洋者、照例治罪、等語。而(3)刑部律例內、只有黃金銅鐵銅錢出洋治罪之條、

the treaty; (2) but those upon which the treaty does not touch, one decides according to equity.

3. If Chinese subjects who have committed any offence take refuge on a foreign vessel; immediately that a despatch from a Chinese official arrives, the Consul concerned shall deliver them up at once.

4. As to the export of silver bullion, — a law should certainly be promulgated prohibiting it. (2) One finds it stated in the rules of the Board of Revenue that, if foreign merchants clandestinely export silver bullion, their offence will be punished according to law. (3) But in the laws of the Board of Punishment, there are only clauses concerning the punishment of the offences of exporting gold, copper, iron, and

(2) *chü li êrh tuan*, hold justice and decide [them].

3. 有; [Among] Chinese subjects, *yu*, should there be [any who], having committed an offence, escape, etc..

4. *yin liang*, silver ounces, uncoined silver, bullion. *tzŭ ying*, one naturally ought.

(2) *ch'a*, *vide* Ex. 23. 19. 則, a rule; *tsê li*, *lit.*, rules and regulations.

者; *chê*, is here equivalent to a simple relative, (*vide* Ex. 22. 6); — foreign merchants who take, etc.. But for convenience of translation it is better to say 'if foreign merchants take'. *chih tsui*, deal with, punish, the offence.

(3) *lü li*, the Penal Code, consisting of *lü*, the ancient, fundamental laws, which are always retained, and *li*, the modifications and additions constantly made.

並(4)無銀兩出洋作何治罪明文。查5道光十五年間、臨(2)安府屬、曾有爭界之事、當(3)經奏明、由雲南督撫用文照會該國王、約(4)束匪徒、不得過界滋事、並(5)令該國王妥辦回覆、等因、

copper cash: (4) there is no explicit statement at all as to how the offence of exporting silver bullion should be punished.

5. I find that in the fifteenth year [of the reign] of Tao Kuang, (2) in the jurisdiction of Lin-an Fu, there were some frontier quarrels. (3) Thereupon a report was made to the Emperor; and the Governor-General and the Governor of Yunnan sent a written communication to the King of the said country (Annam), (4) [requesting him] to restrain his disorderly subjects, [and saying] that they must not come across the frontier and create disturbances. (5) At the same time they desired the King of the said country to deal satisfactorily with the matter and give them a reply. (6) After that the

(4) *tso ho*, doing what, how.

5. (2) 屬, *shu*, to belong to.

tsʻêng yu, there were, *shih*, affairs, *chih*, of, *chêng chieh*, quarrelling about the boundary.

(3) 當, at [that time], thereupon.

由. *vide* Ex. 22. 8.

督撫, *tu fu*, for *tsung-tu*, a Governor General, and *hsün-fu*, a Governor. The Provinces of Yunnan and Kueichou are under the rule of the same Governor General, and have each their separate Governor.

yung wên, using a despatch, *chao hui*, addressed officially.

(4) *yüeh-shu*, to control, to keep in order.

fei tʻu, vagabonds, bad characters, disorderly people.

(5) 等因, *lit.*, such reasons. This expression, like *têng yü*, and *têng chʻing*, marks the close of a quotation. It is a polite form, used after what has been written by a superior, or, by courtesy, after what has been written by an equal.

其(6)後該國匪徒不敢過界多事、相安至今。各6種布疋、此三年中進口之數無甚增減、本(2)年忽然增多、值價一萬三百萬兩。

disorderly folk of the said country did not dare to cross the frontier and make trouble; and [the people on either side] have been at peace with each other up to the present time.

6. Of all kinds of cotton piece goods, the number [of pieces] imported during these three [last] years did not very much increase or decrease. (2) In the present year they suddenly made a great increase, and were worth one hundred and three million taels.

(6) 其, that, 後, after, — after that. *to shih*, to meddle, to interfere.
6. *tsêng chien*, increase and decrease.

EXERCISE 60.

VOCABULARY.

强 *ch'iang*^{2}, strong, violent.
戰 *chan*^{4}, to fight.
軍 *chün*^{1}, an army; military.
餉 *hsiang*^{3}, rations, pay; revenue.
歷 *li*^{4}, to calculate; the calendar; to pass through.
周 *chou*^{1}, to surround; everywhere.
險 *hsien*^{3}, difficult; dangerous.
房 *fang*^{2}, a house; a room.
屋 *wu*^{1}, a room; a house.
輪 *lun*^{2}, a wheel; a revolution.
碰 *p'eng*^{4}, to knock, to collide.
限 *hsien*^{4}, a limit; a boundary.
賠 *p'ei*^{2}, to pay damages.
款 *k'uan*^{3}, an item; a clause; a sum of money.
假 *chia*^{3}, false.
混 *hun*^{4}, muddy; to confuse.

[1] 昔之論富强也、以耕戰爲務、而(2)西人謀富强也、以工商爲先。

[2] 西洋軍餉全出於商稅、商(2)人經商萬里、涉歷重洋、收境外之利、以養本國之民、故(3)國日富而兵亦日强、華(4)商則不然。

[3] 或謂鐵路以運貨爲要、

TRANSLATION.

1. In the discussions of former times concerning [national] wealth and power, men held agriculture and fighting to be the essential points. (2) But Europeans, when making plans for [obtaining] wealth and power, place manufactures and commerce first.
2. The war funds of western nations all come from duties on commerce. (2) Their merchants trade [with places] ten thousand *li* away, and make voyages across many seas, reaping the profits of foreign regions, whereby they support the people of their own land. (3) Therefore their country daily becomes more wealthy, and their army likewise daily becomes more powerful. (4) With Chinese merchants this is not the case.
3. Some one [may] say that in railways one looks upon the transportation of merchandise as the important point; (2)

2. (2) 經, to pass through; *ching-shang*, to trade. *shê-li*, to ford and go through, to traverse. 重, *ch'ung²*, in folds or layers, successive; *ch'ung yang*, sea after sea.

(4) 不然, [it is] not so.

3. (3) 而. Notice this use of *êrh*, before the verb. It is a common idiom, of which we have already had instances in Ex. 59. 2. One can force a meaning for the *êrh*, if one wishes, by making 以 into a verb, 'use gradualness and complete them'.

若[2]造一道、則火車所到者十之一、不能到者十之九、各處商貨依舊不能周通矣、不[3]知西洋各國、鐵路雖多、皆以漸而成、從[4]未聞數道並舉。且[4]外洋保險、不但保海險而已、凡[2]房屋則保其火險、輪車則保其碰險、甚[3]至人身、則保其病險、如限內人死、則家屬得領賠款。

that if we construct a line, then [the places] which the trains will reach, will be [only] one out of ten, and those that they cannot reach will be nine out of ten; [so that] the mercantile commodities of any place will, as of old, be unable to pass everywhere. (3) [But he who says so] does not know that in every western country, though the railways are many, they were all made by degrees. (4) One has never heard of several lines being undertaken together.

4. Moreover, foreign insurance is not confined simply to insurance against the dangers of the sea. (2) In the case of all buildings one insures against the danger of fire. In the case of trains one insures against the danger of collision. (3) The system even includes men's persons, which are insured against the danger of sickness. If the man dies within the limit of time, then his family will receive a sum of money in compensation.

(4) 從未, *lit.*, hitherto one has not.

4. *pao hsien*, to guarantee or protect against danger, to insure. 不但, *etc.*, does not solely insure against sea dangers and nothing more: *êrh i*, and [then] stop, = 'and nothing more'.

(2) *ch'i huo hsien; ch'i*, their, *i. e.* 'the buildings'. *lun-ch'ê*, trains. This term is evidently formed in imitation of *lun-ch'uan*, wheel-ships, *i. e.* paddle-wheel vessels, steamers.

(3) *shên chih*, in extreme cases reaches to = even goes as far as. *chia shu*, those belonging to his house, his family.

5 該處土貨毫無銷路、(2)由於貪圖微利、以假混眞、以及不肯留心工作。

5. That there is no market whatever for the productions of the said place (2) is because that [the people], in their covetous desire for petty gains, are given to adulterating their goods; in addition to which they will not take pains with their work.

5. *hao wu*, have not the least, *hsiao lu*, road for consumption; *cf.* Ex. 53. 15. (2) *t'an t'u*, coveting and desiring, *wei li*, petty profits, *i*, they take, *chia*, the false, *hun chên*, and mix [it with] the true. 以及, *vide* Ex. 58. 8 (2). *pu k'ên*, do not choose, *liu hsin*, to pay attention; *kung tso*, work, or, to work.

EXERCISE 61.

VOCABULARY.

竊 *ch'ieh*[4], to steal.
吏 *li*[4], a government *employé*.
役 *i*[4], to serve; an official servant.
郡 *chün*[4], a prefecture.
源 *yüan*[2], a spring; a source.
普 *p'u*[3], universal.
專 *chuan*[1], single, special, express.
裕 *yü*[4], abundant, to enrich.
致 *chih*[4], to cause to go to; to cause; to result in.
絕 *chüeh*[2], to cut off; decidedly.
太 *t'ai*[4], too; extreme.
荒 *huang*[1], uncultivated; wild.
糧 *liang*[2], grain; rations.
擾 *jao*[3], to trouble, to harass.
了 *liao*[3], to finish.

1 竊思安民之道、必先除害、

TRANSLATION.

1. It is my humble opinion, that, to give tranquillity to the people, one must first do away with hurtful things. (2) Of

1. 竊, *lit.*, to steal, is in common use as a self-depreciatory term: *ch'ieh ssŭ*, I humbly think. 安, *etc.*, [with reference to] the ways of quieting the people.

今(2)天下之害民者、莫甚於州縣之書吏差役。

天[2]下亂發於一郡一縣、天下者郡縣之積也、故(2)清亂之源必自郡縣始。

夫[3]山海之利、公之於人、則普而多、私(2)之於官、則專而少、公(3)之於人、則可以富國而裕民、私(4)之於官、則致於害民而病國。

the things in the world which hurt the people at the present day, there is nothing worse than the clerks and official servants of the Sub-prefectures and Districts.

2. Disorder in the empire springs from some one Prefecture, some one District. The empire is an aggregation of Prefectures and Districts. (2) Therefore, in order to purify the source of disorder, one must begin with the Prefectures and Districts.

3. Now, the natural gifts of the mountains and the sea, — if you throw them open to the public, they will be widely diffused and plentiful: (2) if you keep them private for the government, they will be special and scanty. (3) If you throw them open to the public, they will be able to bring wealth to the country and enrich the people: (4) if you keep them private for the government, they will result in harm to the people and injury to the country.

(2) 書吏, clerks in government offices. *ch'ai i*, official servants, runners, messengers, etc..

2. 者, *vide* Ex. 6. 24. *chi*, to accumulate.

(2) 自, from.

3. 夫, *fu*[2], now. 利, profits, benefits, natural gifts, such as fish in the sea, minerals in the mountains.

4 軍興以來、士與工商、生計或未盡絕、惟(2)農夫則無一人不苦、無一處不苦、農(3)夫受苦太久、則必荒田不耕、軍(4)無糧則必擾民、民無糧則必從賊、賊(5)無糧則必變流賊、而大亂無了日矣、故(6)今日之州縣以重農爲第一要務、病(7)商之錢可取、病農之錢不可取。

4. Since the beginning of the war the men of letters and the artisans and traders perhaps [have found] their livelihood not entirely cut off; (2) but among the farmers, there is not one man who has not suffered, there is not one place that has not suffered. (3) If the farmers suffer hardships for too long a time, they must leave their fields barren and not cultivate them. (4) If the army has no corn, then it must harass the people. If the people have no corn, then they must join the rebels. (5) If the rebels have no corn, they must turn into roving brigands; and the anarchy will have no day of ending. (6) Therefore the Sub-prefects and Magistrates of the present day consider the paying of due regard to agriculture to be their most important business. (7) Money, [the loss of] which cripples merchants, may be taken; that which cripples farmers may not be taken.

4. (3) 荒, here a verb — leave uncultivated.

(4) 從, to follow, to join.

(5) *liao jih*, day of ending.

(7) 病 is here a verb, — to make sick, to injure.

EXERCISE 62.

VOCABULARY.

英 *ying*¹, illustrious; England.
懲 *ch'êng*³, to punish.
虐 *nüeh*⁴, to oppress; to ill-treat.
審 *shên*³, to try a case; to examine judicially.
均 *chün*¹, even, level; all, both.
球 *ch'iu*², a ball, a globe.
獨 *tu*², alone; only.

英[1]國條約第十
五款內言、英國
屬民相涉案件、
不論人產、皆歸
英官查辦、(2)約內
又言、英國民人
有犯事者、由英
領事懲辦、(3)中國
人有欺虐擾害
英民者、由中國
地方官查辦、

TRANSLATION.

1. In the fifteenth article of the British Treaty it is said that law suits, in which subjects of Great Britain are involved with each other, no matter whether [they concern] persons or property, shall all be dealt with by British authorities. (2) It is also said in the Treaty that, if British subjects commit any offence, they shall be punished by the British Consul; (3) that, if Chinese defraud or ill-treat British subjects, the case shall be dealt with by the Chinese territo-

1. *an chien*, legal cases, law suits. *an chien* is the subject of the sentence, and the six preceding words form a participial phrase attached to it, 'people subjects of Great Britain mutually concerned'. In translating into English it is necessary to add a relative pronoun and a verb, — law suits *in which* people subjects of Great Britain *are* mutually concerned.

皆, *etc.*; all, *kuei*, belong to British officials to examine and deal with.

(2) 有, *etc.*; Among British subjects, *yu*, should there be, *chê*, those who, *fan shih*, have committed an offence.

(3) *ch'i*, cheat, *nüeh*, oppress, *jao*, harass, *hai*, injure.

若(4)有兩國交涉事件、彼此均須會同公平審斷、等語。

洋[2]人居中國、不歸中國官管理、夫(2)商民居何國何地、即受治於此地之有司、亦(3)地球各國通行之法、獨(4)中國初定約時、洋人以中西律法差遠、始(5)議華人治以華法、歸華官管理、洋人治以洋法、歸洋官管理、

rial authorities; (4) and that, if there be cases in which the two countries are concerned together, they must act conjointly and try them and decide them impartially.

2. Foreigners dwelling in China do not come under the jurisdiction of the Chinese authorities. (2) Now, that merchants and people, in whatever country, in whatever locality they may dwell, should be governed by the authorities of that locality, (3) is the system universally prevailing in every country [on the face] of the globe. (4) In China, alone, at the time when the treaties were first made, foreigners took up the point that the legal systems of China and western nations differed widely, (5) and then proposed that Chinese should be governed according to Chinese law and be under

(4) *pi tz'ŭ*, the one and the other, *sc.* the representatives of the two countries, *chün hsü*, both of them must, *hui-t'ung*, uniting together, *kung-p'ing*, impartially, *shên tuan*, try and decide.

2. *kuan li*, to take charge of and manage.

(2) 受; *shou chih*, are governed, *yü*, by, *yu ssŭ*, those who have authority.

(3) 亦, also. But one does not see how to assign any value to it here. *ti ch'iu*, the globe. *t'ung hsing*, going throughout, universal.

(4) 以, using the fact that, on the grounds that. *lü fa*, statutes and laws.

差, *ch'a*, different.

(5) 始, *shih*, then.

(6)然居此地而不受治於有司則諸事難辦、(7)且中國之法重、西洋之法輕、(8)有時華人洋人同犯一罪、(9)而華人受重法、洋人受輕法、已覺不均。

the jurisdiction of the Chinese authorities, and that foreigners should be governed according to foreign law and be under the jurisdiction of foreign authorities. (6) But if [people] dwell in this land and are not governed by those who have authority [there], then all matters become difficult to deal with. (7) Moreover, the laws of China are severe, and those of western nations are mild. (8) Sometimes a Chinese and a foreigner have committed the same offence together; (9) and the Chinese has received severe treatment, the foreigner light treatment; so that the unfairness has already been manifested.

(8) 有時, there have been times when, = sometimes.

(9) *chung fa*, severe [application of the] law, severe punishment. *i chüeh*, [people] have already perceived, *pu chün*, that it is not equal.

EXERCISE 63.

VOCABULARY.

執 *chih*², to hold, to grasp.

印 *yin*⁴, a seal, a stamp.

程 *ch'êng*², a rule; a journey.

遭 *tsao*¹, to experience, to suffer.

遞 *ti*⁴, to hand to, to deliver to.

送 *sung*⁴, to send; to escort.

救 *chiu*⁴, to save; to help.

職 *chih*², office; official position.

責 *tsê*², duty, responsibility; to hold responsible.

預 *yü*⁴, to prepare beforehand.

政 *chêng*⁴, government, administration.

[1] 領事首務應保護本國船商以免受屈。[2] 水手人等有逃往內地者、(2) 由領事請地方官查拏交還。[3] 出口船隻、船主當報明領事前往某口、路經何處、(2) 將海關所發執照等件、呈交領事查驗蓋印、(3) 方可起程。[4] 本國水手人等、如有不法情事、

TRANSLATION.

1. The most important duty of a Consul is that he ought to protect the ships and merchants of his country, so that they do not suffer injustice.

2. If any sailors run away into the interior, (2) the Consul will request the local authorities to arrest them and give them up.

3. [In the case of] vessels leaving port, the master ought to report to the Consul the name of the port to which he is going, and what places he will pass (*i. e.* touch at) on the way. (2) [He ought also] to take the pass and such papers issued by the Custom-house, and present them to the Consul, [who will] examine them and stamp them; (3) after which he can commence his voyage.

4. If sailors of his nation commit any unlawful acts; (2) [in the

1. 首務, chief matter. *i mien*, so that they avoid.

2. *jên têng*, merely puts *shui shou*, into the plural. 有, *etc.*, *cf.* Ex. 62. 1. (2); among the sailors should there be any who run away.

(2) 交, *chiao*, give, 還, *huan*, return, — surrender.

3. *ch'ien wang mou k'ou*, that he is going to such or such a port.

(2) *chih chao*, *lit.*, a certificate for holding. Its commonest meaning is that of a passport for travellers. Here presumably it is the port clearance; and, as only one document has been mentioned, *têng chien*, must mean 'and other such papers'. *kai yin*, to affix his seal, to stamp.

(3) 方, then, 程; *ch'i ch'êng*, to begin a journey, start.

4. 如有, *etc.*; if they have unlawful matters.

其(2)罪輕者、各國間有准本國領事辦理、其罪重者、不准領事查辦、如(3)本國船主與水手人等有不協之處、多(4)有准領事辦理。遇[5]有遭風難船、其(2)船上水手人等、應由領事遞送回國。本[6]國兵商各船、遇有遭風碰損等情、領事即當設法救護。

case of] those whose offences are small, the Consul is sometimes permitted by his government to deal with them; but in serious cases he is not permitted. (3) If the master of a ship of his country has any disagreement with his crew, (4) the Consul in most cases is allowed to deal with it.

5. In the event of there being a vessel wrecked in a storm, (2) the ship's crew should be sent home by the Consul to their own country.

6. When any man-of-war or merchant vessel of his country happens to have suffered in a storm, or to have been damaged by a collision, (2) the Consul must at once adopt measures to furnish assistance.

(2) 其 . . . 者, those of them who; here, those of them whose — offence is light. 各; *ko kuo*, *etc.*, *lit.*, countries in general sometimes permit their Consul. 間有, there are intervals, occasionally, sometimes.

(3) 協, *etc.*; *vide* Ex. 59. 1.

5. 遇, to meet with, or, intransitively, to happen. *yü yu*, should it happen that there is, in the event of there being. *tsao fêng*, to encounter a gale, suffer in a storm. *nan*[4] *ch'uan*, a vessel in distress; but here, as the context shows, it must mean one actually lost or abandoned.

(2) *ti sung*, to forward, to send.

6. *yü yu*, happens to have, *têng ch'ing*, such things [as], *tsao fêng*, suffering from a storm, *p'êng sun*, or being damaged by a collision.

(2) *chiu hu*, to help, to save.

領[7]事、身係職官、責任非輕、原(2)不應干預彼國政事、若(3)彼國政事有關本國利害者、無(4)論已行未行、領事聞知、即當稟報。

7. A Consul holds an official position, and his responsibility is great. (2) Naturally, he ought not to interfere with the government measures of the country [where he is stationed]. (3) But if any government measures of that country affect the interests of his own country either favourably or unfavourably; (4) no matter whether they have yet been put in force or not, the Consul, when he hears of them, ought immediately to report them [to his superiors].

7. A Consul, as to his person he is an officer of the Government. A *chih kuan*, is an officer occupying an actual post, not merely holding official rank. *tsê jên*, responsibility's burden, 'responsibility'.

(2) 干, to concern; *kan-yü*, to interfere with, to meddle with.

(3) Notice the peculiarity of this sentence, opening with *jo*, if, and concluding with *chê; lit.*, if [there be any] government measures of that country, *chê*, which, *yu kuan*, concern, *pên kuo li hai*, the gain or loss of his country. 有; *yu*, is joined with *kuan*, to have effect upon, to concern; *cf.* Ex. 22. 20.

EXERCISE 64.

VOCABULARY.

茲 *tzŭ*[1], now.

駐 *chu*[4], to reside temporarily.

欽 *ch'in*[1], reverential; imperial.

劄 *cha*[2], to occupy a post; to give orders to a subordinate officer.

兼 *chien*[1], together, additional.

鎭 *chên*[4], to guard.

漢 *han*[4], name of a river.

轉 *chuan*[3], to turn round.

權 *ch'üan*[2], to weigh; authority, power.

勢 *shih*[4], strength; condition, circumstances.

朝 *ch'ao*[2], the Court.

拜 *pai*[4], to make obeisance, to salute; to visit.

邦 *pang*[1], a country, a nation.

轄 *hsia*[2], to govern, to control.

1 玆准該國領事照會內稱、(2)七月初九日接奉本國駐京欽差大臣(3)劄委本領事兼理長江一帶、鎭江九江漢口等處、(4)卽經本領事轉請美國駐劄漢口領事、代理本國通商事務、

TRANSLATION.

1. [The writer] has now received a despatch from the Consul of the country in question, in [which he] says. (2) "On the "9th day of the seventh month I had the honour to receive "from His Excellency the Minister of my country residing "at Peking (3) [a letter of] instructions appointing me in "addition [to my present post] to take charge of the [three] "places, Chinkiang, Kiukiang and Hankow, [in] the Valley "of the Yangtse. (4) Thereupon I in turn requested the "United States' Consul stationed at Hankow to take charge

1. (2) *chieh fêng; chieh*, to receive, *fêng*, to receive from a superior; *chieh fêng*, 'to have the honour to receive'. *chu ching*, residing, or stationed at the capital, *i. e.* at Peking; *ch'in ch'ai*, any one sent by the Emperor, an Imperial Envoy. This expression means, among the Chinese, an Imperial Commissioner, a high officer sent anywhere in the provinces on special duty; but it has been generally adopted by Europeans to translate 'Ambassador' or 'Minister'.

(3) 本; *vide* Ex. 23. 15. 兼理, is said of an officer who takes charge of a second post or office in addition to that which he is already holding. *ch'ang chiang i tai*, [in] the region of the Yangtse; *cf.* Ex. 22. 15. Chinkiang is the southern pronunciation of *chên-chiang*, (guarding the river). Hankow, *han-k'ou*, so called because it is situated at the mouth of the Han River, the largest of the Yangtse's affluents. 等處, these places.

(4) 經, sign of the past tense. 轉, to turn round. It is constantly used with the meaning of passing on a communication, etc., to another person. *mei kuo*,

嗣(5)後凡有本國商人到彼生理、即由美國領事代辦。凡[2]自主之國、除與某國立約議定不得接使外、莫(2)不有接使之權、然(3)非有條約言明、其(4)國並無必接之勢。使[3]臣抵任之後、雖(2)於未經朝見之先、業已私拜各國使臣、

"for me of the commercial affairs of my country [at that "place]. (5) In future, whatever merchants of my country "may go there for [purposes of] business, the United States' "Consul will act on my behalf [with regard to them]."

2. Every independent country, except when it has made a treaty with some nation binding itself not to receive an envoy, (2) cannot but have the power of receiving envoys. (3) But, unless there be a treaty explicitly saying [that it must], (4) the said country is not at all obliged to receive an envoy.

3. After that an ambassador has arrived at his post, (2) although, before he has been received at Court, he [may] have already privately visited the representatives of the various countries,

America Country, the United States. **駐劄**; *cha*, here 'to be stationed at'. *tai li*, to take temporary charge of the post of an absent official.

(5) **凡**, *etc.*, whatever ones there may be, merchants arriving, = whatever merchants there may be who arrive.

2. *tzŭ chu*, master of itself, independent. **除**; *vide* Ex. 27. 15. *i ting*, discussing and fixing, agreeing, *pu tê*, that it must not. **使**; supply **臣**; *shih ch'ên*, an Envoy, Ambassador, Minister, sent to a foreign power.

(4) *Lit.*, that country has not at all the condition of [being] obliged to receive [one].

3. **抵**, *ti*, to arrive at.

(2) **於 .... 之先**, at the before of, previously to, *wei ching*, he has not been, *ch'ao chien*, received at Court. Note the negative, which is not admissible in the English idiom.

然(3)既經朝見、必當再爲官拜。使4臣駐劄外邦、有保護本國人民之責、其(2)隨員人等亦歸使臣管轄、至(3)本國之民、其能否歸使臣管轄、須視駐劄之國律例。

(3) still, when he has been received at Court, he must be sure to visit them again officially.

4. An ambassador, stationed in a foreign country, has the duty of protecting his fellow countrymen. (2) Also, the members of his mission come under the jurisdiction of the ambassador. (3) As to the people of his nationality, — [in order to find out whether] they can or cannot come under the ambassador's jurisdiction, one must look at the laws of the country where he is stationed.

(3) 然, is correlative with *sui*, 'although', above. *chi ching*, after that he has been. *tsai wei*, again do. The *wei*, is quite redundant: *cf.* Ex. 46. 21 (2).

4. (2) 其, *etc.*, *ch'i*, demonstrative; *sui yüan*, accompanying officers; *jên têng*, sign of plural. 亦, though thrown forward in order to be in proximity to the verb, really couples the whole sentence with the preceding one; as is shown in the translation. *kuan-hsia*, to have charge of and control, have jurisdiction over.

(3) 至, 'to come to'. It is often used when the writer, having disposed of one branch of his subject, proceeds to another. In this last sentence the writer is not thinking of ordinary civil and criminal jurisdiction. The next few words in the passage from which the example was taken show that he is referring to the power to marry people, authenticate documents and so on.

EXERCISE 65.

VOCABULARY.

簡 *chien*³, a tablet; to select.

副 *fu*⁴, an assistant; duplicate.

伊 *i*¹, he, etc.; this.

暫 *chan*⁴, for a short time, temporary.

陳 *ch'ên*^{2}, to spread out; to give details.

尋 *hsün*^{2}, to seek; common.

函 *han*^{2}, a letter, a note.

咨 *tzŭ*^{1}, to communicate by letter.

陸 *lu*^{4}, land, as opposed to water.

額 *ê*^{2} (or, *o*^{2}), a fixed number.

租 *tsu*^{1}, to rent.

謹 *chin*^{3}, careful, cautious.

招 *chao*^{1}, to beckon, to invite, to attract.

1 出使各國大臣、擬自到某國日起、約以三年爲期、(2)期滿之前、由臣衙門預請簡派大臣接辦、(3)各國副使亦一律辦理。

2 出使各國大臣、分頭二三等名目、

TRANSLATION.

1. [With reference to the] envoys sent to [foreign] countries, [we] propose that, beginning from the day of [an envoy's] arrival in any country, we should fix on three years as the term; (2) and that, before the term is completed, this Office should request in advance that an officer of high rank may be selected and appointed to succeed him; (3) further that we should do the same in the case of *chargés d'affaires*.

2. The envoys sent to foreign countries are divided into first,

1. 起, beginning, 自, from. 約, *etc.*, *lit.*, that we should agree, or, arrange, to take three years to be the term.

(2) 臣; *ch'ên ya-mên*, *lit.*, Your Servants' Office: the writers of the passage are the Ministers of the Foreign Office, and they are addressing the Emperor.

預, *yü*, to prepare; *yü ch'ing*, to ask beforehand.

(3) 副, an assistant. It is the word by which the 'Vice' in Vice-president, Vice-consul, etc., is always translated: *fu-shih*, *lit.*, assistant envoy.

一律, [according to] the one, *i. e.*, the same, rule.

2. 分, *etc.*; *lit.*, are divided into, *ming mu*, the designations of head, second, third class.

此(2)次辦理伊始、所有現在業經派出各國大臣、擬請均暫作爲二等。使3臣到各國後、除(2)緊要事件隨時陳奏外、其(3)尋常事件函咨臣衙門、轉爲入奏。使4臣應奏事件、不但關係該國之事、即(2)該國議論別國之事、是(3)何意見、使臣亦當入告本國。

second and third class. (2) On the present occasion, in commencing the system, we propose to request that the Ministers who have already been despatched to various countries may all be placed temporarily in the second class.

3. After that a Minister has arrived in any country, (2) — apart from urgent affairs, [which] he will report to the Throne in detail at the time, — (2) those matters [which are] of ordinary occurrence he will communicate to this Office, which will send on a report to the Throne.

4. The matters which a Minister ought to report [are] not only [those which] concern the affairs of the country in question (*i. e.* the country to which he is accredited); (2) but also, when the said country discusses the affairs of another nation, (3) the Minister ought to inform his own country what are the views [expressed by it].

(2) 伊始, its beginning: *tzʻŭ tzʻŭ*, this time, *pan-li i shih*, we are dealing with its beginning, *i. e.*, with the beginning of the system of sending envoys. 所有; *vide* Ex. 26. 15. It agrees, of course, with *ta chʻên*, below: "The Ministers, etc."; *cf.* Dr. Hirth's *Notes on the Chinese Documentary Style*, p. 32. *hsien tsai*, now. *tso wei*, be made to be.

3. (2) *sui shih*, accompanying the time, at the time, *chʻên*, with details, *tsou*, report. (3) 其, demonstrative. *hsün chʻang*, common, ordinary. 函咨; *han*, an informal or private note, *tzŭ*, an official despatch. *han tzŭ*, send a note or despatch, = communicate in writing. 轉; *vide* Ex. 64. 1 (4). 爲, redundant. *ju tsou*, enter a report.

4 *kuan hsi*, to concern, *cf.* Ex. 22. 20.

(3) *shih ho*, it is what, *i chien*, view.

5 須知西洋諸大國律例、(2) 以及戶口、水陸兵額、地丁租稅、等項。

6 本國欲調使臣回國、(2) 若非因兩國不協、必當致書彼國國君。

7 使臣奉命調回本國者、(2) 當即交卸起程。

8 訪問事情、須加意謹慎、(2) 以免招人之疑。

5. It is necessary to know the laws of all the great western nations, (2) and the population, the strength of the army and navy, the land tax, ground rents and customs duties.
6. When a country wishes to recall its Minister; (2) unless it be doing so on account of a disagreement between the two countries, it must be sure to send a letter to the sovereign of the country where he is residing.
7. When a Minister receives orders recalling him, (2) he ought at once to hand over charge and begin his journey.
8. In making enquiries about things, he must be particularly cautious and careful, (2) in order to avoid attracting people's suspicions.

5. (2) *hu k'ou*, households and mouths, population. 額, fixed number, regulation number, of the *shui ping*, men-of-war's men, *lu ping*, and land soldiers. 地丁, *lit.*, land and men, *i. e.*, land tax and poll tax; but the latter having been long ago merged in the former, the two words are now used for land tax alone. 租, is to let or to rent; and here must mean receipts from occupants of land owned by the government. *têng hsiang*, the above-mentioned items.

6. 調, *tiao*^{4}, to move or transfer; especially of troops or officials: *tiao hui kuo*, to recall.

7. *chê*, who.

(2) *chiao hsieh*, to hand over charge.

8. *chia i*, to add, or apply, thought, to take special pains, *chin shên*, to be cautious and careful.

EXERCISE 66.

VOCABULARY.

享 *hsiang*^{3}, to enjoy.	逐 *chu*^{2}, to drive out.
署 *shu*^{3}, a public office.	答 *ta*^{2}, to reply.
引 *yin*^{3}, to lead, to introduce.	顯 *hsien*^{3}, manifest.
敵 *ti*^{2}, to oppose; an enemy.	訴 *su*^{4}, to tell.

1 不歸地方管轄、亦在使臣所享利益之內、(2)故使臣身居他邦、一如故土、(3)其一切身家財物事故、仍按本國律例辦理、(4)若生子女、亦爲本國之人、(5)至使臣公署、亦不歸地方管轄。

2 按現在常例、某國之人充他邦之使、

TRANSLATION.

1. Not to come under the local jurisdiction, is also among the advantages which an Ambassador enjoys. (2) Therefore an Ambassador, [while] personally living in another country, is altogether as [though he were in] his old land. (3) Everything of his, his person, family, money, property, affairs, is still dealt with according to the laws of his own nation. (4) If he begets sons or daughters, they too are subjects of his own country. (5) As to the Ambassador's official residence, that also does not come under the local jurisdiction.

2. According to the prevailing rule of the present day, when a

1. *li i*, profits and benefits, advantages.

(2) 一如, just as, altogether as.

(3) 其 his. 一切, all: *cf.* Ex. 37. 21. *shih ku*, causes of affairs — often 'causes of troubles', here simply 'affairs'.

2. (2) 以, according to, as. 全權; this is a modern expression, adopted as

其(2)本國之君不以全
權欽使接之、但視爲
辦事大臣、而(3)仍歸本
國管轄。昔3英國查
得日國公使有引敵
入境謀逐君主之意、
是(2)時有將此事間於
法師某人、彼(3)答以凡
使臣於駐劄之國、無(4)
論顯有如何謀害情
事、皆不得治以死罪、

subject of any country serves as the envoy of another country [to his own country], (2) the sovereign of his own country does not receive him as an Ambassador with full powers, but only regards him as a high official [entrusted with] the transaction of business; (3) and he still comes under the jurisdiction of his own country.

3. Once upon a time the English [government] discovered that the Spanish Ambassador had formed the intention of introducing a hostile force into the country with a view to dethroning the sovereign. (2) Thereupon the opinion of a certain legal expert was taken on the subject. (3) The expert replied that any Ambassador whatsoever, in the country to which he is accredited, (4) no matter in what way he has

a translation of our term 'full powers'. *ch'in shih*, a person sent by the Emperor, an ambassador.

3. *jih kuo*, one of the names by which Spain is rendered into Chinese. *kung shih*, a man sent on public business: this term is often used in Chinese official documents for Chinese Ministers sent to foreign countries. 有 governs 意 at the end of the sentence, 'had the intention'. 敵, an enemy, hostile force, *mou chu*, plotting to expel, *chün chu*, the sovereign.

(2) *Lit.*, at that time there was [some one] took this matter and asked [about it] of a certain man, a teacher of law.

(3) 彼, he. 以; the words following *i*, are the words of the reply: *cf.* 告以 in Ex. 13. 6.

(4) *wu lun*, not considering that, *hsien yu*, he has manifestly, *ju ho*, like what (in what way), *mou hai*, plotting to harm, *ch'ing shih*, matters. *ch'ing shih*, is the direct object of *yu*; and *ju ho mou hai*, is in apposition to *ch'ing shih*. *chieh pu tê*,

但[5]可遣之回國、交伊君主代爲懲治、等語、英[6]國乃從此議、於[7]是將該使遣回、派人前往日國以訴其罪。

manifestly plotted against any one's life, in no case can he be put to death: (5) that one can only send him back to his own country, and deliver him to his sovereign, to punish him on one's behalf. (6) The English government, indeed, acted in accordance with this opinion. (7) It thereupon sent the said Ambassador home, and despatched some one to Spain to complain of his offence.

in all [cases] one must not, *chih*, deal with him, *i*, according to, (or, using), *ssŭ tsui*, the death penalty. *Tsui* frequently has the meaning of 'punishment for an offence'.

(6) *nai*, indeed, *ts'ung*, followed.

(7) *yü shih*, upon this.

EXERCISE 67.

VOCABULARY.

式 *shih*^{4}, form, fashion, pattern.

樣 *yang*^{4}, pattern; kind, sort.

板 *pan*^{3}, a board.

陣 *chên*^{4}, to form in ranks; battle.

略 *lüeh*^{4}, a little.

砲 *p'ao*^{4}, a cannon.

需 *hsü*^{1}, to require, to need.

局 *chü*^{2}, a board, an association, an office.

營 *ying*^{2}, a camp; a battalion, a squadron.

登 *têng*^{1}, to ascend.

都 *tu*^{1}, all; a metropolis.

哨 *shao*^{4}, to whistle; a patrol.

雜 *tsa*^{2}, mixed, miscellaneous.

更 *kêng*^{1}, to change; a night watch; *kêng*^{4}, more, still more.

換 *huan*^{4}, to change, to exchange.

長[1]江水師、修造戰船式樣、(2)長龍底長四丈一尺、底中寬五尺四寸、(3)三板底長二丈九尺、底中寬三尺二寸、(4)督陣三板略加長大、(5)長龍設大砲、前後左右六位、(6)三板設大砲前後兩位、左右設車轉小砲兩位。

砲[2]位、大者千餘斤、次者亦數百斤、(2)所需子藥最多、須常設子藥局。

TRANSLATION.

1. In the fleet for the Yangtse, the pattern for building war boats [is as follows]. (2) Long Dragon Boats [must be] forty one feet long at the bottom, and five feet four inches wide amidships, at the bottom. (3) Sampans, twenty nine feet long at the bottom, and three feet two inches wide amidships, at the bottom. (4) Leading Sampans, a little longer and bigger. (5) For Long Dragon Boats, the cannon provided will be six large pieces, [placed] forward, aft, and on the two sides. (6) For Sampans there will be provided two large pieces, one forward, one aft, and at the sides two small pieces, turning on their carriages.

2. Cannon. The large pieces [will weigh] a thousand pounds and more: the smaller pieces, also, some hundreds of pounds. (2) The powder and shot required being a very large [quantity], it will be necessary permanently to provide an ammunition store.

1. 師 army; *shui shih*, water forces, navy. *hsiu*, often, 'to repair'; but here, *hsiu tsao* is simply 'to build'. (3) Sampans, *lit.*, three boards, a name for various kinds of boats in China. (4) *tu chên*, leading the ranks: this is a name given to the boats of the officers in command. 略; this word, like many others ending in *-üeh*, can be pronounced in more than one way. It is read, *lüo*, *lio*, and, very frequently, *liao*. *lüeh chia*, add a little. (5) 砲, as its radical indicates, was originally a machine for hurling stones. 位, *wei*, is the numerative for cannon.

2. (2) 子, balls, shot. *yao*, for *huo yao*, gunpowder.

額[3]兵、副將營、督陣三板船一號、兵二十名、長[(2)]龍船二號、每船二十五人、共兵五十名、三[(3)]板船四十號、每船十四人、共兵五百六十名。

水[4]師官兵皆宜以船爲家、不[(2)]准登岸居住、如[(3)]違例住岸上者、官卽革職、兵卽革糧、自[(4)]都司以下皆係哨官、卽以哨船爲辦公之所、

3. Sailors according to the numbers fixed. A Post-captain's command [consists of] one Leading Sampan, with 20 sailors; (2) two Long Dragon Boats, each with 25 men, altogether 50 sailors; (3) forty Sampans, each with 14 men, altogether 560 sailors.

4. The officers and sailors of the fleet ought all to make their home on board. (2) They will not be allowed to go on shore to live. (3) If any of them break the rule and live on shore, those who are officers will be cashiered, those who are sailors will be deprived of their pay. (4) From a First Lieutenant downwards, all are officers of a patrol, and so [ought] to make the patrol boat their place for doing

3. *ê* is a number fixed upon: *ê ping*, soldiers of, *i. e.* according to, the number fixed upon. It is not 'number of soldiers', which would be *ping ê. fu chiang ying*; the Chinese use the same terms for their military and naval forces: *Fu-chiang*, (*lit.* vice-general), is an officer's title, corresponding with Colonel or Post-captain; in the army a *ying* is a battalion: in the navy one can translate it as 'squadron' or 'command'. 號, *hao*, is here used as a numerative of boats.

4. 以; take the boats and make [them] their home.

(3) 如 . . . 者; *cf.* Ex. 63. 7 (3); *lit.*, if [there be] any who break the rule; *kuan chi*, [if] they be officers, then they will be. *ko chih*, to strip of their rank, to cashier. 糧, *liang*, grain, rations; here, pay of all kinds.

(4) *tu-ssŭ*, a Senior Captain in the army, a Senior Lieutenant in the navy. 哨; a *shao*, or 'patrol', is a subdivision of a *ying*, or battalion. 所, a place.

不(5)准建衙陸居。雜[5]費、酌定長龍戰船每年發銀六十兩。戰[6]船大砲最易損壞、議定每屆三年修理一次、十(2)二年卽行更換。

official business. (5) They are not permitted to build offices and live on shore.

5. Petty Expenses. It has been determined that for Long Dragon War Boats every year there shall be issued sixty taels.

6. The large guns on war boats being very easy to injure, it is arranged that they shall be repaired once every three years, (2) and that after twelve years they shall be changed [for new ones].

5. *cho ting*, to deliberate upon and settle.

6. *sun huai*, *lit.*, to damage and spoil. 屆, *vide* Ex. 48. *hsiu li*, to repair, *i tz'ŭ*, one time.

(2) [After] twelve years, then proceed, *kêng huan*, to change.

EXERCISE 68.

VOCABULARY.

梧 *wu*^{2}, name of a tree.

緒 *hsü*^{4}, end of a thread; to connect.

港 *chiang*^{3}, a creek, a lagoon.

城 *ch'êng*^{2}, a city wall; a walled city.

駛 *shih*^{3}, to sail.

埠 *fou*^{4}, a port.

退 *t'ui*^{4}, to retire.

季 *chi*^{4}, a season.

貿 *mao*^{4}, to trade.

穀 *ku*^{3}, grain.

担 *tan*^{4}, a burden; a picul.

瑞 *jui*, lucky, auspicious.

查[1]梧州口岸、按照和約專
條、自光緒二十三年五月、
開作通商口岸、設關收稅、
該(2)地坐落西江北岸、計(3)到
香港及廣東省城、由海關
所定之河道前往、約七百
里、本(4)口船隻往來尚無阻
礙、夏(5)天大船亦可駛入本
埠、水(6)退之日、船之食水深
至五尺者、亦可到梧、

TRANSLATION.

1. The port of Wu-chou, in accordance with a special clause in the Treaty, was opened as a Treaty Port from the Fifth Month of the 23rd year of Kuang Hsü; and a custom-house was established for the receipt of duties. (2) The said place is situated on the north bank of the West River. (3) I calculate [the distance] to Hongkong and Canton, [if] one proceeds by the water ways fixed by the Customs, as approximately 700 *li*. (4) At this port vessels coming and going have not yet met with any impediment. (5) In summer time large vessels, too, can come up to our port. (6) At the time when the water falls, vessels drawing as much

1. 查 need not be translated. For its use in such passages, *vide* Ex. 23. 19. *kuang hsü*, the name of the reign of the present Emperor.

(2) *tso lao*, to sit and to settle, to be situated.

(3) 到, to. *hsiang chiang*; 'Hongkong' is the Cantonese pronunciation of these two words. For Canton, *vide* Ex. 58. 8. 約, (here an adverb), about, approximately.

(4) 本; the use of this word shows that the writer belongs to Wu-chou.

(5) 亦, too, as well as smaller ones.

(6) *ch'uan chih*, *etc.*, *lit.*, of vessels those eating (*i. e.* drawing) water deep up to (*i. e.* to the depth of) five feet.

然(7)梧州之上河未悉火船能往來否、至(8)河水之長退、全憑天雨、長(9)水時有高於退水時六丈之多、夏(10)季之水常與岸齊、亦有時高於岸也、値(11)此時進口之船、較之岸邊房屋則高、遇(12)此大水居民似多不便、賠本料必不少、孰(13)知居民不以爲災而以爲瑞、

as five feet of water can also reach Wu-chou. (7) But, I am not sure whether steamers can navigate the river above Wu-chou, or not. (8) As to the river's rising or falling, all depends on the rainfall. (9) When the water rises, the river is as much as sixty feet higher than when the water is low. (10) In the summer season the water is frequently level with the bank, and there are times [when it is] higher than the bank. (11) At this time the vessels that enter the port are higher than the houses on the banks. (12) When they meet with these floods, the inhabitants apparently [suffer] many inconveniences. I conjecture that not a few of them must sustain pecuniary losses. (13) Who would think that the people do not regard [the floods] as a calamity, but

(7) 悉, *hsi*, minutely, thoroughly; often combined with verbs meaning 'to know', and not unfrequently used, as here, for 'know thoroughly'.

(8) 長, *chang*^{3}, to grow.

(9) *Lit.*, [at] the time of the rising water, it (the river) is higher than [at] the time of the falling water [by] as much as sixty feet.

(11) 値, *chih*^{4}, to meet, to happen, at the time of. 較, *etc.; lit.*, *chiao chih*, comparing it [with], *an pien fang wu*, the houses on the banks, *tsê kao*, then it is higher.

(12) 似, *ssŭ*, apparently. *p'ei pên*, [those who] lose their capital, *liao*, I conjecture, *pi*, must [be], *pu shao*, not a few.

(13) *shu chih*, who knows?

梧[14]州從前貿易未悉其詳、惟[15]聞年中米穀出口約有一千二百萬担之多、梧[16]州城已歷一千三百年之久、聞[17]未有此城之先、有古城名廣信。

consider them a fortunate occurrence? (14) I am not well acquainted with the particulars of the trade of Wu-chou in the past. (15) But I have heard that the annual export of rice is, approximately, as much as twelve million piculs. (16) The city of *Wu-chou* has already existed for a period thirteen hundred years. (17) I have heard that before the existence of the present city, there was an old city, named Kuang-hsin.

(14) *ts'ung ch'ien*, formerly; here an adjective agreeing with *mao-i*. *mao* to trade, *i* to change, *mao-i*, trade.

(15) 年中, in a year. *mi ku*; *mi* is cleaned rice, and *ku* paddy, *i. e.* rice with the husk still on it. 担, a picul; either a weight of 100 Chinese pounds, or a measure of 100 Chinese pints.

(16) 歷, to pass through. *Cf.* Ex. 60. 2 (2).

EXERCISE 69.

VOCABULARY.

街 *chieh*^{1}, a street.

採 *ts'ai*^{3}, to gather, to collect.

挑 *t'iao*^{1}, to carry by means of a pole on the shoulder.

困 *k'un*^{4}, distress; to be surrounded.

固 *ku*^{4}, strong, firm.

賴 *lai*^{4}, to rely upon.

就 *chiu*^{4}, to go to; according to.

邀 *yao*^{1}, to invite.

監 *chien*^{1}, to superintend; a gaol.

候 *hou*^{4}, to wait.

待 *tai*^{4}, to wait for; to behave to.

質 *chih*^{3}, substance, matter; to confront.

如[1]准商民私造砲船、則(2)强盜亦可造砲船以行刧。

各[2]營之兵勇四路搶刧、刧、生(2)意之人均不敢來城買賣、所(3)以米穀在街收買、無幾、派(4)人赴各鄉採買、挑夫亦怕來城、致(5)阻米穀不能多買積存、縣(6)令眞不敢言、不能與民作主、似(7)此、被困之後

TRANSLATION.

1. If merchants and common people are allowed privately to build gunboats, (2) then robbers will also be able to build them in order to practise piracy.

2. The soldiers from each camp, (or, of each battalion), robbed and plundered on [all] four roads; (2) [so that] no dealers dared to come to the city to trade. (3) Therefore the rice bought on the street (*i. e.* in the market) was not much. (4) Then men were directed to go to the villages and buy supplies; but the coolies also were afraid to come to the city. (5) From these causes it was impossible to buy any large quantity of rice and store it up. (6) The Magistrate really did not dare to speak, and could not exert his authority among the people. (7) Under these circumstances, after

1. (2) *ch'iang tao*, men who rob with violence, = robbers.

2. *ping yung*, *cf.* Ex. 22. 12. (2) *shêng-i chih jên*, the trading men, *chün*, all, *pu kan*, did not dare.

(3) *so i*, *vide* Ex. 8. 18. 幾 *chi*[3], much.

(4) *fu*, to go to, *ko hsiang*, each village, *ts'ai mai*, to collect and purchase. *t'iao fu*, bearers, men to carry the rice bought.

(5) *Lit.*, [which], *chih tsu*, caused a preventing of rice and paddy, [so that there] could not be much bought and, *chi ts'un*, stored up.

(6) *hsien ling* = *chih hsien*, Magistrate. *tso chu*, play the ruler.

(7) *ssŭ tz'ŭ*, [the case being] like this.

合(8)城之人無不害怕、無心固守。

如3有外國無賴流民、或在內地、或在海洋、無(2)論搶刼中外民人客商、銀錢貨物、即(3)由地方官遣派兵役捕拏、由(4)關道就近邀各國領事官、會同審明語音、如(5)係有約之國洋人、即送交本國領事官懲辦、如(6)係無約之國洋人、即由中國究辦、照例治罪。

that [the place] was besieged, (8) the people in the whole town were one and all afraid, and had no heart to make an obstinate defence.

3. If there be foreign vagabonds, who, either inland or on the sea, (2) rob [any persons] of money or property, no matter whether [the sufferers be] Chinese or foreign, common people or travelling merchants; (3) the local authorities will thereupon despatch soldiers and constables to arrest them; (4) and the Customs Taotai will invite all the foreign Consuls who may be nearest at hand to take part with him in examining [them so as to] find out their language. (5) If they be foreigners belonging to a nation which has a treaty [with China], then he will send them to the Consul of their own country for punishment. (6) But if they belong to a nation which has no treaty, then China [herself] will try them, and punish their offence according to law.

(8) *ho ch‘êng*, the whole city. *hai-p‘a*, to be afraid.

3. *wu lai*, worthless folk; *lit.*, men who have nothing to depend on. *liu min*, wanderers, tramps.

(2) *wu lun*, is not connected with the verb *ch‘iang-chieh*, but with all the words following the verb, down to *huo wu*, goods. *yin ch‘ien*, silver bullion and copper coins, = money.

(3) 役, *i*, runners, constables, *pu-na*, to arrest.

(4) *kuan tao; kuan*, customs, *tao*, Taotai, *chiu chin*, according to nearness; *hui t‘ung*, in conjunction with him, *shên ming*, to examine [them so as to] find out, *yü yin*, their words and accent, *i. e.*, their language, (in order to determine their nationality).

(5) *sung chiao*, send and hand to, = send to. *ch‘êng pan*, punish and deal with.

竊[4]查命盜重案、向分首從、定罪輕重不等、(2)如首犯在逃未獲、從犯監候待質、(3)必首犯到案、然後訊供辦結。

4. I would humbly remark that in serious cases [such as] homicide and robbery, [the offenders have] hitherto been divided into principals and accessories, and the one class punished more severely than the other. (2) If the principal offender is at large and has not been captured, the accessories are kept in prison till they can be confronted with him. (3) It is necessary that the principal be brought into court; after which they are interrogated, and the case is brought to a conclusion.

4. 竊, *vide* Ex. 61. 1. 從 *tsung*^{4}, a follower, accessory. *ting tsui*, *etc.; lit.* fix their guilt (or, punishment) light or heavy, not equal.

(2) *chien hou*, to wait in prison. 待, wait for, until. 質 to be present in person, to be confronted with: it may be one prisoner confronted with another, a prisoner with a witness, or, simply, a prisoner with his judge.

(3) *jan hou*, afterwards, *hsün kung*, examine [and get] their statements, *pan chieh*, deal with and wind up, conclude.

EXERCISE 70.

VOCABULARY.

患 *huan*^{4}, trouble, harm.

尤 *yu*^{2}, fault; still more.

堤 *ti*^{1}, an embankment.

淹 *yen*^{1}, to drown; to inundate.

看 *k'an*^{4}, to look at, to see.

庸 *yung*^{1}, to use, to employ.

卹 *hsü*^{4}, to pity.

夾 *chia*^{1}, to squeeze.

鈔 *ch'ao*, vouchers, bank-notes; money.

徵 *chêng*, to levy; proof.

解 *chieh*^{3}, to loosen; to explain; *chieh*^{4}, to send.

另 *ling*^{4}, separate; another.

册 *ts'ê*^{4}, a list; a register.

湖[1]北之水、江爲大、漢次之、而(2)漢之爲患、較江爲尤甚。竊[2]查、治廣東之水、與北省異、北(2)省之水、患在無堤、而廣東之水、則患在多堤、治(3)廣東之水、又與各省異、各(4)省之水、患在害多而利少、治廣東之水、患在利多而害卽因之。至[3]六合縣被水之處、已據該縣稟報、勸捐辦理、

TRANSLATION.

1. Of the rivers of Hupei, the Yangtse is the greatest, and the Han is inferior to it. (2) But the trouble caused by the Han is even greater than that caused by the Yangtse.

2. I would humbly remark that regulating the rivers of Kuang-tung is a different thing from [regulating those of] the northern provinces. (2) In the case of the rivers of the northern provinces, the trouble is in the absence of embankments; but in the case of the rivers of Kuang-tung, the trouble is in the number of the embankments. (3) The regulating of the rivers in Kuang-tung, again, is different from what it is in the other provinces generally. (4) With the rivers of the other provinces, the trouble lies in their doing much harm and little good. In regulating the rivers of Kuang-tung, the trouble lies in the fact that they do much good, and harm at once follows therefrom.

3. As to the places in Liu-ho Hsien which have suffered from

1. Han River, *vide* Ex. 64. 1 (3).

(2) 之; the Han's being a trouble, = the trouble that the Han is. *chiao chiang*, compared with the Yangtse, *wei*, is, *yu shên*, still greater.

2. (4) 因之, is on account of it, follows from it.

3. 已, *i*, sign of the past tense. 據, *vide* Ex. 25. 18. *ch'üan chüan*, exhorting people to subscribe.

其[2]江都縣被淹各處、據該縣稟報、察[3]看民情、目前尚可支持、應請毋庸撫邺。

再[4]查招商局夾板火輪等船、運貨進出通商各口、應納稅鈔銀兩、經[2]總理各國事務衙門、會同戶部議定、按照洋稅徵收、

floods, [I] have received a report from the Magistrate concerned, [to the effect] that he is dealing with the matter by raising subscriptions [for the sufferers]. (2) As to the various places which have been inundated in Chiang-tu Hsien, it is reported by the Magistrate there that, (3) looking at the state of the people, at present they can still hold out, and [he feels that] he ought to request that relief should not be given.

4. Again, I find that, [with regard to] the sums in silver for duties and dues, which ought to be paid by sailing vessels and steamers of the China Merchants Company that carry goods into or out of the various Treaty Ports, (2) the Foreign Office, in conjunction with the Board of Revenue,

(2) 其, goes with *ko chʻu*, — the each place.

(3) 情, matters, circumstances. *chih chʻih; chih*, to prop, to support, *chʻih*, to hold on to; *chih-chʻih*, to hold out, endure. 毋 庸, do not use, *fu hsü*, soothing and pitying, *i. e.* relief. 邺, is merely another form of the *hsü* given in Ex. 50.

4. *chao shang chü*, the Board for attracting merchants. This is the name of the great Chinese, semi-official, steamship company, known in English as the China Merchants Co.. *chia pan*; European sailing vessels have long been called by this name at Canton. The origin of the expression is exceedingly doubtful. It is said that *chia-pan*, in Cantonese *ka-pan*, represents the English word Captain, and that the term was transferred from the Master to the vessel. *huo lun* (*chʻuan*), fire-wheel ships, steamers, *cf.* Note to Ex. 60. 4 (2). *têng chʻuan*, such vessels, vessels of these two classes. 鈔 is the regular term for tonnage dues.

(2) 經, sign of the past tense, — to be taken with *i ting. tsung li, etc.*; we have here the full title of the old Chinese Foreign Office, = the Office for general

仍(3)按三個月一次、核數報解、另造清冊、分明詳報、不(4)得與別項洋稅相混、等因。

has determined that [the Customs Authorities] should levy and collect them on the same system as foreign duties; (3) further, that once every three months they should calculate the amount, report it, and forward [the money to the proper quarter]; that they should separately make out a clear statement, and report the particulars, [with each item] plainly distinguished; (4) they must not mix up [these sums] with other items of foreign duties.

control of affairs with each country. It has now become the Wai Wu Pu, = Board of Foreign Affairs. 按照, in accordance with, *yang shui*, foreign duties (*i. e.* with the duties paid by foreign vessels), *chêng shou*, levy and receive.

(3) *jêng*, further. *an san ko yüeh i tsʻŭ*, according to three months one time, = once every three months. 另, separately, apart from other accounts, *tsao*, make, *chʻing tsʻê*, a clear statement, *fên ming*, distinguishing, *hsiang*, minutely, *pao*, report.

(4) *pu tê*, must not, *hsiang hun*, confuse together. *têng yin*; these words mark the end of the quotation from the Foreign Office's rules.

The above extract is an excellent specimen of the complicated style in which Chinese official documents are frequently written. The whole paragraph is of course governed by the *chʻa*, at its commencement; but this word may be disregarded for our present purpose. We have, then, in the first place about twenty words, from *chao shang chü* to *yin liang*, which form apparently a complete sentence, with subject, verb and object, all in proper order, — vessels of the China Merchants Co., importing goods .... ought to pay .... sums in silver. Reading on, however, we discover that the above, after all, is not a complete sentence, but that it is combined with what follows: that *yin liang*, is not the object of *ying na*, 'ought to pay', but of *chêng shou*, 'levy and collect', far away at the end of the second section. It then becomes plain that *ying na*, and all that precedes it, must be a participial phrase attached to *yin liang*, and that the twenty words mean, 'the .... [by] the C. M. Co.'s vessels .... ought-to-be-paid .... silver', or, 'the silver which ought to be paid by vessels of the C. M. Co.'. The construction would have been much plainer, if 之 had been inserted after *ying na*.

The reason why the Chinese writer has placed these twenty words at the commencement of the paragraph, is partly because they are its logical subject, partly because the insertion in its proper place of so inconveniently long a phrase would have interfered with the sequence of the rest of the passage. And, by taking the liberty of introducing the words 'with regard to', one is able in translating to retain the same order.

If it be asked, why does not one take *yin liang* as the subject instead of as the object of *chêng shou*, "that the duties and dues from the China Merchants Company should be levied and collected on the same system as foreign duties"; the answer is that *chêng shou*, has apparently the same subject as the verbs in section (3) *viz. ho shu pao chieh*, *ling tsao* and *hsiang pao*, and that *yin liang* could not possibly be the subject of these.

EXERCISE 71.

VOCABULARY.

憲 *hsien*⁴, a ruler, an official.	線 *hsien*⁴, a thread; a clue.
札 *cha*², a tablet; to order.	蒙 *mêng*², to receive a favour.
竟 *ching*⁴, end; after all.	封 *fêng*¹, to seal up.
店 *tien*⁴, shop; inn.	押 *ya*¹, to press down.
紬 *ch'ou*², silks.	提 *t'i*², to pick up.
箱 *hsiang*¹, a box.	付 *fu*⁴, to give, to hand to.
冒 *mao*⁴, to feign.	寄 *chi*⁴, to send, to deliver to.

照[1]得本局於光緒十三年間奉廣東釐務總局憲札開、嗣(2)後華商與洋商交易買賣、皆(3)照章責成華商報完釐金、

TRANSLATION.

1. Whereas this Office during the course of the 13th year of Kuang Hsü received instructions from the authorities of the General Lekin Office for Kuang-tung, stating that (2) in future when Chinese merchants deal with foreign merchants, either as buyers or sellers, (3) in all cases, in accor-

1. *chao tê*. These two words are frequently found at the beginning of proclamations. They are a conventional phrase, which it is customary to translate either by 'whereas' or by 'be it known that'. 釐. *sc. li-chin*, lekin: *hsien*, the authorities, *tsung chü*, of the general office, *li wu*, for lekin affairs. The persons issuing the proclamation, from which this Exercise is taken, are the officials of one of the Branch Offices under the control of the General Lekin Office. 札; this character is interchanged with the *cha*, given in Ex. 64. 開, to state, to declare.

(2) *chiao i*, trade. (3) *tsê ch'êng*, to make responsible.

華(4)商將貨賣與洋商、應
由出賣之華商完釐、洋(5)
商之貨賣與華商、應由
收買之華商完釐等因、
當(6)經諭飭各華行一體
遵照、嗣(7)於上年十月間、
竟有逢源店出運土綢
六箱、冒(8)充洋人、希圖走
漏、卽(9)據線人引報拏獲、
稟(10)蒙各大憲飭將土綢
充公、

dance with the regulations, the Chinese merchants will be held responsible for reporting [the transaction] and paying the lekin. (4) When a Chinese merchant sells goods to a foreign merchant, the Chinese seller ought to pay the lekin; (5) when a foreign merchant's goods are sold to a Chinese, the Chinese merchant, who buys them, ought to pay it. (6) Thereupon we issued a notification instructing all Chinese firms that they must without exception comply with [these orders].

(7) Afterwards, in the tenth month of last year, it actually happened that the Fêng Yüan Shop, [which was] exporting six boxes of native silks, (8) pretended to be a foreigner, with the intention of evading [the lekin]. (9) Then, receiving intelligence through an informer, we seized [the goods and men]; (10) and, having made a report, we were favoured [with instructions] from the various high authorities bidding

(6) 當, at [that time]. 行, *hang*, a firm. *i t'i*, one body, uniformly.

(7) 竟, after all, *yu*, there was.

(8) *mao*, to feign; *ch'ung*, to stand for; *mao ch'ung*, to pretend to be; *hsi t'u*, hoping and scheming, *tsou lou*, to evade payment of duty, to smuggle.

(9) *chi*, then, *chü*, getting hold of, *hsien jên*, an informer's, *yin pao*, guidance and information.

(10) *ping*, reporting, *mêng*, we received the favour, *ko ta hsien*, that each high authority, *ch'ih*, should order us. *ch'ung kung*, to make public property.

並[11]將逢源店房屋查封入
官、仍[12]將押貨之華人麥利
仁一名發縣嚴辦、各在案、
茲[13]准南海縣周來函、以提
訊麥利仁、據[14]供去年十月
二十八日、洋人安德散着
伊押貨付寄輪船、被[15]釐金
局查出、連貨拏獲解案、此[16]
貨委係逢源店華人之貨、
等語。

us to confiscate the native silks, (11) and to cause the premises of the Fêng Yüan Shop to be sealed up and forfeited to the state. (12) [We were ordered] further to take Mai Li-jên, the Chinaman in charge of the goods, and send him to the Magistrate to be severely dealt with. All these matters are on record.

(13) We have now received a note from Chou, Magistrate of Nan-hai, to the effect that he had had up and examined Mai Li-jên. (14) According to the man's statement, last year on the 28th day of the tenth month, a foreigner [named] Andersen told him to take charge of the goods and put them on board a steamer. (15) He was discovered by the Lekin Office, was seized together with the goods and was sent before the Court. (16) These goods really were the property of [the owner of] the Fêng Yüan Shop, who was a Chinese.

(11) *Lit.*, at the same time to take the Fêng Yüan Shop's houses and rooms, examine them, seal them up and confiscate them.

(12) 押, to escort, to take charge of.

(13) 以, to the effect that.

(14) 付寄, to send to, to take to.

(15) 連 *lien*, together with.

(16) 委係, to be really.

EXERCISE 72.

VOCABULARY.

素 *su*^{4}, plain; commonly; here-to fore.

殷 *yin*^{1}, abundant.

贓 *tsang*^{1}, booty, plunder.

添 *t'ien*^{1}, to add to.

僻 *p'i*^{4}, secluded, out-of-the-way.

棍 *kun*^{4}, a stick, cudgel.

撞 *chuang*^{4}, to strike, knock against.

驚 *ching*^{1}, to frighten, startle.

攔 *lan*^{2}, to prevent, to stop.

點 *tien*^{3}, a dot; to mark off, check.

光[1]緒十四年九月二十六日、已獲正法之武平武大合、已獲在監病故之張禮、在(2)該縣境內會遇素識獲案之江香陳六、各道貧難、武(3)平知悉事主黃泰山家道殷實、起意搶刧得贓分用、各犯允從、

TRANSLATION.

1. On the 26th day of the ninth month in the 14th year of Kuang Hsü, Wu P'ing and Wu Ta-ho, who have [since] been arrested and executed, and Chang Li, who has been arrested, but died in gaol of sickness, (2) at some place in the said District met with Chiang Hsiang and Ch'ên Liu, who were previously known to them, and who have [since] been arrested [and brought before] the court. They all talked of their poverty and hardships. (3) Wu P'ing, who was well aware that the complainant Huang T'ai-shan was well off,

1. *chêng fa*, to behead, *vide* Ex. 48. 3.

(2) At some place, etc., *lit.*, within the territory of the said District.

(3) *shih chu*, the principal in the affair, the sufferer. *chia tao*, family condition, *yin shih*, was abundant and substantial. 起意 *etc.*, raised the idea that they should plunder and rob, get booty, divide it and use it: each offender assented and complied.

武(4)平又添邀在逃之張成並不識姓名一人入夥、即(5)於是夜在僻處會齊、各犯分執刀棍及徒手不等、一共七人、三(6)更時分、同往事主黃泰山門首、武(7)平令江香陳六、並不識姓名一人、在外把風接贓、自(8)與武大合等撞開大門進內行刧、黃(9)泰山驚起攔捕、被武平用棍拒傷、

proposed that they should rob [his house] and divide the plunder; [to which suggestion] all the party gave their assent. (4) Wu P'ing also invited [two more men] to join the band, [namely] Chang Ch'êng, who is still at large, and a man whose name was unknown.

(5) Then, that [same] night, they assembled in a lonely place, seven men in all, some armed with swords; some with bludgeons, and some without any weapon. (6) At midnight they went together to the gateway [of the house] of the complainant, Huang T'ai-shan. (7) Wu P'ing ordered Chiang Hsiang and Ch'ên Liu, with the man whose name was unknown, to keep watch outside and receive the plunder. He himself, with Wu Ta-ho and the others, burst open the great gate and, going in, proceeded to rob [the house]. (9) Huang T'ai-shan, being aroused by the noise, [tried to] stop them and arrest them, but was hurt by Wu P'ing,

(4) *t'ien yao*, additionally invited. *ju huo*, to enter the band.

(5) *ko fan*, *etc.; lit.*, each offender, *fên* divided, *chih*, holding, swords, sticks, *chi*, and, *t'u shou*, empty-handed, not the same.

(6) At midnight; *lit.*, at the time of the third watch. There are five night-watches of two hours, each, midnight being the middle of the third watch.

(7) *tsai wai pa fêng*, to keep watch out side; *pa fêng*, *lit.*, to catch the wind, = to get news of approaching danger.

(9) *ching ch'i*, being aroused and rising up. *pei wu p'ing etc.*, suffered that Wu P'ing, using a stick, resisting, wounded him.

搶[10]去衣服現錢等物、遞交江香等分帶、一同逃回僻處、正[11]在點贓、因聞有人追捕、各[12]犯隨手取贓逃散。

who resisted and struck him with a bludgeon. (10) [The robbers] took away a quantity of clothes and [copper] money, which they handed to Chiang Hsiang and those with him to carry between them; and all together stole back to the lonely spot. (11) Just as they were counting their booty, they heard that there were people in pursuit of them. (12) [So,] each man took what articles of plunder came first; and they ran off in different directions.

(10) *i-fu*, clothes, and *hsien ch'ien*, ready money, *têng wu*, such, *i. e.* the above mentioned, articles.

(11) *chêng tsai*, exactly when; *yin wên*, because they heard.

(12) *sui shou*, accompanying the hand, = as it came to hand, *ch'ü tsang*, took booty, *t'ao*, ran off and, *san*, scattered.

IV. ALPHABETICAL INDEX OF CHARACTERS.

THE NUMBERS REFER TO THE EXERCISES.

INDEX TO NOTES.

THE NUMBERS REFER TO THE EXERCISES.

Printed in the USA
CPSIA information can be obtained
at www.ICGtesting.com
LVHW051624031123
762999LV00010B/1204

9 781018 68775